Best of the Bruins

Best of the Bruins

*Boston's All-Time Great
Hockey Players and Coaches*

JONATHAN WEEKS

McFarland & Company, Inc., Publishers
Jefferson, North Carolina

LIBRARY OF CONGRESS CATALOGUING-IN-PUBLICATION DATA

Names: Weeks, Jonathan, author.
Title: Best of the Bruins : Boston's all-time great hockey players and coaches / Jonathan Weeks.
Description: Jefferson, North Carolina : McFarland & Company, Inc., Publishers, 2021 | Includes bibliographical references and index.
Identifiers: LCCN 2020054987 | ISBN 9781476683973 (paperback : acid free paper) ∞
ISBN 9781476642253 (ebook)
Subjects: LCSH: Boston Bruins (Hockey team)—History. | Hockey players—Massachusetts—Boston—Biography. | Hockey coaches—Massachusetts—Boston—Biography. | Hockey teams—Massachusetts—Boston.
Classification: LCC GV848.B6 W44 2021 | DDC 796.962/640974461—dc23
LC record available at https://lccn.loc.gov/2020054987

BRITISH LIBRARY CATALOGUING DATA ARE AVAILABLE

ISBN (print) 978-1-4766-8397-3
ISBN (ebook) 978-1-4766-4225-3

Front cover image: Boston Bruins forward Patrice Bergeron (#37) during a game against the New Jersey Devils on February 13, 2009 at Prudential Center in Newark, New Jersey (Wikimedia Commons).

Printed in the United States of America

McFarland & Company, Inc., Publishers
Box 611, Jefferson, North Carolina 28640
www.mcfarlandpub.com

Table of Contents

PREFACE   vi

INTRODUCTION: A BRIEF HISTORY OF THE BRUINS   1

1. Centers   5

*Cooney Weiland, Marty Barry, Nels Stewart, Bill Cowley, Milt Schmidt,
Don McKenney, Bronco Horvath, Derek Sanderson, Fred Stanfield,
Phil Esposito, Gregg Sheppard, Jean Ratelle, Peter McNab, Barry Pederson,
Steve Kasper, Ken Linseman, Craig Janney, Adam Oates, Joe Thornton,
Brian Rolston, Patrice Bergeron, Marc Savard, David Krejci*

2. Right-Wingers   36

*Harry Oliver, Dit Clapper, Bobby Bauer, Johnny Peirson, Leo Labine,
Ed Westfall, John McKenzie, Ken Hodge, Terry O'Reilly, Bobby Schmautz,
Rick Middleton, Keith Crowder, Cam Neely, Glen Murray, Steve Heinze,
David Pastrnak*

3. Left-Wingers   57

*Red Beattie, Woody Dumart, Roy Conacher, Herb Cain, Vic Stasiuk,
Johnny Bucyk, Wayne Cashman, Don Marcotte, Stan Jonathan,
Randy Burridge, Ted Donato, Sergei Samsonov, P.J. Axelsson, Milan Lucic,
Brad Marchand*

4. Defensemen   78

*Lionel Hitchman, Eddie Shore, Flash Hollett, Murray Henderson,
Fern Flaman, Bill Quackenbush, Doug Mohns, Leo Boivin, Dallas Smith,
Ted Green, Gary Doak, Bobby Orr, Rick Smith, Brad Park, Mike Milbury,
Ray Bourque, Glen Wesley, Don Sweeney, Kyle McLaren, Hal Gill,
Zdeno Chara, Andrew Ference, Johnny Boychuk, Adam McQuaid,
Dennis Seidenberg, Torey Krug*

5. Goalies   116

*Cecil Thompson, Frank Brimsek, Jim Henry, Don Simmons, Eddie Johnston,
Gerry Cheevers, Gilles Gilbert, Pete Peeters, Reggie Lemelin, Andy Moog,
Byron Dafoe, Tim Thomas, Tuukka Rask*

6. Hall of Famers Briefly with the Bruins   136

Sprague Cleghorn, Frank Fredrickson, Duke Keats, Mickey MacKay,
Cy Denneny, Billy Burch, Babe Siebert, Bun Cook, Hooley Smith,
Sylvio Mantha, Busher Jackson, Babe Pratt, Terry Sawchuk, Allan Stanley,
Willie O'Ree, Tom Johnson, Bernie Parent, Jacques Plante, Rogie Vachon,
Guy Lapointe, Joe Mullen, Dave Andreychuk, Paul Coffey, Brian Leetch,
Mark Recchi, Jaromir Jagr, Jarome Iginla

7. Coaches   156

Art Ross; Claude Julien; Don Cherry; Harry Sinden; Tom Johnson;
Cooney Weiland; Mike Milbury; Terry O'Reilly; Gerry Cheevers;
Bruce Cassidy

APPENDIX A: LIFETIME STATISTICS OF FEATURED PLAYERS
(THROUGH 2019-20)   161
APPENDIX B: BRUINS PLAYOFF APPEARANCES AND RESULTS   165
CHAPTER NOTES   175
BIBLIOGRAPHY   183
INDEX   191

Preface

Growing up in the Capital District region of New York State, I could easily have ended up a Rangers, Sabres or Islanders fan. But as is so often the case, we don't choose our teams, our teams choose us. During the mid–'70s, the only channel that broadcast hockey in my area was WSBK out of Boston. After watching a handful of games featuring the "Big Bad Bruins," I was hooked.

I remember spending my weekly allowance on Topps hockey cards. And I can clearly recall the excitement I felt when I pulled my first Bobby Orr card out of a wax pack (which came complete with a virtually inedible stick of bubble gum). I can vividly conjure up images from the video segment that preceded Bruins games on WSBK—a montage of memorable moments accompanied by the Ventures' surfer-style rendition of Tchaikovsky's Nutcracker March. The old footage looks so outdated now with the helmet-less players and goalies clad in vintage Jason Voorhees masks.

By the time I attended my first game at the old Boston Garden, most of the stars I had grown up with had retired. A crop of young, dynamic players had taken their place—a list that included two of Boston's all-time greats: Ray Bourque and Cam Neely. I visited the antiquated arena on Causeway Street many times, occasionally craning my neck around metal pillars to follow the action. The glory days of the Bobby Orr era were long gone by then and, though the Bruins would not bring another Cup to Boston until the 21st century, every season brought new hope.

I have followed some very good Bruins teams over the years—especially the ones coached by fashion criminal Don Cherry in the 1970s. I have suffered through some very bad seasons as well. But never at any point in time was my loyalty tested. Win or lose, I will always remain a fan. This book was a labor of love for me and I hope you enjoy reading about Boston's greatest players as much as I enjoyed sharing their stories.

Like most sports, hockey is a game of numbers. In estimating the talents of Bruins players past and present, I relied heavily upon statistical data. When statistics failed to paint a clear picture—as is often the case with defensemen—I utilized the testimonials of coaches, teammates, opponents and sportswriters to determine a player's overall value. Aside from one chapter dedicated to brief appearances made by Hall of Famers, I limited my survey to players who have spent at least four full seasons in Boston. Profiles are arranged chronologically by position since each player has a specific job to do on the ice and comparing goalies to forwards or wingers to defensemen creates an apples to oranges scenario.

I would like to thank McFarland. I would also like to extend my gratitude to Bob Cullum for allowing me to use the vintage Bruins photos in the Leslie Jones collection at the Boston Public Library.

Introduction:
A Brief History of the Bruins

Before the NHL, there was the NHA (National Hockey Association). Founded in 1909, it began with seven teams located in Ontario and Quebec. A series of ongoing disputes between rival owners led to the establishment of the National Hockey League in 1917. Originally a four-team circuit, it was temporarily reduced to three members after a fire destroyed the Montreal Arena, forcing the resident Wanderers club to fold. The league returned to a four-team lineup in 1919.

In the early days, the Stanley Cup playoffs were an interleague competition pitting NHL teams against challengers from the Western Canada Hockey League (WCHL) and the Pacific Coast Hockey Association (PCHA). Aside from the short-lived International Professional Hockey League (which operated from 1904 to 1907), professional play was exclusive to Canada until 1924, when Charles Francis Adams was awarded a franchise.

Born in Newport, Vermont, Adams graduated from Jenney Business College and became president of the First National grocery store chain. An avid fan of hockey, he took a keen interest in the 1924 Stanley Cup finals between the Montreal Canadiens and Calgary Tigers. When the series was over, he enlisted the help of sports promoter Tom Duggan to pressure the NHL for a series of new entries. Duggan, whose interests included horse racing and dog racing, drafted a plan that would allow the four existing NHL clubs to receive $7,000 apiece for three U.S.-based franchises. Applications from New York, Philadelphia and Pittsburgh were put on hold, but Adams got the green light to build a team in Boston. The enterprising grocery mogul reportedly paid a sum of $15,000 for the rights to bring NHL hockey south of the Canadian border.

Upon securing an official charter, Adams hired Art Ross to help assemble a roster. A star defenseman during his playing days, Ross introduced various innovations to the game, including pucks with beveled edges (which prevented them from constantly rolling). He would spend three decades as Boston's GM while logging three separate stints as coach.

Adams held a contest to name the team, specifying that the moniker should correspond to a large animal with speed and power. None of the entries were to his liking and, after consulting with Ross, the Bruins nickname (which was the name of a brown bear in a famous medieval folk tale) was adopted. Adams chose the team colors to match the scheme of his Brookside grocery stores.

The Bruins' inaugural game (the first official NHL game played within the U.S.) took place on December 1, 1924, at the Boston Arena, ending in a 2–1 victory over the

3

Members of the 1939 Stanley Cup winning team. There were 10 Hall of Famers on the squad, including Eddie Shore (#2), Frank Brimsek (#1), Milt Schmidt (#15), Roy Conacher (#9), Bill Cowley (#10) and Woody Dumart (#14). Flash Hollett is #12 but he is not in the Hall of Fame. Courtesy Boston Public Library, Leslie Jones Collection.

Montreal Maroons. It was one the few high points of a dismal season that saw the B's finish in last place—26 points behind the league-leading Toronto St. Patricks.

Before the '26-'27 season, Adams imported a number of players from the Western Canada Hockey League, which was on the brink of collapse. Among them was Eddie Shore—one of the greatest defensemen in Bruins history. By 1928, the B's had lured eight eventual Hall of Famers to Boston. That same year, they bid farewell to their original home and moved into the Boston Garden, where they would reside through most of the 20th century. After posting a 26–13–5 record in '28-'29, they won their first Stanley Cup, defeating the Canadiens and Rangers in the playoffs.

Most knowledgeable fans of Bruins hockey are painfully aware of the extended Stanley Cup droughts in Boston. The club went more than a quarter of a century without an NHL title before capturing two Cups during the Bobby Orr era. More than 30 seasons expired before the next championship run in 2010-'11. But in spite of the extended dry spells, the B's have been in contention more often than not.

As of 2020, the Bruins had made more than 70 playoff appearances with well over a dozen trips to the Stanley Cup finals. Some of the most talented players the game has ever known have skated for Boston over the years. Their profiles are featured on the pages that follow.

1

Centers

COONEY WEILAND
(1928–32/1935–39)

Born in Seaforth, Ontario, Ralph Weiland received the nickname "Cooney" during his childhood. After spending three seasons with his hometown Highlanders, he joined the Owen Sound Greys, helping the club to a Memorial Cup championship. Weiland had intended to enter pharmacy school, but his exceptional hockey skills led him to a career on the ice. He signed his first professional contract with the Minneapolis Millers in 1925 and caught the attention of Bruins scouts when he scored 21 goals in two consecutive campaigns. He was added to Boston's roster prior to the '28-'29 slate.

Weiland had an excellent rookie season. Both of his playoff goals were game-winners as the Bruins captured their first Stanley Cup. Before the '29-'30 campaign, the rules of the game were changed to allow forward passing. Weiland made the most of it, shattering Howie Morenz's single-season record for points. Flanked by wingers Dit Clapper and Dutch Gainor, Weiland put up 73 points in 44 games. His line was dubbed "The Dynamite Trio" (or "Dynamite Line") by sportswriters as the Bruins posted a stellar 38–5–1 record that year. Despite their regular season success, the B's lost to the Canadiens in the Stanley Cup finals.

Weiland was small by today's standards at 5-foot-7, 150 pounds. He was not a trouble-maker, averaging less than 14 penalty minutes per season during his career. He received serious consideration for the Byng Trophy on multiple occasions. Weiland was known for his superb stick-work and face-off skills, and his official Hall of Fame bio describes him as "a magician with the puck."[1] One contemporary referred to him as "master of the poke, sweep and hook checks."[2]

Weiland was among the most resilient players of the era. During the third period of a 1931 game against the Rangers, he was tripped from behind and knocked unconscious after he slid into the boards. He returned to score the winning goal in overtime, getting KO'd again after making the shot. There was no concussion protocol in those days and Weiland missed just two games all season.

As opposing teams adjusted to the forward passing rule, Weiland's offensive production tapered off a bit. He remained an exceptional player nonetheless. In 1932, he was traded to the Ottawa Senators. He led the club in scoring, but couldn't save them from a dismal last place finish. Weiland ended up being traded to the Red Wings shortly into the '33 slate. He made an All-Star appearance with Detroit the following year.

In 1935, Bruins executives arranged a deal with Detroit to re-acquire Weiland in exchange for Hall of Famer Marty Barry. The transaction proved beneficial to both clubs as Barry led the Red Wings to their first Stanley Cup in 1936 and Weiland aided Boston to a championship three years later. Weiland finished his playing career in Boston and was named head coach immediately upon his retirement. He steered the B's to their third NHL title during the '40-'41 campaign. The following year, he became coach of the Hershey Bears.

After several successful seasons in the American Hockey League, Weiland took a job as head coach for the Harvard Crimson, piloting the team to six Ivy League championships. Robert Cleary, captain of the 1960 U.S. Gold Medal hockey team, offered glowing praise for his former coach: "[Weiland] treated us like men. I learned more from him than any Harvard professor."[3]

Weiland was named Coach of the Year by the New England Hockey Writers Association several times. An award bearing his name is still given to the top Harvard player every season. He was elected to the Hockey Hall of Fame in 1971. He received the Lester Patrick Trophy the following year for his contributions to hockey in the United States. He was 80 years old when he passed away in 1985.

MARTY BARRY
(1929–1935)

Born near Quebec City, Barry grew up in Montreal. He became a star in the Mount Royal Intermediate League, where he earned the nickname "Goal-a-Game Barry." He spent the '25-'26 season with the Montreal Bell Telephone team, capturing the attention of New York Americans coach Newsy Lalonde. Signed to an NHL contract in 1927, Barry lasted just nine games before being demoted to the Philadelphia Arrows of the Canadian-American Hockey League. While playing for the New Haven Eagles the following year, he won the Can-Am scoring title.

Looking to add some punch to their already potent offense, the Bruins picked up Barry in the 1929 Intra-League Draft. He collected 33 points as the B's set a record for most wins in a 44-game season. Barry's three goals and three assists in the playoffs helped Boston get past the Montreal Maroons in the semi-finals, but weren't enough to stop the Canadiens from pulling off a major upset in the final round.

Over the next few seasons, Barry became a dominant offensive presence in Boston with four consecutive 20-goal efforts. This included 13 game-winners. In March of 1933, his controversial overtime goal against the Blackhawks prompted Chicago manager Tommy Gorman to assault referee Bill Stewart. After Gorman had been escorted off the premises by police, Chicago players refused to continue without their coach (in those days, there was no sudden death in regular season overtime). The game ended up being awarded to Boston by forfeit.

Despite his many contributions, Barry was traded to Detroit before the '35-'36 campaign. Playing alongside wingmen Herbie Lewis and Larry Aurie, he led the club with 40 points, helping the Red Wings to their first Stanley Cup title. The first game of the semi-final round required six overtime periods to determine the winner. "The rink seemed like it was miles long," Barry later recalled. "Players [on] both teams were praying for somebody to score before we all fell from exhaustion."[4]

In 1936-'37, Barry made an All-Star appearance and won the Byng Trophy for his gentlemanly play. His team-leading 44 points guided the Red Wings to another championship. Commenting on his abundant skills, *Detroit Times* reporter Bob Murphy remarked: "Barry possesses that faculty of mechanical perfection. He sweeps the ice with such smooth, rhythmic strides his play is effortless. He is called hockey's greatest passer."[5] In addition to his reputation as a consummate playmaker, Barry was one of the game's sturdiest players. Between 1929 and 1939, he missed just two regular season games.

After a 41-point season in 1938, the aging Barry was offered to other teams as trade bait. There were no takers and the Red Wings chose to release him. He ended up signing with the Canadiens, but after scoring just four goals in 30 games, he was released. He finished the season with the Pittsburgh Hornets of the International-American Hockey League. Barry's last professional appearance was as a player/coach with the Minneapolis Millers of the American Hockey Association in 1940.

When his playing days were over, Barry coached the Millers for one more season then took a job as a grocery store manager in Nova Scotia. He coached the St. Mary's junior hockey teams in Halifax during the 1940s and '50s. Inducted into the Red Wings Hall of Fame in 1944, he was an inaugural member of the Nova Scotia Sport Hall of Fame when it opened in 1964. He was enshrined at the Hockey Hall of Fame in Toronto the following year. He was 63 years old when he died of a heart attack in 1969.

NELS STEWART
(1932–1936)

Stewart grew up in Toronto. He began his amateur career at the age of 18, joining the Cleveland Indians of the United States Amateur Hockey Association. USAHA teams were small (consisting of nine to 12 players) and typically did not carry back-up goaltenders. Rosters were comprised primarily of Canadian born players. Stewart spent five seasons with the Indians, leading the league in goals scored four times. In 1925, he was signed by the Montreal Maroons.

Stewart made a big splash in his NHL debut, netting a league-high 34 goals and capturing the first of two Hart Trophies. His efforts propelled the Maroons to a championship in their second year of existence. In Montreal, Stewart combined with Babe Siebert and Hooley Smith to form the fabled "S-Line," which averaged more than 90 points per year between 1927 and 1932. During the '31 campaign, Stewart set an unusual NHL record (since broken) with two goals in a four-second span.

As the Great Depression tightened its grip on North America, the Maroons encountered financial difficulty. In 1932, Stewart's contract was sold to the Bruins. He finished second on the club in scoring, helping the B's to a first-place finish. He added a pair of goals in the postseason as the Bruins lost to the Maple Leafs in the semi-final round. Stewart's 39 points in '33-'34 landed him in a tie with Marty Barry for the team lead. Unfortunately, the club finished below .500 and missed the playoffs. In

'34-'35, Stewart's 21 goals were second to winger Dit Clapper as the Bruins finished on top of the American Division. They proved to be no match for the Leafs in the semi-finals, losing three of four meetings.

Stewart was not an exceptionally fast skater and this was sometimes mistaken for a lack of effort. Former referee Bobby Hewitson once remarked: "[Stewart] was big and tall, but awfully lazy ... we used to say that Nels just stood in one spot all the time."[6] Compensating for his lack of speed, Stewart's favorite offensive tactic was to hover around the crease, pouncing on rebounds and netting bad-angle shots. At 6-foot-1, 200 pounds, he had excellent balance and was very difficult to move off the puck. His exceptional shooting ability earned him the nickname of "Old Poison." Referee Cooper Smeaton remarked of Stewart's scoring tactics: "He was terrific in front of the net—a big, strong fellow who had moves like a cat. [He] never seemed to be paying any attention to where the puck was and, if you were checking him, he'd even hold a little conversation with you, but the minute he'd see the puck coming his way he'd bump you, take the puck and go off and score."[7]

Stewart resorted to more than just bumping opponents. In fact, he had a mean streak in him. He regularly fought on behalf of smaller teammates and often used his stick to slash players he felt were being too aggressive. An incessant tobacco-chewer, he would sometimes spit the juice in the eyes of opposing goalies. His dirty tricks did not go unnoticed as he finished among the top five in penalty minutes during four seasons. In spite of his antics, Bruins coach Art Ross referred to Stewart as "the greatest inside player in the game."[8]

Traded to the New York Americans in 1935, Stewart returned to Boston for part of the '36 campaign. He then spent the remainder of his career with the Americans. When he retired in 1940, his 324 goals were an all-time NHL record. The mark stood until 1952, when it was broken by Montreal Canadiens legend Maurice Richard.

Finished as a player, Stewart coached for the Port Colborne Sailors—a junior hockey club affiliated with the Ontario Hockey Association. He lived long enough to celebrate his induction into the Hockey Hall of Fame in 1952. He passed away five years later at the age of 54. Executive Frank J. Selke, who presided over nine Stanley Cup titles with the Maple Leafs and Canadiens, said of Stewart: "I cannot recall any great pro who seemingly put less effort into his play and yet who came up with as much success as the two-hundred pound star.... I would have to rate Nels Stewart the brainiest player I have ever known."[9]

BILL COWLEY
(1934–1947)

Aside from his rookie season, which he spent with the St. Louis Eagles, Cowley wore a Bruins jersey throughout his career. A five-time All-Star and two-time Hart Trophy winner, he retired with exactly one point per game. Though hit his peak between 1941 and 1945, when World War II dramatically thinned out the NHL talent pool, there is no ignoring the fact that he was one of the most prominent stars of his era.

Born in Bristol, Quebec, Cowley was the youngest of five siblings. He received his first pair of skates as a Christmas present at the age of 12 and polished his skills on a frozen pond he created himself in his backyard. By 1933, he was a major star in the Maritime Senior Hockey League. After scoring 50 points in 38 games for the Halifax Wolverines, he signed his first NHL contract with the Eagles. Relocated from Ottawa, the club fared poorly in the standings and ended up folding before the '35-'36 campaign. The Bruins claimed Cowley in a dispersal draft.

Originally used as a left wing, Cowley was assigned to the center position when his exceptional speed and passing accuracy became evident. He was an unselfish player who preferred setting up teammates rather than taking shots himself. Though he was often overshadowed by members of the fabled "Kraut Line," which

Center Bill Cowley won two Hart Trophies during a Hall of Fame career that included 12 seasons with the Bruins. Courtesy Boston Public Library, Leslie Jones Collection.

consisted of Milt Schmidt, Bobby Bauer and Woody Dumart, Cowley turned lesser known players into stars. It was once said that he "made more wings than Boeing."[10] In the first round of the 1939 playoffs, Cowley assisted on all three overtime goals scored by linemate Mel Hill. Hill carried the imposing nickname of "Sudden Death" from that point on. Cowley led postseason skaters with 14 points that year as the Bruins ended a long championship drought.

Nicknamed "Cowboy," Cowley paired with wingers Roy Conacher and Eddie Wiseman to form the short-lived "Three Gun Line." The trio combined for 143 points during the '40-'41 slate, carrying the B's to another Stanley Cup title. Unfortunately, the war began to deplete Boston's roster and, by 1942, both Conacher and Wiseman were gone. Though Cowley continued to be a prolific playmaker, the Cup would elude the Bruins for the remainder of his career and beyond.

Cowley sustained numerous injuries over the years, including a broken hand, broken jaw, torn knee ligaments and a shoulder separation. He sat out more than 30 games in his last two seasons. In 1947, Bruins GM Art Ross arranged an exhibition tour of Western Canada and the United States. Cowley wanted to use the trip as a honeymoon of sorts since his wife was from Vancouver, but when Ross left him out of the lineup, he announced his retirement. He went on to coach the Vancouver Canucks of the Pacific Coast Hockey League.

Cowley owned a hotel in Smiths Falls, Ontario and a tavern in Ottawa. He also held a minority share of the Ottawa 67's—a junior hockey club. He passed away on New Year's Eve in 1993 at the age of 81. He is one of three former members of the St. Louis Eagles to be enshrined in the Hockey Hall of Fame.

MILT SCHMIDT
(1936–1955)

Combining finesse with ferocity and determination, Schmidt has sometimes been compared to Gordie Howe. Among the most gifted players of his era, he guided the Bruins to two Stanley Cups as a player. He later used his wisdom and ingenuity to steer the club to a pair of championships as general manager.

Born in Ontario, Schmidt grew up the German-Canadian community of Kitchener. Though he completed his elementary education, he was forced to drop out of high school to help support his family after his father fell ill. He worked in a shoe factory and played multiple sports on the side. A free-swinger with some power at the plate, he turned down an invitation to try out for the St. Louis Cardinals. Channeling his energies toward hockey instead, he became a major star with the OHA-affiliated Kitchener Greenshirts.

Schmidt formed a lasting bond with teammates Woody Dumart and Bobby Bauer, both of whom ended up signing with the Bruins. Dumart was the first to arrive in Boston with Bauer and Schmidt making their debuts the following year. In the politically incorrect climate of the 1930s, the trio was dubbed "The Kraut Line" in reference to their German roots.

An adept passer and proficient puck handler, Schmidt became known for his crushing body checks and tough defense. His hunched-over skating style invited criticism from veteran defenseman Eddie Shore, who advised him to switch to a more upright position. After consulting with team captain, Dit Clapper, Schmidt chose not to make any major adjustments.

Working alongside his Kitchener pals, Schmidt quickly became one of the league's top scorers. By the end of the Depression Era, the Bruins had assembled a team for the ages, winning Stanley Cup titles in 1939 and 1941. They might have built a legitimate dynasty if not for the onset of World War II. All three members of "The Kraut Line" enlisted in the Royal Canadian Air Force. Hall of fame goaltender Fred Brimsek joined the U.S. Coast Guard. By 1943, few stars remained and the club sank into mediocrity.

The "Krauts" played their last full season together in '46–'47, finishing first, second and third in team scoring with a combined total of 168 points. Bauer decided to go out on top, announcing his retirement at season's end. In his absence, Dumart never had another productive offensive campaign. But Schmidt had not yet reached the height of his career.

A clutch performer, Schmidt scored 39 game-winning goals during his time in Boston (including the postseason). Five of those goals came during the

The fabled "Kraut Line," featuring (from left to right) Bobby Bauer, Milt Schmidt and Woody Dumart. During the Bruins Stanley Cup seasons of '39 and '41, the line collectively averaged more than two points per game. Courtesy Boston Public Library, Leslie Jones Collection.

1950-'51 campaign, when he gathered 61 points and came away with the Hart Trophy. A four-time All-Star, he put up double-digit goal totals in all but three of his NHL seasons. He added no fewer than 25 assists on five occasions.

Schmidt had a remarkably high tolerance for pain. During a late-40s game against the Maple Leafs, he was seriously injured in a collision with center Cal Gardner. Though his left arm hung lifelessly at his side, he refused to return to the bench. Holding his stick with one hand, he continued to hack away at the opposition, winning the respect of the Toronto crowd. As Schmidt grew older, his knees began to deteriorate and had to be heavily taped before every game. He plodded onward in spite of the affliction. Sensing that the end was near, he took over for head coach Lynn Patrick partway through the '54-'55 campaign. He spent a total of 11 seasons at the Bruins' helm, guiding the club to a pair of Stanley Cup finals appearances.

In the late '60s, Schmidt ascended to the GM position. He has been credited with orchestrating one of the savviest trades in Bruins history, wrestling Phil Esposito, Ken Hodge and Fred Stanfield away from the Blackhawks in exchange for three players of lesser ability. Schmidt's Chicago imports had a major impact on the team's fortunes as Boston went on to win two Stanley Cups in a three-year span.

In 1975, Schmidt became GM of the expansion Washington Capitals. The team was absolutely dreadful, compiling the worst record in NHL history and leaving Schmidt with an unfortunate legacy. He was dismissed from his duties the following season. He remained active in Bruins alumni affairs throughout his retirement years.

Elected to the Hockey Hall of Fame in 1961, Schmidt's number 15 was later retired by the Bruins. In 2000, *The Hockey News* assigned him a rank of number 27 among the all-time greatest players. At the time of his death in 2017, he was the last surviving player from the 1930s.

DON MCKENNEY
(1954–1963)

Hailing from Smiths Falls, Ontario, McKenney began his junior hockey career with the Barrie Flyers of the Ontario Hockey Association. Designated team captain, he led the club to a Memorial Cup championship in 1953. He played alongside Don Cherry—who would later become Bruins head coach as well as one of hockey's most colorful ambassadors.

McKenney began his minor league career with the Hershey Bears—the Bruins' AHL affiliate. Though he was beset by injuries that year, he performed well in the playoffs, helping his team to the Calder Cup finals. A multi-sport star, he was scouted by the Brooklyn Dodgers and considered signing with them before choosing a career on the ice.

McKenney spent just one season in the minors before joining the Bruins. He gathered 22 goals and 20 assists in his debut, finishing second in voting for the Calder Trophy. He would finish among the Bruins top scorers for the next eight seasons.

The left-handed shooting McKenney was tall for the era and very slender. A swift skater, he anticipated the moves of opponents adeptly and always seemed to know where to position himself. His style of play has been described by multiple sources as elegant.

During his time with Boston, McKenney demonstrated his durability by leading the league in games played four times. He strenuously avoided penalties, receiving consideration for the Byng Trophy on six occasions. He captured the award during the best offensive season of his career ('59-'60), when he led the league with 49 assists.

McKenney almost always stepped up his efforts during the postseason. In 34 playoff games with the Bruins, he gathered 33 points. Though the B's lost to the Canadiens in the '58 Stanley Cup finals, McKenney and winger Larry Regan combined for six goals and five assists. McKenney scored twice off of Hall of Famer Jacques Plante in Game 4.

Named team captain in 1961, the honor was short-lived as McKenney ended up being traded in February of 1963 to the New York Rangers. A year later, he was dealt to Toronto along with Hall of Famer Andy Bathgate. The timing was perfect as McKenney helped the Maple Leafs to their third straight Stanley Cup title. It was the only Cup he would win during his career.

McKenney spent his final NHL season with the St Louis Blues in 1967-'68. He later played for the Providence Reds of the AHL, leading the team in scoring during the '68-'69 slate. When he was finished as a player, he served as assistant coach at

Northeastern University in Boston. After more than a decade of faithful service, he was promoted to the position of head coach. His teams weren't very good and he ended his stint in 1991. After McKenney's retirement from college hockey, Northeastern University named an award after him. McKenney later scouted for the Colorado Avalanche.

BRONCO HORVATH
(1957–1961)

Joseph Rudolph Horvath was born in Port Colborne, Ontario. His parents were Hungarian immigrants who had moved to Canada from the Ukraine at the end of World War I. Horvath did not reach the NHL until the age of 25. He began his junior hockey career in 1948 with the Galt Black Hawks of the Ontario Hockey Association. After a brief stint in the Eastern Amateur Hockey League, he joined the Springfield Indians of the AHL.

Horvath made his NHL debut with the Rangers in 1955, scoring 29 points in 66 games. Off to a sluggish start in '56, he was shipped to Montreal. He scarcely had time to unpack his suitcase before being reassigned to the Rochester Americans. He took the AHL by storm, gathering 37 goals and 44 assists in just 56 games. He added 13 points in the playoffs as the Americans reached the Calder Cup finals.

In June of '57, the Bruins acquired Horvath via an intra-league draft. The next few seasons were the most productive of his NHL career. Boston was a middle of the road team during Horvath's tenure, finishing higher than fourth place just once. Despite a mediocre 27–28–15 record, the B's eliminated the Rangers in the 1958 semi-final round. Horvath, the club's regular season scoring leader, put up eight points in the playoffs as Boston entered Game 5 of the Stanley Cup finals tied with the powerful Canadiens. The B's took the Habs to overtime at the Montreal Forum, but came out on the losing end, 3–2. Game 6 concluded with a disappointing 5–3 loss for the Bruins.

Hampered by injuries in '58, Horvath managed just 45 regular season appearances. He made the most of it, collecting close to a point per game. He was healthy when the playoffs arrived, contributing two goals and three assists in a semi-final loss to Toronto.

In 1959, Horvath battled with Chicago's young phenom Bobby Hull for the scoring title. When the Blackhawks came to Boston for the final game of the regular season, Horvath held a one-point lead over Hull. This gave fans something to cheer about since the Bruins had already been eliminated from the playoffs. The crowd remained quite lively until Horvath was hit in the face with a shot by linemate Bob Armstrong. Horvath ended up at Mass General Hospital and, in his absence, Hull collected two points, claiming the title for himself. Horvath never came close to duplicating his '59 performance in any of his remaining NHL seasons.

During his time with Boston, Horvath played on a line with Ukrainians Johnny Bucyk and Vic Stasiuk. The trio came to be known as the "Uke Line." From 1957 to 1961, they combined for an average of 158 points per season. In a different era, the Bruins might have dominated the NHL with that kind of production.

No stranger to the penalty box, Horvath wasn't afraid to trade punches with opponents. And he had the skills to match his periodic misbehavior. In a 2015 television interview, Former AHL teammate Don Cherry described Horvath as "confident" and said he would have been a perennial Hart Trophy candidate had he been active in the present day.[11]

Derailed by injuries again in 1960, Horvath was let go at season's end. He played for four NHL teams in a three-year span then established himself as a superstar in the American Hockey League. From 1963 to 1967, he accrued more than 300 points, leading Rochester to three consecutive Calder Cup appearances. He finished his career with the Amerks and was a charter member of the club's Hall of Fame when it opened in 1986. He was inducted into the AHL Hall of Fame in 2015. He passed away in December of 2019 at the age of 89.

Derek Sanderson
(1965–1974)

Sanderson combined exceptional skills with swagger and ferocity. A hockey rebel, he grew his hair long and wore a moustache before the style was popular. Notoriously fond of the nightlife, he eventually sank into the depths of chronic alcoholism, which limited his effectiveness and left him penniless. His victory over the disease has been a source of inspiration to many.

Born and raised on the Ontario side of Niagara Falls, Sanderson was the son of a Canadian Army private. As a boy, he practiced skating on a rink his father built in their backyard. Sanderson recalled his father spending the equivalent of a month's salary on a pair of CCM hockey skates and asking for a Stanley Cup ring in return. It was a request Sanderson would honor.

The young man who would come to be known as "Turk" logged his junior hockey experience with the Niagara Falls Flyers of the OHA. Selected as an All-Star in '65 and '66, Sanderson was awarded the Eddie Powers Memorial Trophy (given to the league's top scorer) in the latter campaign. Mired in last place during the '66 slate, Bruins executives arranged an exhibition game between Sanderson's Flyers and Bobby Orr's Oshawa Generals. Highlights of the game included a fight between the two rising stars—inevitably provoked by Sanderson. The pair became teammates and friends not long afterward.

Sanderson assumed full-time playing status with the Bruins in 1967. He gathered 24 goals and 25 assists, winning the Calder Trophy. He also made a number of enemies around the league as he slashed and brawled with anyone who dared to challenge him. After piling up 98 penalty minutes during his rookie campaign, he averaged 125 per year over the next four seasons. More than just a tactless goon, he scored no fewer than 41 points per year in that span, peaking at 63 in '70-'71.

In 1970, Sanderson's pass to Bobby Orr from behind the net in Game 4 of the Stanley Cup finals set up the most iconic goal in Bruins history. Commenting on Orr's memorable series-clinching score, Sanderson joked: "I made the kid famous."[12] Another Stanley Cup ring came in 1972. As promised, Sanderson gave both of them to his father.

As his popularity grew, Sanderson reveled in his celebrity status, driving a Rolls Royce and buying a nightclub in partnership with fellow playboy Joe Namath. Like Namath, Sanderson dressed flamboyantly when he went out on the town and was often seen with beautiful women on his arm.

In 1972, Bruins fans were disappointed to learn that Sanderson was leaving Boston to play for the Philadelphia Blazers of the World Hockey Association. The contract he signed made him the highest paid athlete in the world. Six games into the season, he sustained a serious knee injury that put him out of action. His snarky remarks to the press prompted the Blazers to let him go, making him property of the Bruins again. Hampered by physical problems, he got into just 54 games between 1972 and 1974. Traded to the Rangers before the '74-'75 campaign, he returned to form, scoring 50 points. He followed with another solid effort, gathering a career-high 43 assists with the Blues in '75-'76.

Off the ice, Sanderson's struggle with alcohol and drugs eroded his talents. A series of bad investments made by his lawyer coupled with his wild lifestyle led him to financial ruin. He made his last NHL appearance with the Penguins during the '77-'78 campaign. Over portions of nine seasons with Boston, he scored 294 points in 389 games.

In 1979, Sanderson's long-time friend, Bobby Orr, came to his aid, convincing him to enter a rehabilitation facility. Though he had failed in numerous prior attempts to maintain sobriety, Sanderson completed the program and has remained abstinent to the present day. His body was in rough shape from years of abuse and nearly a dozen surgeries were required to repair his hips so he could walk without the aid of crutches or a cane.

In 1986, Sanderson was hired to serve as a color commentator for hockey broadcasts on the NESN and WSBK-TV networks. He worked alongside play by play announcer Fred Cusick for 10 years. He later moved on to a career as a financial advisor, serving young hockey players. Explaining his motivation for making the switch, he said: "I wanted to protect athletes from themselves. I wanted to make sure they know what they own, why they own it and what they paid for it."[13]

To date, Sanderson has co-authored two books about his life—one during the height of his career and another after his long road to recovery. His struggles with addiction have served both as a cautionary tale and a motivating factor to those with similar issues.

FRED STANFIELD
(1967–1973)

Hockey was the primary pastime in the Stanfield household in Toronto. A majority of the seven Stanfield brothers played professionally. Fred was the most talented by far, forging a 14-year career that included a pair of Stanley Cups.

Signed by the Blackhawks at the age of 16, Stanfield logged his junior hockey experience with the St. Catharines squad. After putting up 109 points during the '63-'64 campaign, he was called to Chicago. He didn't become a prolific scorer overnight. In fact, he spent a significant amount of time with the Blackhawks' minor league affiliate after making his NHL debut. In spite of his point-per-game status with the St. Louis Braves in '66, he was traded to the Bruins.

The transaction is often cited as the most one-sided in history. Stanfield arrived in Boston along with Phil Esposito and Ken Hodge in exchange for Gilles Marotte, Pit Martin and Jack Norris. A journeyman goalie, Norris ended up defecting to the World Hockey Association when he consistently failed to keep pucks out of the net. Marotte, a defenseman, compiled one of the worst plus-minus ratings of the era. And though Martin had some good years with the Hawks, he was never on the level of Esposito or Hodge.

In the Blackhawks system, Stanfield had been overshadowed by the great Stan Mikita. In Boston, he yielded the spotlight to Esposito and Bobby Orr. Though he rarely grabbed headlines, he quietly emerged as one of the most productive centers in Bruins history.

In 1970, coach Harry Sinden said of Stanfield: "Anywhere else, we would be crowing over what Freddie has been doing. In one sense, he is our team. Orr and Espo are expected to be important key figures, however, we win many of our games on the work of our second line. Our second line is the best second line in hockey."[14]

Sinden's coveted line included wingers Johnny Bucyk and John McKenzie. McKenzie was the agitator, combining physical play with speed and finesse. Bucyk was the sharp-shooter while Stanfield was the play-maker. "We move the puck around pretty well," Stanfield explained. "I can make soft passes or hard ones. With guys who can go like [Bucyk and McKenzie], I throw it to them real hard.... We keep the passes off the ice and that's to our advantage because the puck doesn't get blocked by any-one's stick."[15]

The trio peaked in 1970-'71 with a cumulative total of 269 points. During the B's two championship seasons, they averaged more than 200 points. "Winning the two cups was great," Stanfield recalled fondly. "The first one was especially nice. My first year in the NHL, 1964, I went to the finals with Chicago. We went to the seventh game, but got beat by Montreal."[16]

Stanfield was known for his heavy slapshot. In Game 1 of the 1970 finals, he split the mask of Jacques Plante, putting the Hall of Fame goaltender out for the rest of the series with a concussion. During his six seasons in Boston, Stanfield averaged close to a point-per-game. He netted at least 20 goals every year and his assist totals ranged from 29 to 58. A reliable postseason performer, he put up 16 points in both of the B's Stanley Cup runs.

Traded to Minnesota for goalie Gilles Gilbert before the '73 campaign, Stan-field later landed in Buffalo, where he helped the club to three consecutive playoff appearances. He gave Buffalo GM Punch Imlach a lion's share of the credit for the Sabres' success. "I had a lot of respect for Punch. He had a lot of hockey knowledge. He coached the last Toronto team to win the cup. He knew how to win. He liked to put veterans with young kids. That was a good mix."[17]

Renowned for his clean style of play, Stanfield averaged less than 10 penalty minutes per season during his 14 years in the NHL. Yet somehow, he never received the Byng Trophy. He received consideration for the award just once. He finished his career in the AHL with the Hershey Bears, serving as coach in the second half of the '78-'79 campaign. He coached the Niagara Falls Flyers to an OHL playoff appearance the following year.

Upon retiring from hockey, Stanfield settled in Western New York. He operated a furniture business for many years. Keeping in touch with his former Buffalo teammates, he formed a Sabres alumni group. In a 2006 interview, he cited Bobby Orr as the greatest player he ever skated with and Harry Sinden as the best coach.

Phil Esposito
(1967–1975)

Born in Sault Ste. Marie, Ontario, Esposito came of age in an area known as "The Soo," where minor league hockey was immensely popular. As a boy, he practiced against his younger brother, Tony, who became one of the game's finest goalies. Phil dropped out of high school in twelfth grade and worked at menial jobs until his hockey career took off. While playing for the Sarnia Legionnaires at the junior level in 1960-'61, he scored 108 points in 32 games. He turned professional the following year and made his NHL debut with the Chicago Blackhawks during the '63-'64 campaign.

In his first three full seasons, Esposito averaged 56 points per year. He played on a line with Bobby Hull, who became a mentor and a friend. "Bobby Hull was the instigator," Esposito recalled. "That guy would get me in more trouble than anyone I ever met. But he also taught me more about life and hockey than probably anyone."[18]

Labeled an underachiever by coaches in Chicago, Esposito was traded to the Bruins in 1967. To make him feel welcome, Boston GM Milt Schmidt gave the rising star a substantial pay raise. Before his first practice session, "Espo" delivered a rousing pep talk to teammates and predicted a championship for the B's by 1970. His forecast was spot-on.

Esposito enjoyed his best years with the Bruins, receiving eight consecutive All-Star selections from 1968 to 1975. He won five scoring titles in that span and was named MVP twice. By the time he retired, he was well over a point per game with 36 hat tricks to his credit (30 of them with the B's). Reminiscing about his career years later, he said: "In Boston, I did things I never in my wildest dreams thought I could do."[19]

Esposito was sneaky on offense, positioning himself in hard to cover spots on the ice. A big man at 6-foot-1, 205 pounds, he was difficult to push around. He had an extremely quick release, but admitted that his shots lacked velocity. "I could shoot from sixty feet out all season and not get a goal," he once said. "A player must do what he does best."[20] In 1970-'71, he demonstrated just how good he was by shattering Bobby Hull's record for goals in a season with an incredible total of 76. He was so proficient on offense, he inspired a popular line of bumper stickers that read: "JESUS SAVES, ESPOSITO SCORES ON THE REBOUND."

A colorful character, Esposito was fond of cigars and practical jokes. One reporter dubbed him the "Happy Worrier" in reference to his perpetually distressed facial expressions. A man of rituals, he rigidly adhered to specific game-day routines he believed would bring him success on the ice. He insisted that his sticks and gloves be laid out in front of his locker and was known to become extremely upset with anyone who moved them.

Popular among teammates, Esposito became the subject of an amusing and oft-repeated anecdote. Having been eliminated from the playoffs in 1973, the Bruins scheduled an end-of-the-season party. Esposito had missed the last few weeks with an injury and was recuperating at Mass General Hospital. Insisting that he join the festivities, several Bruins players secretly slipped into the facility and wheeled Esposito's bed (with him in it) to a nearby restaurant known as "The Branding Iron." As the story goes, in order to spring him loose, Espo's liberators had to remove a door from its hinges.

In November of 1975, Esposito was traded to the Rangers along with Carol Vadnais for Brad Park, Jean Ratelle and Jack Norris. Head coach Don Cherry wanted to break the news in person, so he visited Esposito's hotel room accompanied by Bobby Orr.

"Phil, you've been traded," Cherry said, point-blank.

Having just signed a contract with the Bruins for less money than he could have gotten in the WHA, Esposito was genuinely surprised. "If you tell me I've been traded to New York, I'm gonna jump out that window," he replied.

"Bobby, get away from the window," Cherry said sarcastically.[21]

The flamboyant former coach later regretted his flippant remark. "For the life of me, I don't know why I said [it]," he commented in his 2016 book, *Don Cherry's Sports Heroes*. "Here, a guy's life has been rocked and I have to be a smart-ass."[22]

Esposito made the best of his new surroundings, scoring no fewer than 34 goals for the Rangers in four straight seasons. His efforts led the New Yorkers to the Stanley Cup finals in 1979. Years later, he still harbored a grudge against the Bruins for trading him. Interviewed by a writer from *The Toronto Sun* before the 2013 Stanley Cup final, which pitted the Blackhawks against the Bruins, Esposito sniped: "You want to know the truth? This series doesn't mean s—t to me. I have no feeling for these teams. There's nothing emotional about it. They both got rid of me, traded me. So screw them."[23]

Esposito retired after the 1980-'81 campaign. He became assistant coach in New York and later took a job as a TV analyst for the Madison Square Garden Network. In 1986, he was appointed GM of the Rangers. When Tampa Bay entered the league, he accepted the same position with the Lightning. He served as GM in Tampa Bay from 1991 to 1998.

In 1987, the Bruins retired Esposito's number, which was being worn by Ray Bourque at the time. In a touching pre-game ceremony, Bourque removed his number 7 jersey, revealing the number 77 underneath. Esposito was elected to the National Italian-American Hall of Fame in 1981 and the Hockey Hall of Fame in Toronto in '84.

GREGG SHEPPARD
(1972–1978)

Born in North Battleford, Saskatchewan, Sheppard did not begin skating until he was around eight years old. He got his earliest hockey experience in a local midget league. By the time he was 16, he found himself playing against much older men. "You had to keep your head up," he joked.[24]

Sheppard's rise to the NHL began with the Estevan Bruins of the Saskatchewan

Junior Hockey League. His team played in the Memorial Cup twice as he scored more than 80 points in back-to-back campaigns. In 1968, he joined the Oklahoma City Blazers of the Central Professional Hockey League. He attained All-Star status in '70-'71 and was named MVP the following season. He remains the franchise's all-time scoring leader.

During their 1972 Stanley Cup year, the "Big Bad Bruins" decided to add Sheppard to their playoff roster. Since he had missed the regular season, his name was not engraved on the Cup. Bruins owner Harry Sinden gave Sheppard a chance to purchase a ring, but at $1,800, he couldn't afford one.

Sheppard became a full-time player in '72-'73 and admitted to being a bit star-struck. "You're a little bit in awe when you walk into the room with guys like Bobby Orr and [Phil] Esposito," he told a journalist years later. "Previous to that, you see these guys on TV and all of a sudden you're there, so you say 'well, I have a job to do.'"[25]

During Sheppard's rookie season, he netted 24 goals and added 26 assists, receiving consideration for the Calder Trophy. Though his scoring dropped off during the regular season the following year, he was a major offensive presence in the '74 playoffs, gathering 19 points and helping the B's to a Stanley Cup finals appearance against the Flyers. The Bruins lost by a 4–2 margin, but Sheppard's plus-minus rating of 13 was tops among postseason skaters.

Beginning in '74-'75, Sheppard collected 30 goals for Boston in three straight seasons. He added 13 playoff goals during that span. In '75-'76, he captured the Seventh Player Award, which is given annually to Bruins players who perform beyond expectations. Additionally, he received the Elizabeth C. Dufresne Trophy (given to the top performer in home games). Sheppard finished third in team scoring behind Peter McNabb and Jean Ratelle in '76-'77. The B's returned to the finals that year, but ended up being swept by the Canadiens.

In September of '78, Sheppard was traded to Atlanta in a three-way deal that ultimately landed him in Pittsburgh. During his first season with the Penguins, he received consideration for the Byng Trophy and the Selke Trophy. An injury sustained in the wake of a low hit by Denis Potvin of the Islanders prevented him from reaching the 20-goal threshold for the sixth time in his career. He faced his old team in the quarter-finals, which ended with a Bruins sweep.

Sheppard played less often for Pittsburgh in 1980 and '81. Injured during a late-season practice session, he missed the '82 playoffs. He announced his retirement when the season was over.

In his prime, Sheppard was a skilled faceoff man and penalty-killer. He gelled well with teammates, averaging more than 30 assists per year between 1972 and 1980. Though several of the squads he played on were rough and outright dirty at times, he was renowned as a clean player.

While rehabbing from his '82 knee injury, Sheppard completed a real estate course at a Pittsburgh university. He was offered a job as a car-dealer in Boston, but opted to return to the city he grew up in. He underwent two surgeries on his right knee and three on his left to repair the damage from his 10-year NHL career. He spent several seasons as a junior hockey coach for the Battlefords North Stars. In 2015, he told a reporter he had no intention of leaving his boyhood home. "I like hunting and fishing too much," he said. "This is a good spot for that."[26]

Jean Ratelle
(1975–1981)

Ratelle's official Hall of Fame bio states that he "exhibited class and style through-out his career."[27] Recognized for his sportsmanship, he won the Byng Trophy twice. Acknowledged for his skill, he was named to five All-Star teams and finished in the running for the Hart Trophy on four occasions. But despite all that success, he never had his name engraved on the Stanley Cup.

Ratelle grew up in Lac St. Jean, a small Quebec town located to the distant north of Montreal. In two seasons with the Guelph Biltmore junior club, he gathered well over a hundred points. He joined the Trois-Rivieres Lions of the Eastern Professional Hockey League in '59, but ended up being sent back down after just three appearances. In his return to junior hockey, he led the OHA with 61 assists.

A pair of back injuries in '63 and '64 slowed his progress to the higher ranks. At one point, he underwent a spinal fusion operation. He successfully rehabbed and became a regular in the New York Rangers lineup. Originally assigned to a defensive line, his former OHA teammate, Rod Gilbert, insisted that he be placed on the top scoring line. Given the opportunity, Ratelle emerged as a star, recording the first of eight 30-goal seasons in 1967. The line he anchored along with Gilbert and Vic Hadfield came to be known as the GAG ("Goal-a-Game") Line.

Ratelle enjoyed his best offensive season in '71-'72, reaching personal best marks of 46 goals and 109 points. In addition to the Byng Trophy, he received the Lester B. Pearson Award (given to the player voted best by peers). A broken ankle robbed him of a scoring title and hampered his production when the playoffs arrived. Had Ratelle been healthy, the Rangers would have stood a better chance at defeating the Bruins in the Stanley Cup finals.

In 1975, Ratelle was included in a blockbuster trade that sent Boston's Phil Esposito and Carol Vadnais to the Rangers in exchange for Ratelle and Brad Park. The trade was so momentous, news of it actually appeared on the front page of the *New York Times*. Though Ratelle was ambivalent about ending his long career with the Rangers, he grew to accept it. "For me, it was a blessing in disguise," he told a reporter many years later. "I worked for the Bruins for twenty-six years as a coach and scout. It was really good for me and my family."[28]

In his Bruins debut, Ratelle had a major impact, scoring 90 points in 67 games as the B's made it to the semi-final round against the Flyers. Over the next four seasons, he collected no fewer than 72 points, peaking at 94 in '76-'77. The fans grew to love him in Boston and the feeling was mutual. "Their people are very knowledgeable," he said of the Bruins' fan base. "They know the game well. They cheer for you and if you give your best, they will always treat you well. They know when a guy's working hard and when he's not."[29]

Ratelle was so gifted offensively that his defense was sometimes overlooked. Among the smartest positional players of the era, he had a knack for picking off passes in front of the net. Opposing centers rarely scored from the slot with Ratelle on the ice. During his six seasons with the Bruins, he compiled a plus-minus rating of 128. His career total was more than a hundred points higher. Commenting on his uncanny ability to be in the right place at the right time, a writer from the *Boston Globe* once remarked: "Others skate, but Ratelle glides. Others arrive on the scene as if escorted by seventeen motorcycle cops, but Ratelle is already there."[30]

Ratelle played beyond his 40th birthday, retiring in 1981. He ended up just short of a point per game and currently ranks among the top 40 of all time in assists, points, and even-strength goals. He was inducted into the Hockey Hall of Fame in 1985.

Given Ratelle's gentlemanly conduct in a rough-and-tumble era, fellow Hall of Famer Brad Park marveled at his former teammate's on-ice success. "That might be the most amazing thing about Jean Ratelle's career," said Park. "That such a tranquil man could play such an aggressive game and survive…. On an ice surface filled with Marx Brothers madness and Three Stooges shenanigans, he was Fred Astaire in full glide."[31] Bruins great Wayne Cashman echoed that sentiment, commenting: "Jean was the man everyone wanted to be because he was able to maintain such peace in his life. He wasted no time being a jerk, going off on tangents like many of us did."[32]

In 2018, the Rangers retired Ratelle's number. He was the ninth player to be honored as such, joining an elite group that includes Gilbert, Mark Messier and Brian Leetch. Many of Ratelle's old teammates were on hand for the ceremony. Former linemate Vic Hadfield (a 50-goal scorer in '71-'72) offered abundant praise for Ratelle: "Jean was not only an excellent hockey player, but he was an excellent individual. As a team, we all hung out together because we all lived on Long Island…. That's how it was. We won as a team. We lost as a team."[33]

PETER MCNAB
(1976–1984)

Born in Vancouver, McNab spent a majority of his childhood in British Columbia. He moved to California as a teenager when his father was appointed head coach of the San Diego Gulls—a World Hockey Association team. McNab had an accurate shot he attributed to skating by himself in the big arena his father granted him access to. "I'd be alone there and the only thing I could do was practice shooting at the net. And that helped me develop accuracy," he recalled.[34]

A talented baseball player, McNab accepted a scholarship to play for the University of Denver Pioneers. He also made the hockey team, becoming a major star. In an era when college players were seldom drafted by NHL clubs, McNab caught the eye of the Buffalo Sabres and entered their minor league system.

Assigned to the Cincinnati Swords of the American Hockey League, McNab led the team in scoring during the '73-'74 campaign. He made his NHL debut with Buffalo that year, appearing in 22 games. The following season, he established himself as a legitimate offensive presence, posting the highest shot percentage in the league. After two consecutive 20-goal efforts, he was transferred to Boston in compensation for Buffalo's signing of Andre Savard. Though Savard was a top-notch player, he could not come to terms with the Bruins on a contract. Meanwhile, the Sabres had left McNab unsigned. In the end, the Bruins got the better end of the deal.

In the beginning of his Bruins career, McNab lacked confidence and was highly sensitive to criticism. "One of my handicaps early on was that my emotions would take over too quickly," he explained. "When I played a poor game, I would start questioning myself."[35] Coach Don Cherry took a nurturing approach and the results were dramatic. McNab scored more than 30 goals in six consecutive seasons, reaching the 40-goal mark twice. In that same span, he gathered no fewer than 38 assists. Though his goal production dropped off a bit in '82–'83, he gathered a career-high 52 helpers. His postseason contributions were significant as he averaged close to a point per game in playoff action with the B's.

McNab was a bit slow afoot, but he had good puck control. He was excellent on face-offs and power-plays. One of his favorite offensive tactics was to station himself in front of the net looking for tip-ins. His remarkable hand-eye coordination allowed him to redirect the puck adeptly. At 6-foot-3, 210 pounds, he absorbed hits well and knew how to dish them out.

Despite his reputation as a clean player, McNab will forever be associated with an ugly incident at Madison Square Garden during the '79–'80 season. Hostilities began when a Rangers fan hit Boston winger Stan Jonathan. More than a dozen Bruins players went into the stands and McNab was among them. After jostling with a fan, he was fined and suspended.

In February of 1984, McNab was traded to Vancouver. He had two more excellent seasons before his offensive numbers dropped off sharply. Released by the Canucks, he was offered a contract by his father, who had become GM of the Devils. The Devils were a poor team in those days and McNab's plus-minus rating reflected it. He retired before the '87–'88 campaign.

Finished as a player, McNab went on to a long broadcasting career. He called New Jersey games for eight seasons then took a job as a color commentator with Colorado. While serving in that capacity, he became inexplicably star-struck by former Bruins great Ray Bourque. Before Game 2 of the 2001 Stanley Cup finals, McNab waited until Avalanche players had left the dressing room and retrieved Bourque's skate laces (which the Hall of Fame defenseman discarded after every morning skate). McNab brought the laces home and put them on his own skates.

Bourque was not the only Bruins superstar McNab was enamored with. Reflecting on his time with the Bruins, McNab commented: "I love this fact—that Bobby Orr and I will never be separated. Bobby's got 264 goals, I've got 263, so no one can ever come between [us]. We're cemented in Bruins history.... Anytime you can get that close to Bobby Orr, that's unbelievable."[36]

BARRY PEDERSON
(1981–1986/1991–1992)

Hailing from Big River, Saskatchewan, Pederson averaged more than two points per game during his two seasons in the British Columbia Junior Hockey League. He joined the Victoria Cougars of the WCHL near the end of the '77–'78 campaign, helping the club to a league championship in 1981. Chosen by the Bruins in the first round of the 1980 NHL Entry Draft, he made his NHL debut without a shred of minor league experience.

Pederson became a full-time player in Boston during the '81–'82 campaign. Paired with right-winger Rick Middleton, he set a franchise record for rookies with

44 goals (a mark that still stands). He added 48 assists to his totals, finishing second in Calder Trophy voting behind Hall of Famer Dale Hawerchuk.

Pederson followed with another spectacular effort, making the first of two career All-Star appearances. After collecting 46 goals and 61 assists during the regular season, he led the Bruins to the conference finals against the Islanders with 32 points in 17 games. The Islanders eliminated the Bruins in six games then went on to capture their fourth consecutive Stanley Cup.

In '83-'84, Pederson reached career-high marks in assists (77) and points (116), receiving another All-Star nod. The Bruins finished first in their division, but couldn't get past the Montreal Canadiens in the first round of the playoffs. Pederson kept busy over the summer playing for Team Canada, but his career took a turn for the worse when a tumor was discovered in his right shoulder. He ended up missing most of the '84-'85 campaign after undergoing a procedure to remove a four-by-six-inch piece of muscle. By his own admission, he was never the same afterward.

Pederson worked hard to get back into playing shape. He returned in 1985 and, though he put up excellent numbers, his season totals were not on par with his past performances. When the Vancouver Canucks offered Cam Neely and a first-round pick in exchange for Pederson's services, Bruins GM Harry Sinden jumped at the opportunity. Neely forged a path to the Hall of Fame while Pederson slowly faded into mediocrity.

In 1986, Pederson led the Canucks with 52 assists and was named team MVP by the media and fans. He had another solid season in '87, joining a very small group of Vancouver players who have collected 50 assists in consecutive campaigns. By 1989, he was slowing down considerably, prompting a trade to Pittsburgh. Signed by Hartford in '91, he was traded back to the Bruins midway through November. It was his last NHL season.

In his prime, Pederson exhibited good instincts and an exceptional ability to work in sync with his linemates. He recorded seven hat tricks for the Bruins between 1982 and 1984. Fondly recounting his years in Boston, he told a journalist: "I thought maybe we were kind of instrumental in reigniting the Bruins in Boston and getting that fan base behind us. We were an extremely close-knit group of individuals. We hung around together on and off the ice. We had a lot of fun."[37]

During summer breaks, Pederson obtained a business degree. He later became an investment broker. He currently resides in the North Shore region of Massachusetts with his wife, who hails from Marblehead. Pederson now works for a major investment firm in Boston. He has also served on the NESN broadcasting team, providing pre- and post-game analysis for selected games.

STEVE KASPER
(1980–1989)

Kasper grew up in the Montreal area and was a Canadiens fan as a boy. He had no idea he would end up on the other side of the game's most storied (and bitter) rivalry. "I never thought I'd change my loyalties," Kasper told a journalist after his retirement, "but then I got drafted by Boston and played there for nine years."[38]

Kasper began his road to the NHL at the age of 16. He played three full seasons in the Quebec Major Junior Hockey League, getting better every year. During the 1979-'80 campaign, he scored 122 points in 70 games. The Bruins called him up the following season. His 21 goals and 35 assists put him in the running for the Calder Trophy.

Relatively small at 5-foot-8, 175 pounds, Kasper was a preeminent defensive presence. His masterful stick-work, diligent checking and ability to anticipate the moves of opponents frustrated many during his career. After receiving the Selke Trophy in his second NHL season, he was a candidate every year from '84-'85 through '90-'91. Because of his skill as a defender, he was a staple on Bruins penalty kills.

During his time in Boston, Kasper played under four different head coaches. He was a steady performer for all of them. He enjoyed his best all around season in 1987-'88, attaining personal high marks in goals (26) and assists (44). He was a major contributor to the Bruins' playoff run that year, which ended with a disappointing sweep in the finals at the hands of the Edmonton Oilers. Coach Terry O'Reilly assigned Kasper the daunting task of slowing down Wayne Gretzky. "The Great One" managed just three goals in five games, but added 10 assists, capturing MVP honors.

Traded to the Los Angeles Kings partway into the '88-'89 campaign, Kasper got to play alongside Gretzky. He scored a point per game for LA during the '91 playoffs while accruing an incredible shooting percentage of 36.4. Traded to the Flyers before the '91-'92 slate, he sustained a knee injury that limited him to 16 games that year. After a slow start with Philly the following season, he was traded to Tampa Bay, where he ended his playing career. He ranks among the top 100 of all time in short-handed goals.

In 1995, Kasper was appointed head coach of the Bruins. During a mid-season slump, he tried to send a message to players by benching two of the club's most accomplished veterans—Cam Neely and Kevin Stevens. This upset Neely, who griped to a writer: "If [Kasper] thinks that I'm not good enough to play on this team, to help this team win a hockey game, that's his decision and his opinion. But I know my opinion doesn't mean much to him.... I've been through a lot, played through a lot and to be treated like that, it's tough."[39] The Bruins finished in second place that year, but followed with a hasty first round exit from the playoffs. When the team fell to 26–47–9 in Kasper's second year as coach, he was dismissed from his duties.

In 2007, Kasper was named head coach of the Yarmouth Mariners—a junior hockey club based primarily in New Brunswick and Nova Scotia. He later took a job as scouting director for the Toronto Maple Leafs. He was let go after the 2015 season. Kasper has remained friends with former Boston teammate Ray Bourque, but holds no sentimentality for his time with the Bruins. "I enjoyed my time with the Boston Bruins," he told a reporter in 2013. "I have nothing but positive things to say about that. I just don't hold on to it. Maybe that's my personality."[40]

Ken Linseman
(1984–1990)

Born and raised in Kingston, Linseman started his junior hockey career with the Kingston Canadians of the Ontario Major Junior Hockey League. He scored 114 goals in a two-year span, proving he was ready to move up to the next level. In 1977, he filed a lawsuit challenging the WHA/NHL rule that players had to be 20 years old to be drafted. He dropped the suit when the Birmingham Bulls of the World Hockey Association offered him a contract at the age of 19.

Linseman scored 76 points in his pro debut, catching the eye of the Flyers, who sent him to their AHL affiliate—the Maine Mariners. He played 30 games with Philly in 1978, gathering 25 points. Groomed to be an eventual replacement for all-time great Bobby Clarke, Linseman appeared to be up to the task during the '79-'80 campaign, gathering 57 assists.

In 1981-'82, Linseman cemented his reputation as a dirty player with a mind-boggling total of 275 penalty minutes. Clarke gave him the nickname of "The Rat," not only for his scrappy play but also for the quirky way he skated. The nickname stuck and Linseman's line, which included wingers Brian Propp and Paul Holmgren, came to be known as "The Rat Patrol."

At 5-foot-11, 175 pounds, Linseman wasn't the most bruising player in the league, but he often baited opponents into taking penalties with his annoying (and often unsportsmanlike) behavior. He regularly used his stick to slash, cross-check and spear opponents. He was also known for grabbing and holding players during scrums along the boards. His objectionable conduct dated all the way back to his junior hockey days, when he was charged and convicted of assault after kicking Jeff Geiger of the Ottawa 67's in the head with his skate.

Explaining his under-handed strategy, Linseman told a *Sports Illustrated* reporter: "For me, it was a way of surviving. I had to play that way.... Those were the Flyers' 'Broad Street Bully' days and everybody was looking for the big, tough players. I thought I had to play that way to get noticed."[41] His excessive penalties were noticed in a negative way by Philly team executives. Before the '82 campaign, he was traded to the Oilers.

Working alongside Hall of Fame linemate Mark Messier, Linseman scored 142 points in two seasons with Edmonton while significantly reducing his penalty minutes. In the 1984 playoffs, he scored four game-winning goals, helping the Oilers to the finals against the Islanders. Facing a lineup that included hockey luminaries Mike Bossy, Bryan Trottier and Denis Potvin, the Oilers won the series in five games. It was the only Stanley Cup title of Linseman's career.

Linseman joined the Bruins before the '84-'85 slate. He spent five full seasons in Boston, averaging 70 points per year despite missing significant stretches of playing time. During the B's '88 playoff run, he led the way with 11 goals and 14 assists. He always played hard for Boston, racking up points, putting forth a strong defensive effort and stirring up trouble. During a fight with Lee Fogolin of the Oilers, Linseman bit Fogolin on the cheek, necessitating a tetanus shot. He offered no apology for what he had done, mouthing off to the press: "If the league is going to let us fight, I don't see where there are rules about how we should fight."[42]

When Linseman's point production dropped off in '89-'90, he was traded back to the Flyers. He had an encore with the Oilers the following year, making his last NHL appearance with the Maple Leafs in '91-'92.

Though Linseman was universally despised by most opponents, teammates generally had positive things to say about him. Former Philly linemate Paul Holmgren recalled: "Guys on other teams used to ask me: 'What's it like playing with that little jerk Linseman?' I said: 'Great. He got me 30 goals.' When you play with him, you love him."[43]

More than two decades after his retirement, Linseman continues to downplay the extent of his devious tactics. "As my career went on, I used to get penalties—and Terry O'Reilly would attest to this—when I'd be nowhere near somebody getting hit or hurt on the ice, and I'd get a penalty."[44] Numerous other sources found Linseman's assertion laughable. Matt Larkin of *The Hockey News* placed the retired center on his hypothetical "All-Dirty/Skill Team" in 2017, contending that Linseman "blended criminality with talent" better than most players in hockey history.[45]

Linseman currently lives in New Hampshire, where has made a comfortable living in the commercial real estate business. He is an active Bruins supporter, attending several games every year. When he isn't watching Bruins hockey, he skates for Boston's fund-raising alumni team. Commenting on how the game has changed over the years, he said in a 2019 interview: "I think what I like most today is how well everybody in the league passes the puck. The hockey IQ is probably higher overall than it was in my day."[46]

CRAIG JANNEY
(1987–1991)

Janney was one of the most successful American-born players in NHL history. He ranks number 1 among that group in assists per game and number 4 in points per game. He represented Team USA six times in competition, helping the squad to its first-ever medal during the 1986 IIHF World Junior Championships. Recognized for his efforts, he was inducted into the U.S. Hockey Hall of Fame in 2016.

A native of New England, Janney was born in Hartford, Connecticut, and attended high school at Deerfield Academy in Western Massachusetts. Upon graduating, he entered Boston College and spent two seasons with the BC Eagles. In his second campaign, he was a finalist for the Hobe Baker Award after setting Hockey East records for points and assists. He ended up being selected by the Bruins in the first round of the 1986 NHL Entry Draft.

Prior to joining the Bruins, Janney played for the U.S. National team and competed in the 1988 Olympics. He arrived in Boston in time for the playoff stretch. Acclimating very quickly, he scored 16 points in 15 regular season games. He added six goals and 10 assists in the playoffs as the Bruins reached the Stanley Cup finals, bowing to Edmonton in four games.

In his first full NHL campaign, Janney sustained a groin injury that limited him to 62 regular season appearances. He ended up with a point per game, finishing among the top five candidates for the Calder Trophy. Healthy by the time the playoffs rolled around, he was a major contributor with four goals and nine assists. His efforts did not prevent the Bruins from making a second-round exit.

During his 12-year NHL career, Janney used an unusually short stick, which kept him on his forehand. He moved the puck exceptionally well, making accurate tape-to-tape passes while deceiving opponents with a variety of moves. An accomplished playmaker, he was modest about his talents, constantly giving credit to teammates. Asked about his game philosophy, he once said: "My job was to pass the puck. The dancers dance, the diggers dig. Do your job and you'll win."[47]

The Bruins did quite a bit of winning during Janney's Beantown tenure. In 1990, they returned to the finals for a rematch against the Oilers. The end result was the same, but it was no fault of Janney's as he picked up 19 assists in playoff action that year.

In '90-'91, Janney had his best offensive season with the Bruins, reaching a career-high of 26 goals while adding 66 assists. He continued his postseason mastery with 22 points in 18 games. By the time he was traded to St. Louis midway through the '91-'92 campaign, he had accumulated well over a point per game for the Bruins.

In exchange for Janney, the B's received Hall of Famer Adam Oates. Janney was supposed to serve as a set-up man for sniper Brett Hull, but the two never really gelled. Instead, he ended up on a line with Brendan Shanahan, who assembled back-to-back 50 goal seasons.

Janney's lack of physical play coupled with his mediocre defensive skills led many to believe he was "soft." It was a distinction he did not take kindly to. "It's a tag finesse players sometimes get labeled with," he explained. "We take our hits making plays, not by being physical. I'm not going to run over anybody."[48]

When Mike Keenan took over as St. Louis GM in '94, he purged the roster of players he perceived were lacking in toughness. Janney was included on the list along with Shanahan, Curtis Joseph and Steve Duchesne (among others). "It was a difficult situation when I left," Janney recalled years later. "Mike Keenan just didn't want me to play for him."[49]

Janney became a gun for hire, spending time with five different clubs between 1995 and 1998. In that span, he collected no fewer than 38 assists on three occasions. He went to the playoffs with the Sharks, Jets and Coyotes, retiring with 110 points in 120 postseason contests. He was just under a point per game in regular season play. Though he was only 31 years old at the start of the '98-'99 campaign, he was forced to retire due to blot clots.

Janney's shooting percentage ranks among the top 40 of all time. Asked about the statistic, he was characteristically modest, commenting: "That's because I didn't shoot much."[50] In 2007, he had a brief stint as interim coach of the CHL affiliated Lubbock Cotton Kings. He later made appearances for NESN during televised Hockey East games.

ADAM OATES
(1991–1997)

Oates nearly lost his way. A self-proclaimed "punk," he dropped out of high school and found himself working as a gas station attendant at the age of 19.[51] Fortunately, his hockey skills got him back on track as he was recruited to play for Rensselaer Polytechnic Institute in Troy, New York.

Hailing from Weston, Ontario, Oates was an extremely talented indoor lacrosse player. He worked his way up to the Senior-A level before deciding to focus entirely on hockey. In order to play for RPI, he had to complete his secondary studies. He spent three seasons with the Engineers, leading the team to an NCAA championship in 1985. Several teams sought his services and he ended up signing with the Detroit Red Wings.

In his first professional season, Oates bounced back and forth from the NHL to the AHL. He became a full-time player in Detroit by 1986 and his numbers improved every year. During the '88-'89 season, he collected 62 assists—his highest total to that point. In June of '89, he was packaged in a four-player deal that landed him in St. Louis.

Thanks to Oates's stellar puck-work, linemate Brett Hull scored more than 200 goals in a three-year span. During that same stretch, Oates never reached the 30-goal mark. "I never asked him why he didn't want to score more himself," Hull joked. "I was afraid he'd change his mind."[52] Describing his unselfish style of play, Oates explained: "My Dad always said a center man's job was to disperse the puck—share it, get it to the wingers. You've got to make them involved in the game."[53]

In spite of his success in St. Louis, Oates became unhappy with his contract, demanding that it be renegotiated. Rather than accommodating him, the Blues traded him to the Bruins for center Craig Janney and defenseman Stephane Quintal. Assigned to the B's top line alongside Cam Neely, Oates endeared himself to teammates and fans with his multi-dimensional play. "He was not shy to get into the corners and battle for pucks and make plays behind the goal line," said Neely. "He was a guy who competed hard out there."[54]

Oates enjoyed his most successful season in Boston during the '92-'93 campaign, when he led the league with 97 assists. Proving he could put the puck in the net when it counted most, his 11 game-winning goals were tops in the NHL that year. He followed with a 112-point effort in '93-'94, cementing his status as one of the top centers in the game. Between 1989 and 1994, he was the second highest point producer behind Wayne Gretzky.

An injury sustained in the '94 playoffs continued to plague Oates the following year. He resorted to shaving the blades of his sticks so he could get more velocity on passes and shots. The short-bladed stick became his trademark from that point forward.

In portions of six seasons with Boston, Oates averaged 83 points per year. But his contributions could not save the Bruins from compiling their worst record in several decades during the '96-'97 campaign. With 19 games left to go in the season, he was traded to Washington along with goalie Bill Ranford and winger Rick Tocchet.

Oates played for four different teams between 1997 and 2004, enjoying his most productive stretch with the Capitals. Working with sniper Peter Bondra, he became the only NHL center in history to set-up three different 50-goal scorers (Hull and Neely being the other two). By the time he retired, Oates ranked among the top 10 of all time in assists (1,079). He was inducted into the Hall of Fame in 2012.

After his playing career was over, Oates served as assistant coach for the Lightning and Devils. He worked as head coach of the Capitals for two seasons before receiving an unorthodox assignment as co-head coach of the Devils alongside Scott Stevens during the 2014-'15 campaign. He later established his own consulting firm, The Oates Sports Group, which provides assessment and instruction to individual players and teams. The firm's clients have included standouts Jack Eichel, Steven Stamkos, Blake Wheeler and James van Riemsdyck.

JOE THORNTON
(1997–2005)

Few players have surpassed Thornton in terms of longevity. As of 2020, only nine men had appeared in more games. But unlike some veterans who hung around the NHL too long after their prime years, Thornton continued to make an impact throughout his career.

In February of 2019, Thornton moved ahead of Gordie Howe on the all-time assists list. San Jose head coach Peter DeBoer commented: "When you pass Gordie Howe on any list, I don't care what list it is, that's the story of the night. That's an unbelievable accomplishment.... Unbelievable career."[55]

For Thornton, it all began in St. Thomas, Ontario, where he logged his junior hockey experience. After scoring 104 points for his hometown St. Thomas Stars, he joined the Sault Ste. Marie Greyhounds of the Ontario Hockey League. He captured Rookie of the Year honors in his debut then finished second to Marc Savard in scoring during his sophomore season. The Bruins liked what they saw and made him the first overall pick in the 1997 NHL Entry Draft.

Thornton sustained a fractured arm during the '97 preseason, but returned to make 55 appearances, serving mostly on a checking line. In 1998-'99, his production improved exponentially as head coach Pat Burns increased his ice time. Thornton collected 41 points during the regular season then added three goals and six assists in the playoffs. Over the next several campaigns, he developed into a major star.

At 6-foot-4, 220 pounds, Thornton was known around the league as "Jumbo Joe." During his time with the Bruins, he frequently played the role of the enforcer. He averaged more than a hundred penalty minutes per year from 2000 to 2004. Because of his imposing size and physical style of play, he invited trouble from many of the league's toughest players. During a 2004 game against the Rangers, he was cross-checked in the head by notorious trouble-maker Eric Lindros. The two fought afterward and Thornton ended up undergoing facial surgery. Thornton was certainly no choir boy himself, incurring three suspensions for misconduct during the early part of his career. As time wore on, he cleaned up his act considerably. After the 2005-'06 campaign, he never accrued more than 59 penalty minutes in any season. And he was a Byng Trophy candidate on multiple occasions. Nevertheless, he was suspended again during the 2019 playoffs for an illegal check to the head on Tomas Nosek of the Vegas Golden Knights.

During his top offensive years, Thornton was an accomplished playmaker, collecting at least 40 assists during 14 seasons (including a run of 10 straight campaigns). He enjoyed his best season with the Bruins in 2002-'03, when he led the team with 36 goals and 65 assists. He was designated team captain that year—a title he held until his departure from Boston.

Though Thornton was well over a point per game in November of 2005, the Bruins opted to trade him to the Sharks in exchange for three players of lesser value. "I was blind-sided," Thornton told the press. "On one hand, it's disappointing, and on the other it's good to start over again. When you don't win, there's going to be changes."[56] The Bruins had missed the playoffs twice during Thornton's tenure in Boston and never made it past the semi-final round. But the transaction seemed ill-advised when

Upon leaving the Bruins, Joe Thornton had a long stint with the San Jose Sharks. He served as team captain for three seasons in Boston and four in San Jose. Courtesy Aaron Sholl on Visual Hunt/CC BY-ND.

Thornton received the Hart and Ross Trophies at season's end. Lamenting the trade, Canadian rock star Gord Downie (of The Tragically Hip) composed the song "You, Me and the B's." Downie felt that the Bruins were making a major mistake in letting Thornton go and his lyrics reflected it."

Still active as of 2021, Thornton has appeared on six All-Star teams. Over the course of his career, he has received glowing praise for his ability to shut down opponents, protect the puck and make crisp, timely passes to teammates. In 22 seasons, he has led his teams to over a dozen playoff appearances, never winning a Stanley Cup.

BRIAN ROLSTON
(2000–2004/2012)

Rolston was among the most well-rounded players of his era. Appearing at center and both wing positions, he won a Stanley Cup, World Cup and collegiate championship. Though he never experienced postseason glory with the Bruins, he emerged as a prominent scoring threat on penalty kills.

Born in Flint, Michigan, Rolston grew up in Ann Arbor, which is home to the expansive University of Michigan campus. As a youngster, he played in the 1985 and 1987 Quebec International Pee Wee Hockey Tournaments. He later attended Lake Superior State University, helping the squad to a national championship in his freshman year. He scored the game-winner in the deciding contest, earning Most Outstanding Player honors.

Drafted in the first round by the New Jersey Devils, he got his first professional experience with the AHL-affiliated Albany River Rats. He also embarked upon a long career with the U.S. national team. He helped the squad to a Bronze Medal in the 1992 World Junior Championships. Multiple victories with Team USA would follow, including a 1996 World Cup Championship and a Silver Medal in the 2002 Olympics at Salt Lake City.

After winning a Stanley Cup with the Devils in his rookie year, Rolston became proficient at the center and left-wing positions. Completing the rounds, he would appear as a right wing later in his career. He joined the Bruins near the end of the 2000 campaign and began his first stint in Boston at left wing. He was later shifted to center, serving portions of four seasons in that capacity.

The defensive-minded Rolston was a Selke Trophy candidate in five consecutive seasons. A top-notch penalty killer, he led the league in short-handed goals twice while finishing among the top 10 on four occasions. During his time with the Bruins, he netted 16 "shorties," ultimately attaining a rank of number 14 on the all-time NHL list.

Rolston was known for his high-velocity slapshots, which intimidated opposing goalies. He once made Anaheim net-minder Jean Sebastien Giguere duck out of the way. And he was known to use his slapper on penalty shots and shootouts—a highly unusual practice. In March of 2013, *Sports Illustrated* ranked his shot among the 10 best of all time.

Highly durable, Rolston missed just six games during his four full seasons with the Bruins. He averaged 25 goals and 36 assists per year in that span. His best offensive showing came in 2001-'02, when he gathered 61 points and led the league with nine short-handed goals. He had seven game-winners that year, eventually accruing a lifetime total of 72.

Boston never advanced past the first round of the playoffs with Rolston on the roster. Looking to shake things up after the 2003-'04 campaign, the Bruins opted not to re-sign him. He joined the Minnesota Wild, serving as team captain in 2006 and 2007. He made subsequent stops in New Jersey and New York (with the Islanders) before closing out his NHL career as a member of the Bruins.

After his retirement, Rolston opened a hockey academy bearing his name. Located in Oak Park, Michigan, Rolston serves as the school's head instructor. The current staff includes another former Bruins great—Left-winger Sergei Samsonov.

PATRICE BERGERON
(2003–PRESENT)

Born in L'Acienne-Lorette, Quebec, Bergeron grew up following the Nordiques. This gave him something in common with Bruins fans. Both hated the Montreal Canadiens.

Bergeron was selected by the Bruins in the second round of the 2003 Entry Draft. In an unusual turn of events, he made the jump directly to the NHL without any minor league experience. When he first arrived in Boston, he was a green teenager with a limited command of the English language. Veteran winger Martin Lapointe welcomed Bergeron into his home and mentored him on various aspects of NHL life.

In his debut season, Bergeron scored 39 points in 71 games and was selected to play in the NHL YoungStars Game, which was held in Minnesota as part of the 2004 All-Star Weekend festivities. He finished among the top 10 candidates for the Calder Trophy and was chosen to play for Team Canada in the IIHF World Championship event. As of 2020, Bergeron had made seven appearances for the Canadian national team, helping the club to six tournament victories.

When a lockout ended the NHL season in 2004-'05, Bergeron spent the entire campaign in the AHL with the Providence Bruins. He returned to Boston the following year, gradually becoming a fan favorite with his two-way play. A four-time Selke Trophy winner, Bergeron is considered one of the best defensive centers in the league. Often used as a penalty killer, he has wide range and knows precisely where to position himself. An adept stick-handler, he frequently keeps the Bruins out of trouble by poking the puck away from opponents. When that tactic fails, he slows them down with his body.

Offensively, "Bergy" (as he is known to teammates and fans) is one of the top faceoff men in the game. At the end of the shortened 2019-'20 campaign, he had a lifetime success rate in excess of 58 percent. An accomplished playmaker, he is largely responsible for the emergence of linemates Brad Marchand and David Pastrnak. Collectively, the unit is known to sportswriters as "The Perfection Line." Owing much to Bergeron's tireless work on both sides of the puck, Marchand and Pastrnak are considered to be among the NHL's top offensive threats.

A four-time Selke Trophy winner, Patrice Bergeron is one of the most respected two-way players in the NHL. His efforts have carried the Bruins to three Stanley Cup appearances. Courtesy sarah_connors on Visual Hunt/CC BY.

Bergeron's most memorable season with Boston came in 2010-'11, when the Bruins ended a Stanley Cup drought spanning nearly four decades. He scored 57 points during the regular season then added six goals and 14 assists in the playoffs. In 2013, he helped the B's get back to the finals against the Blackhawks. Exemplifying courage and dedication to the team, he continued to play despite a slew of serious injuries that included a separated shoulder and punctured lung. During the Bruins 2019 Stanley Cup run, which ended just one game short of an NHL title, Bergeron played through nagging groin issues sustained in the conference finals against the Hurricanes.

Describing what he likes

most about the atmosphere in Boston, Bergeron remarked: "This is a blue-collar town that expects its team to reflect blue-collar values.... Toe drags and slap shots are great, but Bruins hockey is about more than that. That's one of the things I really love about playing here. Our fans want active sticks. They want battles for pucks. They want a group that will constantly compete and impose its will from the time the game starts until it ends."[57]

In 2018-'19, Bergeron was honored at TD Garden before his 1,000th appearance with the Bruins. He currently ranks third on the all-time list in games played. Additionally, he is among the franchise leaders in goals and assists. Perhaps the most impressive statistic of all, only two players in Bruins history have scored more game-winners—Johnny Bucyk and Phil Esposito. Most everyone would agree that Bergeron now finds himself in pretty good company.

Despite missing more than a dozen games with injuries in 2018-'19, Bergeron posted the highest single-season point total of his career with 79. He recorded his fourth career hat trick that season against the Ottawa Senators. He added a fifth hat trick to his collection against the Rangers in 2019-'20. During the Bruins 2019 Stanley Cup bid, he scored nine goals and added eight assists. Two of those goals were of the game-winning variety. Though Bergeron celebrated his 34th birthday before the 2019-'20 campaign, he may not even have reached his peak yet.

MARC SAVARD
(2006–2011)

Savard still refers to the injury he sustained in Colorado on January 22, 2011, as the worst moment of his professional career. He was racing down the wing at top speed when defenseman Matt Hunwick delivered a clean hit. Savard's head smashed into the glass, dropping him to his knees. Although his eyes were wide open, he was temporarily blinded. As panic set in, he kept repeating the words to his trainer: "Why me?" He knew his career was over.[58]

Prior to then, Savard had sustained several other concussions. The worst of those occurred in March of 2010. The Bruins were in Pittsburgh and the playoffs were right around the corner. Savard had just snapped a wrist-shot when Penguins center Matt Cooke blind-sided him with a high hit. He fell to the ice and lay unconscious for half a minute. When he came to, his vision was cloudy and he was unable to get off the ice on his own power.

Describing the long, painful recovery, Savard wrote: "Imagine waking up and still feeling completely exhausted. Imagine that feeling lingering for almost two months. There's no relief. You're just exhausted and pissed off and confused."[59]

The worst part of the 2011 injury?

Savard was unable to participate in the Bruins Stanley Cup victory over the Vancouver Canucks that year. "We had worked for years to rebuild the team and become a contender," he recalled sadly, "and now my boys were on my TV—hoisting the Cup."[60]

Savard grew up in Ontario and became a star with the OHL-affiliated Oshawa Generals. Within four seasons, he had become the franchise scoring leader—a major accomplishment considering that Bobby Orr had also worn a Generals jersey.

Selected by the Rangers in the '95 NHL Entry Draft, Savard was called to New York in October of '97. Before his first game, he got lost on the way to Madison Square Garden and was forced to ask a policeman for directions. Savard spent a majority of his first season with the Hartford Wolfpack. He played in 98 games for New York before a trade sent him to Calgary.

With the Flames, Savard found his scoring touch, collecting 42 assists during the 2000-'01 campaign—his highest total to that point. Traded to the Atlanta Thrashers in November of 2002, he reached his full potential. After putting up 97 points in 2005-'06, the Bruins offered him a four-year contract worth $20 million.

With Boston in 2006-'07, Savard gathered 74 assists—the highest mark of his NHL career. He added 63 helpers in each of the next two seasons. In 2008, he made his first playoff appearance—a first round loss to Montreal. The Bruins had their revenge the following year as Savard scored 13 postseason points and led the NHL with an incredible 35.3 shooting percentage.

Savard was obsessed with the condition of his sticks throughout his career. He spent a great deal of time before and during games applying tape to repair various imperfections he felt negatively affected his ability to control the puck. Addressing his neurotic behavior in a television interview, he said: "I've always been adamant about my sticks being perfect and if I take care of [them], they'll take care of me."[61]

Savard exhibited some fancy moves on occasion. He handled the puck well and was an accurate passer. By his own account, his game was less about artistry and more about creating opportunities for linemates. "I'd rather set up a teammate than score myself," he once said.[62]

In October of 2009, Savard broke his foot blocking a shot. An examination at Mass General Hospital revealed that the foot had been injured earlier during training camp. He returned to the lineup in late November and signed a seven-year extension. But he would never play again after 2011.

Savard waited until 2018 to officially announce his retirement. Interestingly, he was traded to the Panthers in 2015 despite being inactive. A trade to the Devils occurred the following year. Though Savard didn't play in the 2011 Stanley Cup final, the Bruins pulled some strings to have his name engraved on the Cup. To this day, he still suffers from anxiety and short-term memory loss—lingering effects of his multiple concussions.

DAVID KREJCI
(2006–PRESENT)

Describing Krejci's status with the Bruins in March of 2019, ESPN writer Greg Wyshynski wrote: "David Krejci's name isn't always evoked when discussing what makes the Bruins a consistent contender in the NHL. Perhaps it's because he's a center playing in [Patrice] Bergeron's shadow, or because we don't heap praise on middle-men who have hit 70 points only once in their careers."[63] Wyshynski spoke too soon as Krejci finished the 2018-'19 campaign with 73 points then added 16 more during a playoff run that ended one victory short of an NHL title.

Though he rarely steals the spotlight, Krejci has quietly become one of Boston's most reliable performers. The 2019-'20 campaign was his 14th season with the Bruins. And he was slowly working his way to the top of the franchise leader board. At the time of this writing, he had attained a rank of number 8 on the all-time points list, surpassing Ken Hodge. Asked about his success, he typically defers to his teammates, pointing out how he has been lucky to play alongside some of Boston's best and brightest.

Krejci was born in Czechoslovakia and raised in a small town known as Sternberk. As a teenager, he played for the HC Trinec team and eventually caught the eye of a Bruins scout, who recognized his play-making ability. Selected by Boston in the second round of the 2004 NHL Entry Draft, he moved to North America and joined the Gatineau Olympiques of the Quebec Major Junior Hockey League. In his second season, he put up 81 points in 55 games, earning a promotion to the Providence Bruins.

Krejci's stellar play with Providence warranted a call to Boston in January of 2007. But just a few seconds into his third NHL shift, he sustained a serious concussion. He ended up playing in only six games with the B's that year. Injuries have plagued Krejci throughout his career. His laundry list of ongoing ailments includes a broken wrist and torn MCL in his left knee along with nagging hip issues that have required surgery. In spite of his relative fragility, he has consistently finished among the Bruins top scorers.

Krejci's best all around effort came in 2008-'09, when he won the Seventh Player Award. His 73 points and league-leading plus-37 rating made him an ideal candidate. Named alternate captain alongside teammate Zdeno Chara in 2013-'14, Krejci rose to the occasion, leading the NHL once again with a plus-39 rating.

Serving primarily on the Bruins second-line, Krejci is great on the rush, weaving elaborate serpentine routes through the offensive zone. Among the best passers in the NHL, he is tremendously creative with the puck, constantly generating scoring chances. He has collected no fewer than 40 assists on five occasions while reaching the 20-goal mark during four seasons.

In addition to NHL action, Krejci has skated in many tournaments for the Czech Republic. He was most recently active during the 2018 IIHF World Championship tournament. The Czech National Team has placed third on three occasions with Krecji on the roster.

In 2018-'19, Krejci made his tenth playoff appearance with the B's, helping them reach Game 7 of the finals. During the Bruins' Stanley Cup year of 2010-'11, Krejci led postseason skaters with 23 points. Four of his goals were game-winners that year. When the B's returned to the finals in 2013, Krejci again led the way with 17 assists and 26 points—tops in the NHL. He is currently signed through the 2020-'21 campaign with a no-trade clause. He'll be in his mid–30s when he becomes a free agent. If he continues to play as well as he has to this point in his career, the Bruins are likely to keep him on board.

2

Right-Wingers

HARRY OLIVER
(1926–1934)

There was no formalized hockey in Selkirk, Manitoba, when Oliver was a boy. He taught himself the basics of the game competing against neighborhood kids. "We just went outside and played," he recalled, "sometimes on an indoor rink, but mostly on the river."[1]

Organized hockey arrived eventually and Oliver skated for his hometown Selkirk Fishermen. In 1919, he helped the club to an Allan Cup appearance against the Hamilton Tigers. The following year, he joined the Calgary Canadians of the Big-4—a top-level amateur league. In those days, there was no forward passing allowed and offensive numbers were modest by modern standards. Oliver's 20 points in 16 games were considered outstanding for the era.

Oliver was a bit under-sized at 5-foot-8, 155 pounds. This earned him the nickname of "Pee Wee." He compensated for his diminutive stature with remarkable speed and tenacious stick-work. He had an accurate shot and was known for his sportsman-like conduct on the ice.

In 1921, Oliver signed with the Calgary Tigers of the Western Canada Hockey League. The Tigers won a league championship in '23-'24, earning the right to battle the Montreal Canadiens for the Stanley Cup. Calgary was badly outmatched, losing by a combined score of 9–1. Oliver didn't figure into his team's only goal of the series.

From 1923 through 1926, Oliver averaged more than a point per game for the Tigers. He was designated an All-Star twice in that span. By the time the '25-'26 campaign was underway, WHL teams were selling off their best players to NHL rivals in order to remain financially solvent. Attendance suffered and the NHL board of directors bought up all the WHL contracts. Oliver ended up with the Boston Bruins.

Working on a line with winger Percy Galbraith, Oliver led the B's in scoring for three straight seasons. His efforts propelled the club to three Stanley Cup finals appearances in a four-year span. Boston captured its first Cup during the '28-'29 campaign, but lost the other two bids. Oliver's point production was tops among postseason skaters during the '27 playoffs. His overtime goal in Game 1 of the 1930 semi-finals lifted the B's to a 2–1 victory over the Montreal Maroons. Boston won that series then lost to the underdog Canadiens in the Stanley Cup finals. It was the first time the Bruins had dropped consecutive games all season.

Oliver's offensive production tapered off considerably in 1934 and he was sold to the New York Americans. He had one more excellent campaign, collecting 25 points in '35-'36 (the second highest total of his career). He retired the following year.

When his playing days were over, Oliver returned to his home in Selkirk and worked as an electrician. He later moved to Winnipeg and served the Canadian government in the Weights and Measures Department. Largely forgotten today, he was elected into the Hockey Hall of Fame in 1967. He is also a member of the Manitoba Hall of Fame.

DIT CLAPPER
(1927–1947)

Clapper's election to the Hall of Fame was inevitable. In fact, the standard waiting period was waived after he retired. Among an elite group of players to make the All-Star team as a forward and a defenseman, Clapper competed for 20 seasons—a record since broken. He spent his entire career with Boston and his name was engraved on all three Stanley Cups the Bruins won prior to 1970.

Born in Newmarket, Ontario, Clapper grew up in Hastings. A childhood speech impediment prevented him from correctly pronouncing the nickname his parents had given him ("Vic") and he became known as "Dit." He began playing minor hockey at the age of 13 and logged his junior experience with the Toronto Parkdale club in 1925. He turned professional the following season, joining the Boston Tigers of the Canadian-American League.

Acquired by the Bruins in 1927, Clapper became an integral part of the so-called "Dynamite Line," a potent offensive combination that included Cooney Weiland and Dutch Gainor. In '28-'29, the trio combined for 53 points (including the playoffs), leading the Bruins to a Stanley Cup title. With the advent of forward passing in 1929, the "Dynamite Line" earned its nickname, exploding for 183 points. The Bruins seemed destined to repeat as champions that year before the Canadiens pulled off a shocking upset in the finals. Gainor left the Bruins in 1931 and the fabled threesome never skated together again.

Standing over six feet tall and weighing roughly 200 pounds, Clapper was a physical player who hit hard and took a lot of punishment in return. He was highly durable, missing only a handful of games between 1931 and 1938. Though he used his size primarily to prevent fights, he was not afraid to trade fists with opponents. During a brawl in Ottawa, he reportedly knocked down three men—each with a single blow. And he once delivered a shot to the head of referee Clarence Campbell, who had allegedly called him a "dirty son-of-a-bitch."[2] Campbell admitted that he had failed to do his job properly and, instead of incurring a suspension, Clapper received a $100 fine and a lecture from NHL president Frank Calder.

Clapper's best offensive showing came in '29-'30, when he scored 41 goals in 44 games. He never came close to matching that total in any other season. Appointed team captain in 1932, he began to appear as a defenseman during the '36-'37 campaign. His intricate knowledge of the sport made him one of the best blue-liners in the NHL. "Clapper diagnosed the plays like a great infielder in baseball," Bruins goalie Tiny Thompson remarked. "He put himself where the puck had to come."[3]

Dit Clapper served as team captain for 14 seasons. His name was engraved on all three Stanley Cups the Bruins won prior to 1970. Clapper is pictured here at left with teammates Cooney Weiland (center) and Red Beattie. Courtesy Boston Public Library, Leslie Jones Collection.

With Clapper and Eddie Shore anchoring the defense, the Bruins captured a Stanley Cup title in 1939. Another championship followed after Shore's departure. Clapper remains the only Bruins player to have skated for three championship squads.

Designated player-coach in '45-'46, Clapper guided the B's to a series loss against the Canadiens in the finals. He played in his last game the following year then remained at the Boston helm until 1949. Explaining his motivation for retiring, he said: "To be a really good coach you have to drive the guys. I couldn't really do that because I liked them too much."[4] His number 5 was retired by the Bruins in 1947, the same year he became a Hall of Famer. Since then, he has been compared to all-time greats Jean Beliveau and Wayne Gretzky.

BOBBY BAUER
(1936–1947/1952)

A native of Waterloo, Ontario, Bauer had 10 siblings. His brother Frank later became mayor of the city. Like so many Canadians, young Bobby learned to skate on a backyard rink. He played youth hockey in Kitchener-Waterloo before moving to

Toronto and attending St. Michael's College School. In 1933-'34, Bauer guided the St. Michael's Majors to a Memorial Cup championship. He formed a lifelong friendship with his future NHL linemates—Milt Schmidt and Woody Dumart—while skating for the Kitchener Greenshirts the following season.

Bauer began his professional career with the Boston Cubs of the Canadian-American Hockey League. He joined the Providence Reds in 1936, making his first appearance on a line with Schmidt and Dumart. Providence coach Albert Leduc dubbed his three stars the "Saurkrauts" in reference to their German roots. In Boston, the trio came to be known as the "Kraut Line."

Bauer, Schmidt and Dumart attained full-time status with the Bruins in 1937. Together, they averaged more than 100 points per season between 1937 and 1941, helping the B's to a pair of Stanley Cup titles. Reflecting on his days beside Bauer in Boston, Schmidt commented: "Bobby was our team. He was my right arm."[5] Dumart had positive memories as well, remarking: "[Bauer] had a good shot, was a good skater and stick handler and he had a way of finding holes. He and Milt would pass the puck back and forth. I got the garbage goals."[6] Marveling at the tightness of the unit, a writer from *Sports Illustrated* proclaimed: "They were the stuff of devoted boyhood chums scaling the heights together, all for one and one for all."[7]

When anti–German sentiment reached a peak during World War II, the so-called "Kraut Line" was briefly referred to as the "Buddy Line" or the "Kitchener Kids." All three players joined the Royal Canadian Air Force and were called to active duty in January of 1942. In the game preceding their departure, they combined for eight points and were carried off the ice on the shoulders of both teams. "The ovation, at the height of my youth, sort of grabbed me," Bauer recalled fondly.[8]

Bauer served as a radio technician during the war and was sent to the UK, where he joined a bomber squadron. He was transferred back to Canada when a hockey injury began to hamper his activities. In '45-'46, the "Kraut Line" was reunited. Bauer's contributions were minimal that year, but he returned to form with a career-high 30 goals the following season. Despite the 168 points generated by the "Krauts" in '46-'47, the Bruins lost to the Canadiens in the first round of the playoffs. Bauer announced his retirement at season's end. He was the first player to call it quits after a 30-goal season.

In his prime, Bauer was listed at 155 pounds. His dexterous skating allowed him to avoid hits and outmaneuver opponents. Renowned for his clean play, he was awarded the Byng Trophy on three occasions. He also received four All-Star selections.

Following his retirement as a player, Bauer returned to Kitchener to work for his family's business (known then as the Bauer Skate Company). He coached in the Ontario Hockey Association and also played portions of four more seasons for the Kitchener-Waterloo Dutchmen. He returned to Boston to skate with his old pals on "Milt Schmidt-Woody Dumart Appreciation Night," which was held on March 18, 1952. Bauer assisted on Schmidt's 200th career goal that evening and added a goal of his own in a 4–0 win over the Maple Leafs.

During the 1950s, Bauer served as GM and coach of the Kitchener-Waterloo Dutchmen, guiding the team to a pair of Allan Cup victories. The club was chosen to represent Canada in the 1956 and 1960 Olympics. With Bauer at the helm, the Dutchmen captured a Bronze and a Silver medal.

After leaving hockey behind, Bauer made a living off of multiple business partnerships. He died in 1964 of a heart attack. He was only 49 years old at the time.

Johnny Peirson
(1946–1958)

Peirson did not consider himself an exceptional player. Modest about his abilities, he referred to his skill set as "above average" and claimed that his career was marked by "complete accidents."[9] Regardless of those pronouncements, he helped guide the Bruins to eight playoff appearances—a fact that can hardly be viewed as accidental.

Born in Winnepeg, Peirson played for the Montreal Junior Canadiens and served in the Army during World War II. With his sights set on a career in business, he enrolled at McGill University. A chance encounter with Don Penniston, head coach of the Hershey Bears, led to a minor league promotion in 1946. When a gambling scandal forced several players out of the NHL, Peirson was called to Boston, where he would remain for portions of 11 seasons.

Described by one source as "a cerebral player in the Selke mode," Peirson was a tenacious back-checker who didn't shy away from the rough stuff.[10] He averaged more than 40 penalty minutes per year between 1948 and 1954, frequently finishing among the team leaders. Proving his worth offensively, he netted 20 or more goals on four occasions. He added no fewer than 20 assists the same number of times—excellent stats for the era. Recognized for his efforts, he played on two All-Star teams.

Despite his success on the ice, Peirson admitted there were aspects of his game he would have liked to improve. "I wish I had worked more diligently on my upper body strength because I would have been a better player," he once said. "I lost a lot of battles and wasn't able to do what I would like to have done from the viewpoint of strength."[11]

The Bruins missed the playoffs just twice during Peirson's career, making three appearances in the finals. Peirson was characteristically modest in his evaluation of the squads he played on. "We never had a powerhouse, but we had some representative teams," he said. "Nobody blew us out of the building."[12] In his first three playoff runs, Peirson averaged close to a point per game. His highest postseason total came in 1952, when he gathered three goals and six assists in 11 games. He tied for the team lead in the semi-final round against Detroit that year.

As the years wore on, Peirson's, knees began to weaken, slowing his offensive production. He was out of action during the '54-'55 season, but returned the following year. He saved his last great offensive effort for the '56-'57 campaign, when he gathered 26 assists and aided the Bruins to a berth in the Stanley Cup finals. It was Boston's 13th consecutive playoff loss—a skein dating back to the '41-'42 campaign. Limited to just four points in his final NHL season, Peirson decided to call it quits rather than languishing in the minors. He took a job in his father's furniture manufacturing plant, where he worked for several years.

In 1969, former B's coach Lynn Patrick got Peirson a job doing color commentary alongside Boston broadcasting icon Fred Cusick. The two developed a rare chemistry

Johnny Peirson (at left) with Bruins pals (from left to right) Fleming Mackell, "Sugar Jim" Henry and Leo Labine. Courtesy Boston Public Library, Leslie Jones Collection.

while calling games on WBZ radio. "Johnny and Fred never looked at each other," said one contemporary. "When the play stopped, Fred just pointed to Johnny and Johnny talked. Fred started again when the puck dropped no matter what Johnny was saying."[13]

After two years in radio, Cusick and Peirson began calling games on the WSBK television network. Cusick praised Peirson's remarkable ability to recall precisely what happened on the ice and repeat it to viewers without the benefit of instant replay. In all, the two men worked together for 20 years. When Peirson retired from broadcasting, Derek Sanderson took over color commentary. Peirson settled in Wayland, Massachusetts. As of 2020, he was still alive at the age of 94.

Leo Labine
(1951–1960)

Labine has drawn comparisons to Derek Sanderson with his spirited style of play. An incorrigible agitator with a cheeky sense of humor, he made more than a few enemies on the ice. When he finally retired from hockey in 1967, he joked that he was "lucky to make it out alive."[14]

Labine's roots can be traced to Haileybury, Ontario, which is located in the northeastern region of the province. His path to the NHL began with the Toronto-based St. Michael's Majors. Other prominent Bruins to skate for the club include Bobby

Bauer and Gerry Cheevers. After two seasons with St. Michael's, Labine joined the Boston-affiliated Barrie Flyers. He helped the team to a Memorial Cup championship in 1951.

Labine developed a reputation as an instigator and a wise-guy early in his career. Invited to the Canadiens' training camp in 1948, he stirred up so much trouble he ended up being released. Not only did he verbally harass the established veterans, but he offered unsolicited managerial advice to director Frank Selke, Jr. Though Selke was somewhat amused by Labine's brashness, he knew he couldn't keep the youngster around without inviting a host of problems.

After a successful run with the Barrie Flyers, Labine was promoted to the Hershey Bears. He gathered close to a point per game and was called to Boston near the end of the '51-'52 campaign. Though he never developed into a superstar, he endeared himself to the Beantown faithful with his aggressive play. He remained one of the most popular sports figures in Boston for nearly a decade.

Acting as an enforcer, Labine averaged over a hundred penalty minutes in a three-year span. He found his scoring touch in '54-'55, tying with center Don McKenney for the team lead in total points. Labine put up double-digit assist totals in nine straight seasons, gathering 20 or more on four occasions. He won the Elizabeth C. Dufresne Trophy (given to the team's most valuable player at home) in 1955. He also made consecutive All-Star appearances in '55 and '56.

Often playing on a line with McKenney and Real Chevrefils, Labine gave opponents fits with his ferocious checks and incessant wisecracks. During a game in Toronto, his antagonistic behavior inspired Maple Leafs bad boy Eric Nesterenko to break a stick over his head. Instead of dropping his gloves, Labine laughed it off and taunted Nesterenko as he headed to the penalty box. On another occasion, after absorbing a dirty hit from an opponent, Labine snarled: "You've got thirty-two teeth, would you like to try for sixteen?"[15]

The Bruins made seven playoff appearances with Labine on the roster but never won a cup. Reflecting on the Montreal Canadiens domination of the Bruins throughout his career, he remarked: "I made a lot of Frenchmen famous by losing to them. I just wish we had better players on our teams."[16]

After putting up a personal-best 47 points in '56-'57, Labine's production took a nose-dive the following year. Off to another slow start in 1960, he was traded to the Red Wings with Vic Stasiuk for three players. He played his last NHL game in 1962, moving on to the Western Hockey League. He became a major offensive presence for the L.A. Blades, averaging 63 points per year over five full seasons. Only two L.A. players (Norm Johnson and Willie O'Ree) surpassed Labine's lifetime total of 317 points.

Labine made his retirement home in Ontario. He developed cancer during his later years and died in 2005. He was 73 years old.

ED WESTFALL
(1961–1972)

Westfall was among those fortunate players who experienced success with more than one team. After hoisting the Stanley Cup with the Bruins in 1970 and 1972, he helped build a dynasty in New York. He is fondly remembered for his contributions in both of the NHL cities he called home.

Born in Belleville, Ontario, Westfall played junior hockey for the Barrie and Niagara Falls Flyers—both of which were Bruins affiliates. After three brief stints in the Eastern Professional Hockey League, he was promoted to Boston. He appeared at nearly every position before finding a permanent job at right wing. "The next move is to get myself some goalie equipment," he joked one day. "I've never been in the nets before but that opportunity may arise any day and I should be ready for it."[17]

During Westfall's first six NHL seasons, the Bruins missed the playoffs every year. The pieces of a championship puzzle were gradually assembled with the arrival of Bobby Orr, Phil Esposito and Wayne Cashman. Iconic left-winger Johnny Bucyk was already in residence when Westfall arrived.

At six-foot-one, 200 pounds, Westfall was a representative member of the hard-hitting squads known as the "Big Bad Bruins." But after serving a career-high total of 65 penalty minutes during the '64 campaign, he cleaned up his act, averaging less than 30 minutes per year from that point forward. A persistent checker, team-mate Ted Green said of Westfall's defensive abilities: "He's the big spoke out there ... he does so many things to stop the other team from scoring you can't name them if you spent all night trying."[18]

Westfall benefited tremendously from the sharp-shooters around him, gathering no fewer than 20 assists in seven straight seasons with Boston. He was a 20-goal scorer three times during his career, reaching a high of 25 during the '70-'71 slate. In February of '71, he combined with Johnny Bucyk and Ted Green to score three goals in 20 seconds off of Blues goaltender Dunc Wilson—an NHL record at the time.

In two trips to the Stanley Cup finals, Westfall collected a cumulative total of 15 points. This included three goals of the short-handed variety. He was a sniper on penalty kills, finishing among the top 10 in short-handed goals on six occasions. Very few Bruins players have netted more during their careers.

Looking for a multi-dimensional player with leadership abilities, the Islanders claimed Westfall in the 1972 expansion draft. He became the first captain in franchise history and represented the club in three straight All-Star games. Though the Islanders lost more than a hundred games in their first two seasons, Westfall fostered a cohesive environment by hosting team parties and offering guidance to rookies. In their third year of existence, the Isles overcame a 3–0 deficit in the quarter-final round against Pittsburgh. "That shocked the heck out of [owner] Roy Boe," Westfall said years later. "Nobody expected the team to get to that point so quickly."[19] By the time Westfall retired in 1979, the Islanders were on the brink of a dynasty with four Hall of Famers on their roster (Denis Potvin, Bryan Trottier, Clark Gillies and Mike Bossy). Westfall was there for the arrival of each.

In 1977, Westfall received the prestigious Bill Masterton Memorial Trophy. Established in 1968 to honor the fallen North Stars center (who is the only hockey player to have died from injuries sustained during a game), the award is given annually to the player who "exemplifies the qualities of perseverance, sportsmanship and dedication to hockey."[20] Other former Bruins to receive the honor include Jean Ratelle, Brad Park and Cam Neely.

After hanging up his skates, Westfall took a job as a color analyst for the SportsChannel group—precursor to the Fox Sports Network. He worked alongside play-by-play announcer Jiggs McDonald, who dubbed him "18" in reference to the number he had worn on his Islanders jersey. Westfall retired after 20 successful years in broadcasting. In 2011, he was inducted into the Islanders Hall of Fame on "Ed Westfall Night." He returned to the microphone along with McDonald to call the second period of an Islanders-Bruins game that evening.

JOHN MCKENZIE
(1966–1972)

McKenzie was a hockey nomad. Including the time he spent at the junior level, he wore more than a dozen uniforms during a career that spanned a quarter of a century. But of all the teams he played for, he is best remembered for his time with the Bruins.

Born in High River, Alberta, McKenzie got his start in the Western Canada Junior Hockey League. He was promoted to the minors briefly in 1955, appearing in one game with the Calgary Stampeders. After scoring 99 points for the St. Catharines Teepees during the '57-'58 campaign, he joined the Chicago Blackhawks. By the time he was traded to Boston in January of '66, he had spent portions of six seasons with the Hawks, Red Wings and Rangers.

McKenzie's teammate, Gerry Melnyk, nicknamed him "Pie Face" for his alleged resemblance to a character appearing on a popular Canadian candy bar wrapper. The colorful wrapper pictured a rosy-cheeked depression-era figure with a red bowtie and bowler's hat. Eventually shortened to "Pie," the moniker stuck with McKenzie throughout his NHL career.

Though McKenzie was only 5-foot-9, he was known for his feisty temperament. One of his favorite tactics was to lay a big hit on an opponent during his first shift to stir things up. He often paid the price for his aggressive behavior. In a 1963 game against Toronto, he suffered a ruptured spleen. In 1971, he separated his shoulder and fractured his skull. A bad boy in the '70s Bruins mold, he accrued 710 penalty minutes in 454 games with Boston. Though he was often the agitator, he usually skated away before the gloves came off. Reminiscing about his career with a *Boston Herald* reporter in 2014, he recalled a comical incident in which he got tangled up with Canadiens enforcer John Ferguson. On the verge of fisticuffs, McKenzie glowered at Ferguson, who was much bigger, and said fiercely: "Don't let my size scare you." There was a brief pause before both men burst into laughter then headed back to their respective benches.[21]

McKenzie offered no apologies for his rough style of play. In the spirit of baseball icon Leo Durocher, he once remarked that he would flatten his own mother if she played for an opposing team. A maverick off the ice, McKenzie herded cattle in the Western Canadian countryside and competed in rodeo events until Bruins GM Milt Schmidt decided it was too risky and made him stop.

Before arriving in Boston, McKenzie accumulated just 78 points in 238 NHL games. Paired with Johnny Bucyk and Fred Stanfield, he became a legitimate offensive threat, averaging 29 goals and 38 assists in a four-year span. Asked about the chemistry he established with his linemates, McKenzie commented: "After awhile, it got so that in any given situation I knew where Fred was and we both knew what 'The Chief' [Bucyk] had in mind."[22]

McKenzie made the most of his scoring chances, burying more than 20 percent of his shots during four seasons. He led the league with a healthy 23.6 percentage in '68-'69. His efforts helped propel the Bruins to a pair of Stanley Cup titles. He gathered 17 points in both championship runs.

After the Stanley Cup season of '71-'72, McKenzie was traded to the Philadelphia Blazers for cash. The Blazers were among the inaugural lineup of the short-lived World Hockey Association, which operated from '72 to '79. The WHA was the first major league to compete with the NHL since the Western Hockey League folded in 1926. McKenzie coached the Blazers briefly in '72, but resigned when the team lost six of seven games under his watch. He served as interim coach the following year after the club moved to Vancouver.

McKenzie played for four different WHA teams over the course of seven seasons. He made the most of a rather sparse talent pool, averaging 23 goals and 36 assists per year in that span. He retired after the '78-'79 campaign, gathering a hefty total of 115 penalty minutes in his final season. He was later inducted into the WHA Hall of Fame.

McKenzie struggled with alcoholism off the ice, which contributed to a pair of failed marriages. He eventually cleaned himself up and made amends. He once joked that retirement wasn't all it was cracked up to be since he still had so many things to do. He served in the American Collegiate Hockey Association and New England Hockey Conference as head coach of the Berklee Ice Cats. He was also director of development for Bay State Hockey. McKenzie died at his Wakefield, Massachusetts, home in 2018. He was 80 years old.

KEN HODGE
(1967–1976)

Despite all his success, Hodge was one of those unlucky players who never really gelled with coaches or fans in Boston. As of 2021, he ranked among the Bruins top 10 in goals, assists and points per game. He also helped the club to a pair of Stanley Cup titles. But because of his imposing size, he was expected to be an enforcer—a role he never fully embraced. As a result, he opened himself up to scathing criticism.

Hodge was among a handful of players born in the UK. Though he hailed from Birmingham, England, he grew up in Toronto, Canada. Signed as a teenager by the Blackhawks, he led the Ontario Hockey Association with 123 points in 1964. He found a permanent roster spot in Chicago the following season.

In 1967, Hodge was involved in a blockbuster trade that kept the Bruins in contention for many years. He arrived in Boston with centers Phil Esposito and Fred Stanfield. All three players had an immediate impact as Esposito led the team in scoring while Hodge finished behind Stanfield at number 5. During his years in Boston, Hodge's accomplishments were overshadowed by the brighter stars around him, which also included Bobby Orr and Johnny Bucyk.

At 6-foot-2, 210 pounds, Hodge was expected to throw his body around. It was a responsibility he disliked immensely. "It was my job and I did it," he told a reporter, "but it cost me offensively.... I don't like to play the bully and it hindered my development as a player."[23] Initially, Hodge was a slightly deficient skater, but he worked hard to improve his skills so he could be on the top line with Cashman and Esposito.

As Hodge peaked offensively, his physical play declined. This did not sit well with coaches Harry Sinden and Don Cherry, who hen-pecked him about it. Booed by fans for his inconsistency, Hodge defended himself to the press. "Sometimes I feel like telling them all to go to hell," he once said. "But I figure the boos come from people who just don't understand.... I don't think you have to run around crashing into people to qualify as a hockey player."[24]

There is undeniable truth in that statement. And Hodge's numbers should have been enough to silence his critics. In nine seasons with the B's, he scored more than a point per game. He gathered 30 or more assists eight times and netted at least 25 goals on seven occasions. During Boston's two Stanley Cup seasons, he scored 12 goals and 18 assists in 29 playoff games. His career plus-minus rating is among the top 40 NHL marks of all time. Even so, a fan once hung his number 8 jersey in effigy from the rafters of the Boston Garden. After his trade to the Rangers in '76, coach Cherry accused Hodge of being a one-way player and quipped sourly: "I would have traded him for the Rangers' trainer just to get rid of him."[25]

In spite of any damning statements made by his detractors, Hodge received two All-star selections and finished among the team scoring leaders every year he was in Boston. His 47 game-winning goals place him among the franchise leaders. He led the NHL in that category during the '73-'74 campaign.

Hodge made a comfortable living playing hockey. During his years with the Bruins, he lived in Lynnfield, Massachusetts—an affluent community in the North Shore region. Lynnfield was also home to Bucyk, Esposito and Jean Ratelle. Hodge's house was identifiable by the large backyard pool in the shape of the number 8.

Hodge played his last NHL season in '77-'78, finishing the campaign with the New Haven Nighthawks of the AHL. He moved on to a career in broadcasting. He has remained active in Bruins alumni affairs. Three of Hodge's sons played professionally. Ken Jr. scored 30 goals for the Bruins in '90-'91 before fading into obscurity. Dan and Brendan both played in the minors, later moving on to coaching roles.

Terry O'Reilly
(1971–1985)

O'Reilly was the type of player who made coaches guilty of favoritism. During his prime years with the Bruins, Don Cherry remarked: "Terry typifies our team. He's tough, really tough, and that's the way I like them. I know a coach isn't supposed to like one player more than another, but I can't help it in regard to Terry O'Reilly."[26] Sportswriters were partial to O'Reilly's spirited play as well. According to one writer, "O'Reilly was the heart and soul of the Bruins. He out-hustled every opponent, crashed and banged with reckless abandon and played every shift as if it was Game 7 of the Stanley Cup Finals."[27] Though his numbers don't exactly leap off the page, there have been few players in franchise history more dedicated to the Bruins' cause.

O'Reilly was born in Niagara Falls, Ontario. His family moved to Oshawa when he was in elementary school. He took an interest in hockey early on and played as a goalie until the age of 13. His awkward skating style led many to believe he would never make it as a professional. Yet somehow he muddled through, ascending to the junior hockey level with the Oshawa Generals. He established a solid offensive presence in '70-'71, collecting 65 points in 54 games. The Bruins were impressed, selecting him in the first round of the '71 amateur draft.

O'Reilly spent most of the '71 campaign with the Boston Braves. He joined the Bruins for one game that year and became a permanent fixture in the lineup the following season. In his early days with Boston, he spent a lot of time on the Bruins' checking lines. Fiercely protective of teammates, he was charged with over 200 penalty minutes in five straight seasons. Various press members referred to him as "Bloody O'Reilly" for his rough style of play. But Phil Esposito came up with a less menacing nickname, calling him "Taz" in reference to a hyper-kinetic Looney Tunes character.

O'Reilly had a nasty temper that got the best of him at times. In December of 1979, he was involved in one of the most unfortunate incidents in Bruins history. After an overzealous fan hit forward Stan Jonathan, several Boston players went into the stands at Madison Square Garden and brawled with spectators. O'Reilly led the charge, receiving an eight-game suspension for his actions. It wasn't the first time he was punished by league officials and it would not be the last. In 1977, he received a three-game suspension for throwing his gloves at referee Dennis Morel. And in '82, he sat out 10 games after taking a swing at official Andy van Hellemond.

Off the ice, O'Reilly was far more refined. An avid reader, chess player and antique collector, he made numerous visits to sick children in Boston hospitals. He studied part-time at Boston University and the University of Toronto during his playing days. He was also known for his self-deprecating sense of humor.

O'Reilly eventually found his scoring touch, clicking with Peter McNab and Jean Ratelle. "If I was out there with Peter, anything I gave him, he put it in the net," O'Reilly recalled. "If I was out there with Jean, anything he shot off my backside went in the net."[28] O'Reilly collected at least 20 assists in 10 straight seasons. He was a 20-goal scorer four times, peaking at 29 in '77-'78—his finest offensive season. Elven Bruins players reached the 20-goal mark that year, setting a new NHL record.

O'Reilly served as captain of the B's during his last two years as a player. He was appointed head coach in 1986 after Butch Goring was fired. The following season, O'Reilly guided the Bruins to the finals against the Edmonton Oilers. In the divisional playoff, Boston ended a string of 18 consecutive postseason defeats against the Canadiens. "It was very satisfying, but it was very stressful," O'Reilly said. "We were up three goals with twelve seconds to go with a faceoff. I was still worried.... When the final buzzer rang, it was a wonderful feeling to finally send them home and to the golf course."[29] His efforts were recognized as he was named Coach of the Year by *Hockey Digest*.

O'Reilly left the Bruins staff in 1989 to spend more time with his son, Evan, who was suffering from a serious liver ailment. He later served as assistant coach for the New York Rangers. His uniform number was retired and hung from the rafters in 2002 on "Terry O'Reilly Night" at the Boston Garden. In typical self-admonishing fashion, O'Reilly joked: "I think we would all agree it's a little bit of a deviation from the norm of the players who have been raised to the roof. Bobby Orr and Ray Bourque both could skate a little bit faster than me."[30] Bourque referred to O'Reilly as the "ultimate Bruin" and said to the crowd: "[his number] hangs next to mine, protecting me again. That's awesome."[31]

O'Reilly ran a construction business in the 1990s. After his second stint as an NHL coach, he moved to the Boston area and made a living in real estate. He has been very active in raising funds for the American Liver Foundation. Sadly, his son Evan died from complications of liver disease in 2018.

Bobby Schmautz
(1974–1979)

A writer from the *Boston Herald* described Schmautz as a "wiry, long-haired crooked-nosed, hyper-kinetic forward known for a high wrist shot that goalies hated, stick work that earned him the moniker 'Dr. Hook,' and a maniacal glare that would have scared the devil."[32] While some of those statements are somewhat exaggerated—others are not. His ruthless style of play provided the inspiration for an iconic movie character.

Born in Saskatoon, Schmautz's road to the NHL began in the Saskatchewan Junior Hockey League. He scored 55 goals in his sophomore season while being charged with over 100 penalty minutes. Promoted to the Western Hockey League in 1964, he seemed overwhelmed, barely making an impact with the L.A. Blades. But in spite of his deficiencies, he was signed by the Blackhawks. He became a full-time player with Chicago in 1968.

Unable to establish an offensive presence, Schmautz's contract changed hands multiple times between '69 and '71. He had a break-through season with the Canucks in 1972, leading the team in scoring. He was among the club's top point producers when the Bruins acquired his contract in February of 1974. Coach Don Cherry was always partial to players who weren't afraid to get their hands dirty and Schmautz fit the mold nicely.

Relatively small at 5-foot-9, 170 pounds, the ferocious Schmautz often antagonized larger opponents. One of his favorite targets was Canadiens enforcer Larry Robinson, who was seven inches taller and more than 40 pounds heavier. One night, Robinson got fed up and started pummeling Schmautz in front of the Bruins' bench. Though several Boston players wanted to step-in, Cherry held them all back, believing he was protecting Schmautz's pride. The under-sized winger later admitted that Cherry was mistaken—he would gladly have accepted the help.

On another occasion, Schmautz got into a jousting match with tough guy Paul Stewart, who later became a referee. Stewart hit Schmautz with an elbow, knocking the wind out of him and Schmautz retaliated. "I could have taken his chin off, but I didn't," Stewart recalled. "So he came back at me with his stick and we had a stick fight. It was ugly." The two had a mutual animosity for one another after that. "He was a gutless puke," Stewart remarked bitterly. "He had no code and no honor."[33] There were plenty of players who agreed as Schmautz's extracurricular activities earned him the derogatory nickname of "Dr. Hook." Former Edmonton coach

Craig MacTavish recalled the rough-and-tumble era of the late '70s. "There were some wicked stick men when I started," he said. "Guys were proud of it. It was: 'Hey, if you screw around with me, I'm gonna carve your eyes out.' There's an expression you never hear anymore."[34]

Schmautz and Philadelphia Flyers bad boy Dave Schultz became the mold for the Hanson Brothers—legendary brawlers from the classic hockey comedy *Slap Shot*. But unlike Schultz, Schmautz actually knew how to put the puck in the net. Over portions of seven seasons with Boston, Schmautz scored 295 points. He netted 26 goals in six playoff appearances—matching the lifetime total of Bobby Orr. Three of those goals were game-winners. In Game 4 of the '78 Stanley Cup finals vs. Montreal, his overtime goal against Ken Dryden tied the series at two games apiece. During the '77 playoffs, he led the NHL with 11 goals. Only Jean Ratelle scored more postseason points that year.

Schmautz was known for his powerful shot. He liked to put the puck in the high corners of the net. When he missed, he missed big, creating booming rebounds off the back boards. He had four hat tricks during his Bruins career, one of which came during the '77 playoffs.

The itinerant Schmautz was traded eight times during his professional career, which was spent with nearly a dozen teams. Dealt to Edmonton in 1979, he played for the Colorado Rockies before returning to Vancouver for a final curtain call. Upon leaving hockey behind, he moved on to a career as a roofer.

Schmautz remained sentimental about his time with the Bruins, telling a reporter: "The people in Vancouver and Boston treated me so well, but those Bruins years were special. [Don Cherry] and I were great friends. He was in it to win it and we both were so outspoken about it."[35] Schmautz has participated in multiple Bruins alumni events over the years.

RICK MIDDLETON
(1976–1988)

During his 12 seasons in Boston, Middleton established himself as one of the most versatile offensive threats in Bruins history. As of 2021, only two Boston players had scored more goals and only three had accrued more points. Recognized for his efforts, Middleton's number 16 hangs from the rafters of the TD Garden.

A native of Toronto, Middleton played youth hockey in Wexford. He showcased his developing skills in the 1966 Quebec International Pee Wee Hockey Tournament. He emerged as a major star at the junior level, collecting 207 points in two seasons with the Oshawa Generals. He was the OHL's top scorer in '72-'73.

Selected by the Rangers in the first round of the '73 Entry Draft, Middleton was assigned to the Providence Reds of the AHL. He proved his worth, helping the club to a Calder Cup finals appearance. He was named Rookie of the Year at season's end. Called to New York in 1974, he sat out more than 30 games with injuries. Though he finished fourth among teammates in scoring the following year, the Rangers weren't satisfied with his defense. He ended up being traded to the Bruins in exchange for veteran sniper Ken Hodge.

Middleton underwent a remarkable transformation in Boston. He later credited coach Don Cherry for "getting him out of [his] comfort zone" and "teaching [him] both sides of the game."[36] An apt pupil, Middleton earned the nickname "Nifty" for his superior puck control and deceptive moves. He evaded defenders adeptly, sometimes leaping through the air on his way to the net. One writer proclaimed: "he was like a 'Wild Mouse' carnival ride or a lightning bug as he zipped across the ice."[37]

Middleton had one of the most accurate shots in NHL history. His 19.7 lifetime shooting percentage is among the top totals of all -time. He was extremely dangerous on penalty kills, collecting 25 short-handed goals during his career—a team record that stood until 2019. Former Providence Reds teammate Alex Kogler said of Middleton: "He wasn't big, he wasn't fast, but no one could take the puck away from him. And he could score to the top corner lying on his back."[38]

Asked about his favorite linemates several years after his retirement, Middleton commented that center Barry Pederson had a lot to do with his success on the ice. That success extended to the postseason—a time of year when heroes are made. Middleton turned in an epic performance during the 1983 playoffs, collecting 11 goals and 22 assists in 17 games. This included a 19-point showing in a clash with the Sabres. No one—not even Wayne Gretzky—has equaled that mark in a single round of the playoffs.

Middleton's regular season accomplishments were numerous. A three-time All-Star, he was Boston's top goal scorer from 1979 through 1984. In that span, only Gretzky, Mike Bossy and Marcel Dionne exceeded Middleton's totals. The Bruins recognized "Nifty's" efforts by appointing him co-captain in 1985 along with Ray Bourque.

When helmets became mandatory for new players in 1979, Middleton exercised his right as a veteran not to wear one. He paid the price in February of '86 when he was hit in the head by a puck during practice. He sustained a concussion and suffered from recurring headaches after that. Though his production dropped off considerably, he still managed to collect 44 goals and 56 assists in his last two seasons. In his final trip to the playoffs, he netted three game-winners while accruing a robust shooting percentage of 29.4.

Middleton came up just short of 1,000 points during his career. He went to Switzerland to get in shape for a comeback, but ultimately decided against it. After hanging up his skates for good, he became president of Bruins Alumni Affairs. He also served as a studio analyst for the New England Sports Network.

In 2001, Middleton was appointed coach of the U.S. National Sled Hockey Team. He had never worked with disabled athletes before and described it as an "eye-opening" experience. "They were so able, it was scary," he said.[39] Before Middleton's arrival, the U.S. team had never won a medal. Thanks to Middleton's efforts in restructuring the offense and defense, the squad captured Gold at the 2002 Paralympic Games in Salt Lake City.

In 2018, Middleton was thrilled to learn that his number was being retired by the Bruins. "For any athlete in any sport, to be recognized by your team and your organization, to have your name prominently exhibited with all those other great names over a hundred years so my family and my family's family and generations to come will always see it is the greatest honor," he said proudly.[40] As of 2020, Middleton had yet to be elected to the Hockey Hall of Fame, though a compelling argument can be made in favor of his induction.

KEITH CROWDER
(1980–1989)

Crowder came from a hockey family. His older brother, Bruce, spent three seasons with the Bruins and his younger brother, Craig, played at the collegiate level. Born in Windsor, Ontario, Keith and his siblings grew up in nearby Essex. Keith got his start in organized hockey at the age of nine. With an assortment of skills, he eventually ascended to the Junior C level with the Essex 73s. He scored 87 goals in two seasons with the club, leading his squad to an OHA championship in 1975.

Crowder considered attending the University of Michigan before joining the Class A Peterborough Petes in 1976. The club went on to win three consecutive league championships with Crowder participating in two of those efforts. Demonstrating the toughness that would characterize him throughout his career, Crowder played with a broken wrist in the '79 Memorial Cup finals. In spite of his injury, he gathered 18 postseason points that year.

Crowder joined the World Hockey Association briefly in '79, getting into five games with the Birmingham Bulls. The league folded at season's end and he wound up being drafted by the Bruins. He played for three minor league teams before arriving in Boston during the '80-'81 campaign. Skating on a line with rookie center Steve Kasper and veteran left-winger Wayne Cashman, Crowder put up 25 points in 47 games. He also set a franchise record for rookies with 172 penalty minutes. His ferocity and two-way abilities made him an instant crowd favorite in Boston.

At six-foot, 190 pounds, Crowder was not an easy man to push around. He rarely backed down from a challenge, mixing it up with anyone bold enough to drop the gloves. A frequent visitor to the penalty box throughout his career, he logged no fewer than 100 penalty minutes in each of his nine seasons with Boston. Carrying his weight offensively, he reached the 30-goal plateau on three occasions and netted 26 game-winners during his Beantown tenure. He also gathered 20 or more assists in seven straight campaigns. His best offensive effort came in '85-'86, when he led the team with 84 points. He won the Seventh Player Award the previous season.

Crowder eventually paid the price for his rough style of play. During his last few seasons, he suffered shoulder, rib, abdominal and hand injuries. In 1989, he signed as a free agent with the Los Angeles Kings. Placed on a checking line, he lost his passion for the sport and retired at season's end.

Crowder bought into the Tim Horton's restaurant franchise and made a comfortable living after hockey. Acknowledged for his on-ice success, he was inducted into the Windsor-Essex Hall of Fame in 2000. His son, Cam, later became head coach of the Essex 73s.

CAM NEELY
(1986–1996)

Neely was born in Comox, British Columbia, which is located on the eastern coast of Vancouver Island. One of four siblings, he spent a significant portion of his childhood in Moose Jaw, Saskatchewan. Taking an interest in hockey at a young age, he grew up as a fan of the Maple Leafs and Canucks. Some of his fondest memories of the game include skating on backyard rinks and getting placed on the same team as his older brother, Scott, who was two grades ahead of him in school.

Neely ascended to the junior level with the Portland Winter Hawks and helped the club to a Memorial Cup championship in 1983. In the final game, he got a hat trick while scoring the deciding goal. He was selected by the Canucks in the NHL Entry Draft shortly afterward.

Though Neely showed promise during his three seasons with Vancouver, he didn't blossom into a star until he was traded to the Bruins in 1986. The transaction was bittersweet for the big right-winger. Though he reached new personal-highs in nearly every statistical category and finished second to Ray Bourque in team scoring, both of his parents were diagnosed with cancer a few months into the season. "I go three thousand miles across the country and my career takes off, but my personal life falls apart," he recalled sadly. "It teaches you an awful lot about your priorities, about what really counts."[41] After losing his parents to the disease, he founded the Cam Neely Foundation for Cancer Care, which has raised tens of millions in funds to support patients and their families over the years.

Aptly describing Neely's style of play, one sportswriter wrote that he was "the ultimate power forward of his time. His hands were as soft as a feather when he handled the puck yet hard as a rock when he handled an enemy."[42] Neely had a soldier's mentality when it came to hockey, sacrificing his body for the good of the team. Opponents were wary about going into the corners after the puck when Neely was in pursuit. And anyone who challenged him to a fight got all that they could handle. Over the years, Neely outpunched the game's toughest competitors, including Ulf Samuelson, Lindy Ruff and Adam Burt. In one of the defining games of his career, Neely took an Allen Pedersen slapshot to the head, opening a gash that later required 16 stitches. After receiving medical attention, he returned to the ice and got into a fight with Canadiens winger Shayne Corson, re-opening the wound. Neely later admitted it was a foolish thing to do, though it cemented his status as a hockey god in Boston.

Including the 36 he netted in his Bruins debut, Neely compiled a string of five consecutive 30-goal efforts. He made four straight All-Star appearances and reached the 50-goal plateau in back-to-back campaigns—a rare feat. His contributions helped guide the Bruins to a pair of berths in the Stanley Cup finals. Though the B's lost both times to the powerful Edmonton Oilers, it was no fault of Neely's as he added a total of 45 playoff points in those two seasons. He was over a point per game in seven trips to the postseason with Boston.

During the '91-'92 campaign, a borderline dirty hit by Penguins defenseman Ulf Samuelsson left Neely with a debilitating knee injury. He played just nine games that year and 13 the following season. He returned to form in '93, putting up 50 goals in 49 games. His performance earned him the Masterton Trophy. Marveling at the accomplishment, a writer from the *Boston Globe* remarked: "He persevered. He scored. He lived to play a game he sometimes thought was over for him and regained his status as the game's most potent and feared power forward."[43]

Unfortunately for Neely, the injuries kept coming. In '94, he lost a chunk of his finger after receiving a hard slash during a game against New Jersey. He returned to action soon afterward but later tore the collateral ligament in his right knee. Though he missed nearly a third of the season, he led the league in game-winning goals that year. A degenerative hip condition eventually put him out of action for good in 1996. He was only 31 years old when he retired.

Though his playing days were behind him, his hockey career was far from over. In 2007, he was named Bruins VP. He ascended to the team presidency three years later. As of 2021, the B's had made three appearances in the Stanley Cup finals during Neely's front office tenure. Recognized for his contributions to the sport, he received the Lester Patrick Award, which is given annually for outstanding service to hockey in the United States. He is currently enshrined at the Hockey Hall of Fame in Toronto.

GLEN MURRAY
(1992–1995/2001–2008)

Growing up in Bridgewater, Nova Scotia, Murray competed in multiple sports. Not only did he excel at hockey, but he also showed promise as a swimmer and high-jumper. As he got older, his 6-foot-3, 220-pound frame slowed him down a bit. During his time in the NHL, his skating style was described by multiple sources as lumbering. Still, he managed to become one of the Bruins' top point producers for several seasons.

Murray got his junior hockey experience with the Sudbury Wolves of the Ontario Hockey League. Entering the 2019 campaign, the Wolves had the longest championship drought of any team in the OHL. They made three first-round playoff exits during Murray's tenure. But in spite their postseason failures, Murray ended up as Boston's first round choice in the '91 entry draft.

Murray joined the Bruins at the tail-end of the '91-'92 regular season. He put up four points in five games, earning a spot on the playoff roster. The B's made it through two rounds before losing to the Penguins in the conference finals. Murray scored four goals and added a pair of assists along the way.

After spending a majority of the '92-'93 campaign with Providence, Murray assumed full-time status in Boston the following season. Because of his imposing size, he was expected to be a successor to Cam Neely. When he failed to dominate the opposition as Neely had in his prime, the Bruins traded him to Pittsburgh. A subsequent trade to the L.A. Kings in March of '97 altered the trajectory of his career.

A middling offensive player in Pittsburgh, Murray had a breakout year with L.A. during the '97-'98 campaign, reaching personal highs in goals (29) and assists (31). He had another outstanding season in '99–2000, finishing third in team scoring behind Luc Robitaille and Ziggy Palffy. Feeling that Murray had finally "arrived," the Bruins reacquired him in a four-player deal shortly into the 2001 campaign. For the next six seasons, Murray would figure prominently into the Bruins offensive scheme.

Appearing on a line with consummate play-maker Joe Thornton, Murray reached the pinnacle of his career, recording back-to-back 40 goal seasons. He added 32 goals in '03-'04, making his second straight All-Star appearance. Commenting on Murray's remarkable skills, former coach Jacques Demers said: "There's a guy who never cheated the system. He brought the maximum of his abilities and was a very, very respected hockey player.... He wasn't the greatest skater, but he could score from anywhere."[44]

Murray averaged 34 goals and 30 assists per year from 2001 to 2007. But the strain of 14 NHL seasons began to take its toll. Battling hip problems and various foot ailments, he was forced out of action after the '07-'08 campaign. He was placed on waivers the following season.

Finished as a player, Murray landed a job as a development consultant with the L.A. Kings. By then, his right foot was in rough shape after multiple surgeries and he was unable to actually take the ice with the young prospects he was working with. Addressing the problem, members of the Kings staff designed a special skate for him. "I thank them every day for helping me out and getting me back on the ice," he told a writer. "I'm not going to out-skate anyone—that's for sure," he added jokingly.[45] Murray's hard work and dedication were recognized in 2018, when he was promoted to director of player development for the Kings.

STEVE HEINZE
(1991–2000)

Born in Lawrence, Massachusetts, Heinze grew up in North Andover and played a majority of his hockey career in New England. After scoring 105 points for Lawrence Academy—a prestigious boarding school located in Groton—he became a member of the Boston College Eagles. Paired with center David Emma and winger Marty McInnis, Heinze earned All-American honors during the 1989-'90 season. The line came to be known as the "HEM Line" with Emma, Heinze and McInnis finishing first, second and third respectively in Hockey East scoring that year. Emma made brief NHL appearances over the course of five seasons while McInnis forged a 12-year career. Heinze didn't fare so poorly himself, remaining at the game's highest level for over a decade.

Confident in Heinze's skill-set, the Bruins selected him in the third round of the 1988 Entry Draft. After a stint with Team USA, he was called-up near the end of the '91 campaign. He wanted to wear the number 57 in reference to the popular brand of ketchup, but the Bruins politely denied the request. In his NHL debut, Heinze scored seven points in 14 games then added three postseason assists, strengthening his chances of earning a permanent roster spot. He became a full-time member of the B's the following year.

A fast skater, Heinze became a valuable asset on penalty kills, scoring eight short-handed goals in a five-year span. He played primarily on the Bruins' third line and his high energy level earned him a reputation as a grinder. He was a virtual stranger to the penalty box, never accruing more than 54 penalty minutes in any season. He averaged just 30 minutes per year over portions of nine campaigns with Boston.

In 1996-'97, Heinze was limited to 30 games with knee and abdominal injuries. He came back strong the following year with his best offensive season to that point, netting 26 goals. His efforts eventually caught the attention of the Columbus Blue Jackets, who claimed him in the 2000 Expansion Draft. During the Jackets inaugural season, Heinze finished third in team scoring. Instead of rewarding him with tenure, Columbus executives shipped him to Buffalo near season's end as part of a youth movement. He finished the year with 27 goals and 27 assists—the highest marks of his career.

In 2001, Heinze signed with the L.A. Kings as a free agent. He was among the club's top scorers that season. He was off to a decent start the following year before suffering a concussion on a vicious hit by winger Brad May, who was suspended for his actions. Heinze returned to action briefly, sustaining a second concussion on a hard check by Jody Shelley of Columbus. The 230-pound Shelley ran up a league-leading total of 249 penalty minutes that season. His hit ultimately ended Heinze's career. After absorbing the blow, Heinze finished the game, but knew something was terribly wrong. "I was scared," he recalled. "I couldn't think. I didn't know what was going on."[46]

For the next three years, Heinze suffered from extreme lethargy and recurring headaches. He spent a majority of his time in bed or on his couch. Though most of the symptoms eventually faded, he has experienced ongoing memory lapses. Upon leaving hockey behind, he moved to Santa Barbara to raise his two children. Wary of what happened to him, he hasn't pressured his kids into playing hockey. "We push the books harder than we push athletics," he told a reporter in 2016.[47] Doing his part to battle post-concussive syndrome, Heinze placed his name on the Brain Donation Registry.

Heinze has served as an instructor at youth hockey camps since his retirement. He returned to the ice along with some of his old teammates during the 2016 Bruins Alumni Game, which was held at Gillette Stadium in Foxboro. Interviewed after the game, he admitted that he missed the thrill of NHL action. Hampered by injuries in three of his eight complete seasons in Boston, he still managed to collect 239 points as a Bruin.

DAVID PASTRNAK
(2014–PRESENT)

Pastrnak was born in Havirov, which is among the largest cities in the Moravian-Silesian Region of the Czech Republic. He lost his father to cancer when he was in his teens and has credited his dad for giving him the inspiration to become a professional hockey player. As of 2021, his career was off to a magnificent start.

In 2011-'12, Pastrnak led the Czech under–18 league with 41 goals and 68 points. He later joined the Czech national team, skating in multiple international tournaments. Entering the 2021 campaign, he had been honored with the Golden Hockey Stick (given annually to the top Czech player) in four consecutive seasons. Other prominent countrymen to win the award include Jaromir Jagr, Dominik Hasek and David Krecji.

Selected by the Bruins in the first round of the 2014 Entry Draft, Pastrnak attended camp that year and was assigned to Providence. After collecting 28 points in 25 AHL games, he was called to Boston. He has remained a staple in the Bruins lineup ever since.

Pastrnak's abundant offensive skills became evident early on, but he was a bit under-sized at 170 pounds. Larger opponents quickly learned that they could push him off the puck. Responding to the challenge, he worked hard to add some muscle and upgrade his physical game. Those efforts paid great dividends.

From 2016 through 2019, Pastrnak's point production placed him among Boston's elite. He set a team record for most goals by the age of 23 (passing Barry Pederson) and was also the youngest Bruin to become a 30-goal scorer on three occasions. His four goals against Anaheim on October 14, 2019, tied another Bruins franchise record. In response to those accomplishments, Ken Campbell of *The Hockey News* referred to him as "the man with the golden stick."[48]

Pastrnak brings a lot of energy to the Bruins bench. He is well-liked by teammates, who refer to him as "Pasta" not only because it's a shortened version of his name but also because it's his favorite food. Showcasing his jovial personality, he was featured in a series of comedic Dunkin' Donuts TV commercials. In one ad, he carried an iced coffee to the penalty box and taunted an official: "Hey, ref—check your voice mail! You missed some calls!"[49]

In reality, Pastrnak is noted for his clean play. During his first five NHL seasons, he averaged just 26 penalty minutes per year. But he has been known to act out of character on occasion. In 2015-'16, he was suspended for an illegal hit on Rangers defenseman Dan Girardi. And in March of 2018, he recorded a "Gordie Howe Hat Trick," getting a goal, an assist and a major fighting penalty (the first of his career) against the Tampa Bay Lightning.

A creature of habit, Pastrnak is particular about the way he prepares for games. During one productive streak, he got in a habit of using three strands of white tape on the top of his stick and three strands on the bottom. Explaining his ritualistic behavior, he told a reporter: "I don't like to change things that are working."[50] Whatever the underlying cause, he received Boston's Seventh Player Award in 2015 and 2017. He was named MVP of the 2020 All-Star Game in spite of his squad's loss to the Pacific Division. In the 2019 All-Star showcase, he won the accuracy shooting competition.

A hand injury sustained in a fall following a Bruins team function kept Pastrnak out of action for well over a month during the 2018-'19 campaign and limited his effectiveness in the playoffs. He got off to a hot start the following season, compiling a 13-game point streak from October 8 through November 5. At the time of the coronavirus shut down in 2020, "Pasta" was leading the league with 48 goals. Singing his praises, a writer from Boston.com proclaimed: "Pastrnak has the perfect combination of skill, speed, strength, balance and ice vision. He deserves his place amongst the NHL elite."[51] Barring a major injury, Pasta may very well be destined for even bigger and better things.

3

Left-Wingers

RED BEATTIE
(1930–1937)

Nicknamed for the color of his hair, John "Red" Beattie was born in Ibstock, England—a small village located in North West Leicestershire. During his formative years, Beattie's family moved to Edmonton, Alberta, where he developed an affinity for hockey. He ascended to the senior level with the Edmonton Superiors and turned pro with the Vancouver Lions of the PCHL. Beattie's contributions helped the Lions to consecutive league championships in 1929 and 1930.

Though the Rangers initially won the rights to Beattie's contract, Bruins GM Art Ross was determined to sign him. He shelled out a reported sum of $25,000—an enormous figure in the Depression Era—to bring Beattie to Boston along with defenseman Joe Jerwa. In his rookie season, Beattie became on overnight sensation, making 32 appearances and gathering 21 points.

Before the start of the '31-'32 campaign, Beattie broke his leg. He appeared in just one game that year as Boston placed last in the American Division. Beattie worked hard to get back into playing shape and, by 1932, he was ready for action. In fact, over the next five years, he didn't miss a single regular season game—an amazing accomplishment considering the roughness of the era.

Beattie was a bit under-sized at 5-foot-9, but he played a very physical game. With exceptional speed, he was often asked to shadow opponents on top lines to neutralize their effectiveness. His stick-handling skills made him a reliable playmaker and penalty killer. Often eclipsed by the brighter stars around him (such as Dit Clapper, Cooney Weiland and Eddie Shore), his durability and persistence were greatly appreciated by fans.

Beattie reached his prime between 1932 and 1936, finishing among the Bruins top scorers every year. His best offensive showing came in '35-'36, when he led the club with 32 points (14 goals/18 assists). Despite his tireless efforts, the Bruins never made it past the first round of the playoffs during his time in Boston.

In the summer of '37, Beattie came down with a serious case of the flu and wound up in the hospital. He returned to action that season, but slumped badly. Fans in Boston began booing him as team executives gradually lost their patience. In December of that year, Beattie was traded to the Red Wings. At the time of the transaction, he held a rank of number 5 among Bruins forwards in all-time point production. The change of scenery failed to bring him out of his offensive doldrums and he ended up in New York, where he finished his NHL career.

Beattie is on a very short list of players from the United Kingdom to experience success in the NHL during the 1930s. Aside from winger Tom Anderson, who won a Hart trophy with the Brooklyn Americans, Beattie was the most offensively productive member of that group. After falling from the NHL ranks, he played at the semi-pro level for two seasons. He died in 1990 at the age of 83.

WOODY DUMART
(1935–1954)

Dumart's name is inextricably linked to the linemates who helped make him famous—Milt Schmidt and Bobby Bauer. The trio carried Boston to Stanley Cup titles in 1939 and 1941, averaging well over a hundred points per season in a seven-year span. While Schmidt and Bauer were the playmakers, Dumart was the most physical of the unit, digging in the corners and picking up rebounds in front of the net.

Red Beattie is on a short list of British-born players to be successful in the NHL. Extremely durable, he went five straight seasons in Boston without missing a single game. Courtesy Boston Public Library, Leslie Jones Collection.

Dumart was born in the primarily-German community of Kitchener, Ontario, which was known as Berlin prior to World War I. He was named after U.S. president Woodrow Wilson. As a boy he lived about a mile from Schmidt. Bauer lived across the Grand River in Waterloo and the youths became acquainted playing local sports. Though all three skated for the Kitchener Greenshirts at the junior level, they did not appear on a line together until they turned pro.

Fairly large for the era at 6-foot-1, 190 pounds, Dumart began his career as a defenseman. He had a breakout season with the Greenshirts in '34–'35, netting 17 goals and adding 11 assists in 17 games. He was signed by the Bruins and sent to Boston's Can-Am League affiliate, where he was converted to the left-wing position. The transition was not an overnight success and Dumart spent a significant portion of time in the minors during the '35 and '36 campaigns.

Schmidt, Bauer and Dumart became linemates while playing for the Providence Reds of the American Hockey League. Coach Albert Leduc, a former defenseman with the Canadiens, referred to them as the "Sauerkraut Line." A writer from the *Toronto Star* remarked that the nickname was created "in recognition of a delicacy that casts its enticing aroma over Kitchener."[1]

The "Krauts" (as they came to be known in short-form) stuck together through thick and thin, sharing a one-room apartment in Brookline, Massachusetts. When contract-time arrived, they negotiated as a collective unit. In fact, Bruins GM Art Ross had no inclination to sign Milt Schmidt until Bauer and Dumart persuaded him to do so. During the Stanley Cup years of '39 and '41, the dynamic trio scored 203 collective points, adding 34 during the postseason.

Dumart typically ranked third among his linemates in scoring, but he was a clutch performer, leading the NHL in game-winning goals twice. He amassed 20 or more assists on four occasions, peaking at 28 in '46-'47. In spite of his physical play, he hardly ever went to the penalty box. His highest single-season total was 16 minutes. He was a Byng Trophy candidate twice, finishing second to Red Kelly of Detroit in 1951.

When World War II arrived, Dumart enlisted in the Canadian military with his "Kraut" pals. The threesome helped the Ottawa Air Force squad to an Allan Cup title in 1942. In all, Dumart lost three of his prime years to the war effort. Discharged in time for the '45 campaign, he surpassed both of his linemates in scoring that season, though Bauer and Schmidt played in fewer games.

After the Kitchener-based line was dissolved with the retirement of Bauer in '47, Dumart enjoyed several more productive seasons. When he reached his mid–30s, head coach Lynn Patrick began to use him as a utility forward. Dumart enjoyed playing a defensive-minded game and was happy to throw his body around for the good of the team. He retired in 1954 as the Bruins' all-time top-scoring left-winger. At the time of this writing, he was still among the top five.

Dumart retired to Needham, Massachusetts, living right next door to Schmidt. He stayed active with various charities and served as coach of the Bruins alumni squad. On his way to Ray Bourque's retirement in 2001, he experienced a heart episode. He was taken to the hospital and later died. He was 84 years old at the time.

Roy Conacher
(1938–1946)

In spite of his many accomplishments on the ice, Conacher shared the spotlight with his older brothers, Lionel and Charlie. Charlie, who played for three NHL clubs, became known as "The Big Bomber" in recognition of his goal-scoring prowess. Lionel won a pair of Stanley Cups with the Chicago Blackhawks and Montreal Maroons. All three Conacher brothers were elected to the Hockey Hall of Fame, becoming the first trio of siblings to be enshrined.

The Conacher family included 10 children—four boys and six girls. Hailing from Toronto, they came of age in Davenport, a financially repressed neighborhood northwest of the city's downtown area. Benjamin, the family matriarch, was a teamster whose earnings were scarcely enough to support the clan. All of the Conachers were encouraged by their principal at Jesse Ketchum School to participate in sports. Nearly half of them excelled.

As a boy, Roy had no aspirations of forging a career on the ice. In fact, he was far more interested in softball. But it was hard to escape the allure of hockey growing up in Toronto. During his teen years, Roy sold programs at Maple Leaf Gardens on game nights. He logged his junior hockey experience with the Toronto Nationals. After two mediocre seasons, he had a breakout year in '35-'36, leading the Ontario Hockey Association with 12 goals. His efforts lifted the club to a victory over the Saskatoon Wesleys in the Memorial Cup finals.

Signed by the Bruins, Conacher failed his initial tryout. In 1937, B's head coach Art Ross assigned him to the Kirkland Lake Hargreaves of the Northern Ontario Hockey Association. He had a spectacular year, earning an invitation to Boston the following season.

Conacher began his Bruins career on a line with Pat McReavy and Mel Hill. They failed to generate much offense and, when Hall of Famer Bill Cowley returned from an injury, he was inserted as a replacement for McReavy. The new pairing produced dramatic results as Conacher led the NHL with 26 goals during the regular season. He remained productive throughout the playoffs. In Game 4 of the Stanley Cup finals, he lit the lamp twice, putting the Bruins on the verge of a long overdue championship. In Game 5, he netted the series-clincher. Years later, he remarked that his Game 4 performance was the highlight of his playing days. "It wasn't so much that I was fortunate to score," he said, "but because Charlie and Lionel were in the audience."[2] The season might have been even more magical had Concacher come away with the Calder Trophy, but teammate Frank Brimsek's 10 shutouts and miserly 1.56 goals against average garnered more support from sportswriters.

The 1930s and '40s were a violent era for hockey. Conacher was big enough to handle himself at 6-foot-1, 180 pounds, but avoided fighting unless absolutely necessary. His highly accurate shot made him a menace to opposing goalies. He finished among the NHL's top 10 in even-strength goals during each of his nine full seasons. His 37 points in '41-'42 led the Bruins.

With the outbreak of World War II, Conacher joined the Royal Canadian Air Force. He was shipped to England and put to work as a physical training instructor. He also skated for the Durham air base hockey team. By the time he was discharged, he had sacrificed three of his prime seasons to military duty.

In 1946, Conacher was traded to Detroit for right-winger Joe Carveth. Carveth scored 21 goals in his Bruins debut, but the rest of his career was less remarkable. In contrast, Conacher netted a career-high 30 goals in '46 (second only to Maurice Richard of the Canadiens) and remained a scoring threat until his final NHL season.

Before the '47 campaign, Conacher got into a salary dispute with Detroit GM Jack Adams. He was traded to the Rangers, but refused to report, nullifying the deal. Two weeks later, he came to terms with the Blackhawks. The Hawks never made it to the playoffs during Conacher's five-year residency, but at least he carried memories of two championship seasons with Boston in '39 and '41. The highlight of his Chicago career came in '48-'49, when he won the Art Ross Trophy as the NHL's points leader.

During Conacher's last few seasons, he lived in Midland, Ontario, which is located in the picturesque Georgian Bay 30,000 Islands region. He remained there after his NHL retirement and coached Midland's junior hockey team to a provincial championship. He later moved to Victoria, British Columbia. He died of cancer in

1984 and followed his brothers into the Hall of Fame posthumously in 1998. Several of Conacher's nephews played in the NHL.

HERB CAIN
(1939–1946)

Cain was among the many players of hockey's golden era who deserved a much better fate. Two years after setting a new NHL record for points in a season, he held out for more money. This was not a common practice at the time and Bruins GM Art Ross (in one of the low points of his career) buried Cain in Boston's farm system. Completing an ignominious end to a very bright career, Cain remains the only eligible scoring champion of his era to be excluded from the Hall of Fame.

Born and raised in Newmarket, Ontario, Cain made his junior hockey debut with the Newmarket Redmen in 1931. He moved quickly up the ranks, ascending to the NHL with the Montreal Maroons in 1933. The Maroons captured two championships during their 14-year existence and Cain was a major contributor to the latter effort. Skating on the club's "Green Line" with Bob Gracie and Gus Marker, he gathered 27 points during the '34-'35 regular season then helped the Maroons eliminate the Black Hawks, Rangers and Maple Leafs on the road to the Stanley Cup.

Traded to the Canadiens in 1938, Cain placed fourth in team scoring, but couldn't prevent the squad from finishing in sixth place. He ended up being shipped to Boston the following year in exchange for forwards Charlie Sands and Ray Getliffe. The transaction proved beneficial to both clubs as all three players maintained steady production over the next several seasons.

Cain has been described as an "enthusiastic and gifted skater."[3] On occasion, that enthusiasm got him into trouble. While playing for the Maroons, head coach Tommy Gorman decided he didn't want players skating behind the net at the start of offensive rushes. To discourage the habit, he roped off the end boards during a practice session. The ambitious and energetic Cain, who was often among the first to hit the ice, didn't see the ropes until it was too late. He ended up lying flat on his back—unconscious but not seriously injured.

In his Bruins debut, Cain proved his worth to the team with seven game-winning goals—tops in the NHL. He added six game-winners during the Bruins successful Stanley Cup run in '40-'41. Two of those goals came during the playoffs.

Cain was among a select group of players who stuck around during the war years. He made the most of a diluted talent pool, averaging 26 goals and 22 assists per year between 1942 and 1946. He reached the peak of his career in '43, claiming the Art Ross Trophy with an unprecedented total of 82 points. He finished his career with seven hat tricks, six of them with Boston.

Before the start of the '46-'47 campaign, Cain got into a contract dispute. Ross decided to "punish" him by demoting him to the Bruins' AHL affiliate in Hershey. Other teams inquired about Cain's services, but Ross had planned for that eventuality by imposing a no-trade policy. Instead of rebelling against the system, Cain played four full seasons with the Hershey Bears, collecting 190 points in 198 games. His reliable offense helped carry the club to a Calder Cup championship in 1947.

Reflecting on the raw deal he was dealt by the Bruins, an embittered Cain told a sportswriter: "The NHL was like a little house league then. The six owners simply made up their own rules, called each other up and made the deals, and settled things among themselves. The players had no clout, no say in anything."[4]

Cain's story took another turn for the worse when he was diagnosed with Hodgkin's Disease in 1955. On a positive note, he agreed to experimental treatments and survived for another 30 years. He made a living as a sheet metal worker when his days on the ice were finished. He died in 1982 at the age of 69. Members of his family lobbied strenuously for his election to the Hall of Fame, but as of 2020, those efforts had produced no results.

Vic Stasiuk
(1955–1961)

Hailing from Alberta, Stasiuk got his earliest hockey experience playing pick-up games on an outdoor rink in his hometown of Lethbridge. He remembered being inspired by a one-armed rink attendant, who would skate with the local kids in spite of his handicap. "Without two arms for balance, hockey is really tough," said Stasiuk. "And there he was, up against a lot of youngsters, just for the love of it."[5]

Stasiuk grew to love the sport himself, joining the Lethbridge Native Sons junior hockey club at the age of 17. Signed by the Blackhawks, he began his minor league career with the USHL-affiliated Kansas City Pla-Mors. He was called to Chicago during the '49-'50 campaign then traded to the Red Wings the following season.

Though Stasiuk never captured a Stanley Cup during his years in Boston, he won a pair of them with Detroit—in '52 and '55. The Wings were loaded with talent in those days and Stasiuk spent a significant period of time in the minors. When he scored 80 points in 48 WHL games during the '52-'53 campaign, it became evident to Wings executives that they couldn't keep him in their farm system for much longer.

Stasiuk got his break in 1955, when he was traded to the Bruins in a blockbuster deal involving eight other players. He led the team in scoring during his Boston debut, later joining the fabled "Uke Line" with Johnny Bucyk and Bronco Horvath. Keeping pace with his talented linemates, Stasiuk reached the 20-goal mark in four straight seasons. He collected no fewer than 30 assists every year from '57 to '61.

The garrulous Stasiuk was fond of chatting with opposing players and referees to distract them. He was also an incorrigible bench jockey, keeping up the dialog when he wasn't on the ice. One day, an opponent who had heard more than enough snapped at him: "What are you leading the league in—conversation?"[6] During his days in Detroit, Stasiuk drew praise from Gordie Howe, who told a reporter: "I don't know where [Stasiuk] gets all the energy from, but he sure has a lot of pep and go."[7]

Stasiuk's best offensive season came in '59-'60, when he gathered 29 goals and 39 assists. Bucyk and Horvath added 132 points, but the Bruins failed to make the playoffs. The "Uke Line" was broken up and Stasiuk's production dropped off sharply. Multiple sources reported that the disbanding of the line was due to poor defense—a claim that Stasiuk objected to. His disenchantment eventually led to a trade back to

Detroit in January of 1961. Skating on a line with Gordie Howe, he gathered 23 points in the same number of games to close out the season.

During the '62-'63 campaign, Stasiuk was demoted to the minors. It turned out to be a blessing in disguise as he aspired to the position of player-coach with the AHL's Pittsburgh Hornets. He finished his playing career with the Memphis Wings in '66 and continued coaching for the Quebec Aces, leading them to consecutive Calder Cup finals appearances.

In 1969, Stasiuk returned to the NHL as head coach of the Philadelphia Flyers. The team missed the playoffs in his first season at the helm but made it to the quarter-finals in '70-'71. It wasn't enough to save his job as Philly GM Keith Allen dismissed him from his duties. "Personally I think he's a dedicated guy," Allen told an Associated Press reporter. "I want him to stay in the organization."[8] Stasiuk turned down Allen's offer to join the Flyers scouting staff, becoming head coach of the California Golden Seals instead.

Considered a player's coach, Stasiuk was tough but fair. He made a point of skating with the team in practice. "I never ask them to do what I wouldn't do myself," he said, "and when I give them a chance to take some whacks at me in practice, I think it helps them work out that anger they might have."[9] Stasiuk could be fiery at times, directing streams of profanity at referees. The Seals were not enamored with his style and let him go after the '71-'72 campaign. He took over the Vancouver Canucks the following season, but was dismissed after the club failed to make the playoffs.

Upon leaving the NHL, Stasiuk coached at the junior hockey level. He was elected to the Alberta Sports Hall of Fame in 2009. Reflecting on his playing days, he offered the following advice to posterity: "You have to have enthusiasm and a love of this game to play ... if you're not enthusiastic, you've got no business out on the ice."[10]

JOHNNY BUCYK
(1957–1978)

Born in Edmonton to Ukrainian parents, Bucyk lived in the poorest section of Alberta. He lost his father at the age of 11 and worked in a drugstore with his older brother, Bill, to help the family stay afloat. Without much money to spare, Johnny and his brother settled for makeshift hockey equipment, stuffing old magazines in their socks for protection. On occasion, they even used frozen horse manure in place of pucks.

During his Pee-Wee Hockey years, Bucyk demonstrated a passion for the sport, but his skating ability was sorely lacking. By the time he reached the junior level, there was still room for improvement. While playing for the Edmonton Oil Kings, he was ordered by head coach Ken McAuley (a former NHL goalie) to take figure skating classes. Bucyk felt that figure skating was effeminate but conceded. The practice paid off as he soon became one of the team's brightest stars. During the '53-'54 campaign, he collected 67 points in 33 games, earning a promotion to the Edmonton Flyers of the Western Hockey League.

In Bucyk's only full season with the Flyers, he netted 30 goals and added 58 assists, helping the team to a league championship. By 1955, he was skating for the

Nicknamed "Chief," Johnny Bucyk is among the Bruins' all-time leaders in nearly every major statistical category. He had 88 game-winning goals during his career. He is pictured here fulfilling his duties as Bruins ambassador. Derek Sanderson is on the left and Bobby Orr is next to him. Courtesy Dan4th on Visualhunt/CC BY.

Detroit Red Wings. A first-round playoff exit in '57 inspired the Wings to make some changes. Bucyk was traded to the Bruins in exchange for Hall of Fame goaltender Terry Sawchuk. Both players enjoyed more than a decade of success in the wake of the transaction.

In Boston, Bucyk joined center Bronco Horvath and winger Vic Stasiuk on what would come to be known as "The Uke Line." The moniker was a reference to Stasiuk and Bucyk's Ukrainian roots. Horvath was actually of Hungarian descent, but he liked the nickname and indulged the press. Bucyk's primary objective was to dig the puck out of the corners and feed it to linemates. Horvath became known as "The Colonel" for the way he parked himself in front of the net and shouted at Bucyk to chase down the puck. Bucyk was assigned the handle of "Chief" because (according to Horvath) he used his stick like a tomahawk to snare the puck and center it. "The Uke Line" skated together for nearly four years as Bucyk gathered 30 or more assists in three of those seasons. By 1961, Horvath and Stasiuk were gone and the Bruins were in a rebuilding phase.

Though Bucyk put up impressive statistics every year, Boston remained absent from the playoffs for eight consecutive seasons. With the addition of Bobby Orr, Phil Esposito and Wayne Cashman (among others), the team reversed its fortunes. During the early '70s, Bucyk was placed on a line with Fred Stanfield and Johnny McKenzie. As a result of the pairing, Bucyk's numbers soared to new heights. He reached a personal high of 51 goals during the '70-'71 campaign and added 46 playoff points in a three-year span as the Bruins won a pair of Stanley Cups. During the 1970 championship run, the B's honored Bucyk (who served as an alternate captain) by allowing him to be the first to hoist the cup at the Boston Garden.

Bucyk was a nervous type who became extremely jittery before games. By his own admission, he used to "cough and choke" in the dressing room before taking the ice. It became a running joke that, if Bucyk reported feeling "lousy," it meant he was going to have a good game.[11]

Among the heavier players of the era at 220 pounds, Bucyk was a master of the hip-check. "I threw my weight around and always played a physical game," he recalled. "The other players respected me because they knew if they had their head down, I'd hit them pretty hard. I just tried to stay out of the penalty box."[12] He did a pretty fair job of that, averaging less than 20 penalty minutes per season during his long career. In acknowledgment of his fair play, he was awarded the Byng Trophy twice.

Often used on power plays, Bucyk routinely positioned himself off the left post. He had a very quick release and a strong back-handed shot. He was also an accurate, crisp passer. "He could thread the needle with the pass," said teammate Brad Park. "He could put it through your skates, under your stick, over your stick, and he'd just put that big body between you and the puck, protect it, shovel it off."[13]

Bucyk had 30 or more assists during 17 seasons and remains the Bruins all-time goals leader with 545. A remarkable 16 percent of those goals were game-winners, making him one of the most clutch performers in Bruins history. Despite his iconic status in Boston, he was always very modest about his abilities. "I've thought of myself as a spear-carrier, not a star really," he told one writer. "I'm not a glamour guy and I've just gone along getting what I could out of every game."[14]

Bucyk played beyond his 42nd birthday. He gained entry into the Hockey Hall of Fame in 1981. After his retirement, he remained affiliated with the Bruins as a broadcaster and front office advisor. He also served as director of the team's road services. In 2011, the B's honored him again by engraving his name on a third Stanley Cup. He was in his 53rd year of service to the organization at the time. As of 2019, he was still listed as a Bruins team ambassador.

WAYNE CASHMAN
(1964–1983)

One element of being a good hockey player is knowing your own limitations. Wayne Cashman once told a reporter: "I knew at an early age I'd never be a fifty-goal scorer so I spent my career doing what had to be done."[15] Cashman carried that lunch-pail philosophy into more than a thousand games with the Bruins. And by the time his career was finished, he had two Stanley Cup rings to show for it.

Born in Kingston, Ontario, Cashman led his midget team to a championship in 1961. He later joined the Oshawa Generals, sharing the ice with Bruins icon Bobby Orr. Cashman spent four seasons with Oshawa before ascending to the professional level with the Oklahoma City Blazers. By 1969, he held a permanent roster spot in Boston, where he would remain for the next 13 seasons.

Widely known as a grinder, Cashman always yielded the spotlight to the higher-profile stars around him. Hall of Famer Gerry Cheevers commented: "[Cashman] didn't have the flair of a Bobby Hull, but championships aren't won only by the flashy guys. They're won in the corners and along the boards."[16] That's exactly where Cashman made his living—digging for pucks, protecting teammates and even brawling when necessary. It has been said that, during the era of the "Big Bad Bruins," Cashman was the biggest and baddest. "You could see a guy go into a corner after the puck, and just before he got to it, he stopped and flinched when he saw Cash," remarked former Calder Trophy winner Derek Sanderson.[17]

A policeman on the ice, Cashman once said he would match any transgression committed by opponents, even if it included spearing. He traded fists with the roughest players of the era, including legendary Flyers bruiser Dave Schultz. Schultz later claimed that, during one such encounter, Cashman literally threatened to cut his eyes out. As could only be expected, Cashman served a fair share of penalties, accruing no fewer than a hundred minutes in four straight seasons.

More than just a one-dimensional player, Cashman put forth his best offensive effort in '73-'74, gathering 89 points. He had at least 30 assists in nine seasons, twice reaching the 50-mark. In 16 trips to the playoffs, he scored 31 goals and added 57 helpers. He led postseason skaters with a 29.4 shooting percentage during the B's championship season of 1970. As of 2021, he held a rank of number 7 among Boston's all-time point-producers.

During his first few years with the Bruins, Cashman was quiet and reserved. But as he matured, he assumed a leadership role, serving as captain for six seasons. During the '77-'78 campaign, Boston goalie Ron Grahame remarked: "Cash is a real team player. On the ice he's leading by example and off the ice, he's more vocal than anyone else, yapping at us to keep it going."[18] Cashman could be very supportive, but he wasn't afraid to offer criticism if he felt it would help a player and the team.

Though Cashman was all business when it came to hockey, he had a unique sense of humor away from the rink. In an often-repeated anecdote, he was taken into custody by Massachusetts police for a driving infraction one day. After granting him his obligatory phone call, officers at the station were taken off guard when a delivery man from a local Chinese restaurant showed up with a large bag of food for Cashman shortly afterward.

Following his retirement as a player in 1983, Cashman served as an assistant coach with the Rangers, Lightning, Bruins and Sharks. In 1997, he finally ascended to the head coach position with the Philadelphia Flyers. In spite of the team's respectable 32–20–9 record, he was demoted to assistant status again as part of an organizational restructuring movement.

DON MARCOTTE
(1965–1982)

Marcotte was born in Asbestos, Quebec—a small town named for the material that was once mined there. The area has a snowy period lasting more than six months and Marcotte experienced a fair share of glacial weather. The roads were often frozen during the winter and he routinely traveled to school on skates.

Like most boys from Quebec, Marcotte developed an interest in hockey before he became a teenager. He played at the junior level with the Niagara Falls Flyers, participating in the squad's successful Memorial Cup bid in 1965. His journey through the lower ranks lasted several years. He was called to Boston on three separate occasions while playing for the Hershey Bears. He earned a permanent roster spot with the Bruins during the '69-'70 campaign.

Marcotte reached the peak of his Bruins career early on. Skating on Boston's third line with Ed Westfall and Derek Sanderson, he helped the club breeze through all three rounds of the 1970 playoffs with a 12–2 record. His line contributed 27 postseason points that year as the B's ended a ponderous Stanley Cup drought. The memories had scarcely faded before they claimed another Cup in '72. "I was lucky," Marcotte told a reporter. "I won two in my first three years and thought I was going to get all kinds of them. [But] that was it."[19] Though the Bruins would wait nearly four decades to hoist Lord Stanley's coveted prize again, the rest of Marcotte's career was remarkable nonetheless.

Known for his solid body-checks and two-way play, Marcotte carried a well-deserved reputation as a grinder. "I would go up and fore-check and come back and back-check. That kept me going and I loved it. I had a job to do and I took pride in it," he said.[20] His hard style of play won him the respect of coach Don Cherry, who gushed: "No one knows the fundamentals of the game better than Don. If you were going to send a hockey player to Mars, it would be Marcotte. They could watch [him] play and manufacture perfect players. He skates, he checks and gets his share of goals. That's the perfect hockey player."[21]

One of Cherry's favorite strategies was to assign Marcotte to superstars like Bobby Hull and Guy Lafleur to curtail their production. Lafleur once said that Marcotte was the hardest checker he ever faced. And teammate Terry O'Reilly marveled at Marcotte's tenacity. "He never takes his eyes off of his winger and he never stops skating," said O'Reilly. "What he lacks in speed and finesse, he compensates for with hustle and disciplined play."[22]

Though Marcotte's peers were more apt to talk about his defense, there was another side to his game. He netted 20 or more goals during seven seasons, adding no fewer than 20 assists the same number of times. A potent threat on penalty-kills, he scored 21 short-handed goals during his Bruins career, giving him a rank of number 4 among the franchise leaders behind Brad Marchand, Rick Middleton and Derek Sanderson. Though he played hard, Marcotte never accrued more than 76 penalty minutes in any season. An asset to any line he appeared on, he retired with a plus/minus rating of (+) 191.

Marcotte is associated with one of the most unfortunate moments in Bruins history. On May 10, 1979, Boston was leading Montreal, 4–3, at the Forum with 2:34 remaining in Game 7 of the Stanley Cup semi-finals. During an awkwardly executed line change, referee John D'Amico noticed that the Bruins had too many men on the ice. Marcotte recalled that Boston had six skaters for five full seconds though he was not among them, having successfully returned to the bench before the call was made. Guy Lafleur scored on the ensuing power play to tie the game and Yvon Lambert clinched the series with an overtime goal. For

Marcotte and other members of the '78-'79 squad, it remains one of the most painful on-ice memories.

Marcotte's career continued undaunted. As he got older and wiser, he worked with young players to assist in their development. In particular, he worked closely with Steve Kasper on a penalty-killing unit. Owing much to Marcotte's guidance and support, Kasper quickly became one of the best defensive forwards in the NHL.

Marcotte settled in Massachusetts early in his career and helped raise four children there. After his NHL retirement in 1982, he played with the Bruins alumni team in charity games. He later became manager of the Boston Garden Club at TD Banknorth Garden. Reflecting on his prime years as a player, he said: "I am very proud of the style I played.... I thought hockey was played at both ends of the ice."[23]

Stan Jonathan
(1975–1983)

Though Stan Jonathan was renowned for his ability to pound opponents into submission, he didn't feel he should be characterized as a fighter. "We took care of our business," he said during a 2014 interview. "We took care of the Ricky Middletons and Jean Ratelles—our goal scorers—and we played as a team. That's the way the Bruins always were."[24]

Regardless of Jonathan's refusal to accept the label of "goon," it is an irrefutable fact that he was pretty handy with his fists. He demonstrated his pugnacity during his rookie year when he knocked tough-guy Keith Magnuson senseless in his first career fight. He later cemented his reputation as a man not to be trifled with during Game 4 of the 1978 Stanley Cup finals, when he rearranged Pierre Bouchard's face, leaving the Montreal defenseman (who was several inches taller and 30 pounds heavier) with a broken nose and shattered cheekbone.

A full-blooded member of the Tuscarora Tribe, Jonathan was the sixth child in a family of 14. He grew up on the Six Nations Reserve in Ontario. His clan struggled to make ends meet and Jonathan took a job as a high steel worker at the age of 16. He served as a rigger in the construction of apartment and office towers south of the Canadian border. Though he admitted to being nervous when he first started the job, he grew accustomed to working at high altitudes.

Jonathan spent his junior hockey seasons with the Peterborough Petes. He was discovered accidentally in 1975, when Harry Sinden and Don Cherry went to Oshawa to evaluate the skills of defenseman Doug Halward. Halward sustained an injury during the game and Cherry's attention was drawn to Jonathan instead. Sinden was not as impressed with Jonathan's performance and waited until the fifth round of the '75 Amateur Draft to sign him. Jonathan was sent to the Dayton Gems of the IHL. Within a year, he was skating for the Bruins.

To Jonathan's credit, he was not an entirely one-dimensional player. He could rack up the points when he was on a hot streak, but he also had periods in which he temporarily lost his scoring touch. At 5-foot-8, 175 pounds, he worked hard to gain the respect of opponents. One writer remarked that he "played the game like a human bowling ball. He loved to hit anything in sight and loved to get hit as well."[25]

Jonathan's intensity won over head coach Don Cherry, who wrote in one of his books: "Stanley reminded me of my pet dog, Blue, a bull terrier. They were both relatively small but enormously tough. I liked Stanley so much that I took a beautiful painting of Blue from home and had it hung directly above Jonathan's locker."[26]

During his rookie year, Jonathan ended up on a line with Jean Ratelle. He was in awe of Ratelle's skating ability and deceptive moves. Though it was Ratelle who put the puck in the net more often than not, Jonathan made his shots count that season—accruing a handsome shooting percentage of 23.9. He maintained that accuracy throughout his career, retiring with a lifetime mark of 18.8—a figure that would have placed him among the all-time NHL leaders had he taken enough shots to officially qualify.

Jonathan reached the peak of his offensive abilities in '77-'78, gathering 52 points (27 goals/25 assists). In recognition of his performance, he received Boston's Seventh Player Award. His aggressive style ultimately shortened his career as he missed significant portions of time in all but two of his six full NHL seasons. In spite of his frequent injuries, he had a knack for delivering in the clutch. His hat trick against Hall of Famer Ken Dryden in the '79 semi-finals forced a Game 7. The Bruins took the Canadiens to overtime at the Forum, but came out on the losing end, 5–4. Jonathan's efforts helped lift the B's to Stanley Cup finals appearances in consecutive seasons ('77 and '78).

In November of 1982, Jonathan was traded to the Penguins. He spent a significant portion of the season with the AHL-affiliated Baltimore Skipjacks. By '83, his career was more or less over, though he did play in one OHA game during the '86 campaign.

Jonathan has participated in various Bruins alumni events over the years. His retirement has been less than peaceful. In 2012, he was charged with criminal negligence in a hunting accident that left a man from Hamilton, Ontario, dead. While hunting on the Six Nations Reserve, Jonathan reportedly discharged his rifle from a roadway into a line of trees, accidentally killing a bow-hunter named Peter Kosid, who was not wearing any protective colors. Though the crown attorney ultimately dropped the charges, the case dragged on for several years.

RANDY BURRIDGE
(1985–1991)

Burridge was born and raised in Fort Erie, Ontario, which is located directly across the Niagara River from Buffalo. He grew up around the corner from Sabres winger Rick Martin. According to Burridge, he and his friends would knock on Martin's door constantly to pester him with questions. The seven-time All-Star was always very accommodating to neighborhood kids. It taught Burridge a valuable lesson he carried into his own career—to be gracious to fans.

Burridge started skating in a house league when he was 11 years old. He led his team to a championship in his first year and was picked for the All-Star team. He later joined the Fort Erie Meteors of the Golden Horseshoe Junior Hockey League. During the '82-'83 season, he collected 88 points in 42 games, earning a promotion to the Peterborough Petes. He was selected by the Bruins in the eighth round of the '85 Entry Draft and summoned to Boston that same year.

Burridge made 52 appearances in his Bruins debut, gathering 17 goals and 25 assists. His performance earned him Boston's Seventh Player Award. But his follow-up campaign was a disaster. After inadvertently failing to attend a practice session in L.A. one day, he was summoned to Harry Sinden's office, where he learned that he was being sent back down to Moncton. Atoning for his mistake, Burridge produced 67 points in 47 AHL games that season and never incurred another demotion during his Bruins career.

Growing up as a fan of the Canadiens, it was a major adjustment for Burridge to be on the opposite side of the storied rivalry. "As soon as I got drafted, the first year in Boston, the rivalry was huge," he recalled. "Petr Svoboda, Chris Chelios, I hated them. But then I found out ninety-nine percent of the players were great guys."[27]

As a boy, Burridge admired Flyers superstar Bobby Clarke, who was known for his toughness. Burridge was no slouch himself, grinding hard every game. Describing his high-energy style of play, a correspondent from *The Washington Post* wrote in 1993: "Burridge charge[s] into situations, churning his short, muscular legs fast enough to collect a loose puck in the corner, deny an opponent a scoring chance or gain position to register one of his 131 regular season National Hockey League goals or 159 assists."[28] For the record, Burridge significantly padded those totals by the time he retired.

Burridge's short, stocky frame inspired Bruins teammate Keith Crowder to saddle him with the nickname of "Stump." Not only did the moniker stick, but it gave rise to another expression—the "Stump Pump," which was used to describe the signature windmill-pump salute Burridge executed after cashing-in on scoring opportunities. During his junior hockey years, Burridge carried the handle of "Garbage" because he was so adept at grabbing loose pucks in front of the net and stuffing them in.

After being exiled to Moncton, Burridge enjoyed his best seasons in Boston. He collected 27 goals and 28 assists in '87-'88, adding 12 points during the B's road to the finals against Edmonton. He reached the pinnacle of his Bruins career the following season with 31 goals and 30 helpers—numbers good enough to win his second Seventh Player Award. He also received the Elizabeth C. Dufresne Trophy for outstanding performances in home games. When his offense dropped off sharply during the '90-'91 campaign, he was traded to the Capitals for winger Stephen Leach. Leach had a handful of productive seasons in Boston as Burridge continued to prosper in the nation's capital. He was off to an epic start in '91-'92 before blowing his knee out in the All-Star Game. He finished the season with 23 goals and 44 assists, but it was the beginning of the end.

Burridge played for three teams between 1994 and 1998. He had his last great season with the Sabres in '95-'96, claiming the team's Tim Horton Memorial Award (given to the club's unsung hero) and Punch Imlach Memorial Award (for dedication and leadership). He made his last NHL appearance in '97-'98. Not quite ready to hang up his skates yet, he played in the International Hockey League with the Las Vegas Thunder. He also appeared in 14 games for the Hannover Scorpions—a German-based team affiliated with the Oberliga—a third tier professional league.

After retiring as a player, Burridge entered the real estate business. He also coached youth hockey in Las Vegas. Asked about his biggest influences in Boston, he credited Ray Bourque, Cam Neely and Rick Middleton for teaching him how to play the game properly. During an interview with *The Hockey News* in 2015, he described his mantra in hockey and in everyday life as follows: "Just try and look for the best in every person. Treat people like you like to be treated."[29]

TED DONATO
(1991–1998/2003–2004)

Some players make names for themselves in the NHL. Others arrive with a pre-established reputation. Ted Donato was definitely in the latter category. By the time he appeared in his first game with the Bruins, he had already distinguished himself as a winner.

Born in Boston, Donato grew up in the suburb of Dedham. He played youth hockey with the Hyde Park Eagles and later skated for Catholic Memorial School, which is located in West Roxbury. After breaking the high school's all-time scoring record, Donato was selected to play for Harvard University.

The Crimson squad was loaded with talent during the late '80s and Donato was among the best and brightest. Over four seasons, he collected more than a point per game as the club dominated the Ivy League and captured an NCAA championship. Donato was named Most Outstanding Tournament Player in 1989.

After graduating from Harvard with a degree in history, Donato was selected for the U.S. national team. He joined the Bruins after playing in the 1992 Winter Olympics, which were held in Albertville, France. Donato arrived in Boston with a history of delivering in the clutch. He had scored the deciding goal for Catholic Memorial in the prestigious Super Eight Tournament. He had also netted the game-winning goal for Harvard in the '89 NCAA championship showdown. In Boston, he became part of the club's secondary power play unit, lighting the lamp 29 times with a man advantage. He accrued a fair share of game-winners as well, peaking at five during two seasons ('92-'93/'97-'98).

Donato had speed and an advanced hockey I.Q.—one of those immeasurable traits that seem to be lacking in many players. A hard-worker, his hockey acuity allowed him to read opponents and anticipate their moves to break up plays. This made him a valuable asset on penalty kills. Joined by former Olympic teammate Steve Heinze, Donato's short-handed unit was among the team's best during the 1990s.

Though he played for eight NHL teams over the course of his career, Donato put forth his best offensive efforts with the Bruins. He averaged 17 goals and 20 assists per year during his seven full seasons in Boston, peaking at 25 goals in '96-'97. He collected a career-high of 32 assists in '93-'94.

Off to slow start in '98, he was traded to the Islanders for winger Ken Belanger. This was the beginning of an extended tour of duty that included stints with the Rangers, Kings, Blues, Senators and Ducks. He re-signed with the Bruins in 2003, finishing his NHL career where it had started. Completing the circle, he took a job as head coach of the Harvard Crimson in 2004. As of 2021, he was still at the helm.

Donato's job at Harvard has not been especially easy. The school has stringent program rules that prohibit the use of athletic scholarships to recruit players.

Additionally, the Crimson are not allowed to play as many games as other Division 1 schools and must wait until late fall to begin full practices. Commenting on these restrictions, Donato once said: "There are times when I think we have great structure and support and other times where you feel you are a small part of something that is much larger than any sport or any one entity."[30] Donato has made the best of the situation, guiding his squads to multiple ECAC Tournament victories. The year of 2017 was an especially productive year for the Crimson as they won the Ivy League and ECAC regular season championships then marched on to a semi-final appearance in the NCAA Frozen Four playoff.

SERGEI SAMSONOV
(1997–2006)

Samsonov was born in the Russian capital of Moscow, which is the nation's most populous city. He grew up near the end of the Cold War, when the Soviet Union was still a functional unit run by Leonid Brezhnev. Back then, the Soviet hockey team was a force to be reckoned with, winning five world championships and two Olympic Gold Medals between 1972 and 1980. Players trained year-round and were not required to hold jobs outside of hockey. By the time Samsonov skated in the '92 International Pee Wee Hockey Tournament held in Quebec City, the Soviet Union had dissolved though the Russian team continued to fare well in international competition.

At 16 years of age, Samsonov scored an incredible total of 182 points in just 50 games for the Moscow Red Army junior team. He joined the Detroit Vipers of the IHL in '96-'97, capturing the Gary F. Longman Memorial Trophy as the league's top rookie. Impressed with his performance, the Bruins used one of their first-round picks to acquire him in the '97 Entry Draft. It was a bountiful year for Boston as they also picked up Joe Thornton in the first round.

Samsonov came to the NHL as a highly touted prospect. He was among a wave of high-level Russian arrivals during the '90s that included Peter Bondra, Pavel Bure and Sergei Federov. Samsonov was short but stocky at 5-foot-8, 188 pounds. He had slick moves and a powerful, accurate shot. Starting his Bruins career with a bang, he gathered 22 goals and 25 assists. Members of the Professional Hockey Writers Association were sufficiently impressed, awarding him the Calder Trophy at season's end. He is the only player in NHL history to win an IHL rookie of the year award and a Calder Trophy in consecutive campaigns.

Samsonov enjoyed five highly productive seasons in Boston before a serious wrist injury—sustained in a 2002 game against the Blue Jackets—altered the trajectory of his career. During those prime years, he averaged 25 goals and 33 assists per season. Often assigned to the power play unit, he gathered 112 points in man-advantage situations during his Bruins career. He played a fast, clean game, finishing in the running for the Byng Trophy three times while stationed in Boston. In 1999–2000, he spent just four of his 1,200-plus minutes of ice time in the penalty box.

Samsonov missed all but eight games in 2002 and was never quite the same when he returned. In March of 2006, he was shipped to Edmonton in a transaction that brought Milan Lucic to Boston. He signed as a free agent with the Canadiens in

2006, but became unhappy playing under head coach Guy Carbonneau. He was eventually placed on waivers, continuing his NHL tour with the Blackhawks and Panthers. He was a regular with the Hurricanes for several seasons though his numbers never returned to the level of his Bruins days. He made his last NHL appearance during the 2010-'11 season.

In 2014, Carolina GM Ron Francis announced that Samsonov would be joining the club's scouting staff. "I think he's a bright guy," said Francis. "He's a guy who played the game and understands the game extremely well."[31] As of the 2019-'20 campaign, Samsonov was in his sixth year as a scout. Nowadays, he works exclusively with forwards. Outside of hockey, he is married with two daughters.

P.J. AXELSSON
(1997–2009)

Though Axelsson never lit up the scoreboard for Boston, he fit in nicely with the Bruins blue collar philosophy. Described by multiple sources as "gritty" and "defensive-minded," the hard-working winger gave 100 percent every time he was on the ice, winning the respect of coaches, teammates and fans. His unwavering work ethic allowed him to remain in Boston for the entirety of his NHL career, which spanned more than a decade. That's an accomplishment in itself.

Born in Kungalv, Sweden, Axelsson came of age in Frolunda, which is among the 21 boroughs located in the city of Gothenburg. His nickname "P.J." is a shortened version of his birth name—Anders Per-Johan. In Sweden, he carried the nickname of "Pebben." The city of Gothenburg is a soccer mecca with a number of "football" teams in residence there. Axelsson gravitated to hockey instead, joining the Vastra Frolunda junior club at the age of 17. He was chosen 177th overall in the '95 Entry Draft and made his NHL debut without any minor league experience.

Axelsson arrived in Beantown with a variety of skills that often made him seem like the smartest man on the ice. He played a hard, clean game, keeping his mistakes to a minimum. Appearing primarily on the third line, he collected eight goals and 19 assists in his Bruins premiere, finishing among the top 12 candidates for the Calder Trophy. He remained a fan favorite in Boston for many years.

Tall and lanky with strong skating abilities, Axelsson covered a lot of ground. Though he wasn't afraid to throw his body around, he was rarely penalized, averaging just 25 minutes of box-time per season during his career. His persistent stick-work and vigilant play in the defensive zone put him in the running for the Selke Trophy on six occasions.

The Bruins weren't always loaded with talent during Axelsson's career and missed the playoffs four times between 1998 and 2009. Axelsson got a taste of victory with the Swedish National Team during the 2006 Olympics in Turin, Italy. The Swedish squad that year was a virtual All-Star team with Henrik Lunqvist, Mats Sundin, Niklas Lidstrom and Daniel Alfredsson (among others) on the roster. It was the only gold medal Axelsson won during his long career with Tre Kronor, though he did capture two silver medals and a pair of bronze medals in world championship competition.

Axelsson enjoyed his best offensive season with the Bruins in 2002-'03, gathering 36 points (17 goals/19 assists) in 66 games. In his final year (2008-'09), he reached a career-high of 24 assists. When his playing days were over, he joined the Bruins scouting staff, evaluating amateur prospects in Europe and in North America.

Reminiscing about his days on the ice, Axelsson said he felt very blessed to play for Boston. "The tradition, being an original six team, the fans were passionate—it was just awesome and I was fortunate to be here for my whole career."[32] He was equally ecstatic about being a member of the Bruins front office staff. "I wanted to stay in the game so everything fit perfect, being around this town and the sports that are here—[it's a] great time."[33]

MILAN LUCIC
(2007–2015)

Lucic's parents are of Serbian descent. Both immigrated to Canada from Yugoslavia. Young Milan grew up in Vancouver as the middle child of three siblings—all boys. During his teen years, he was diagnosed with Scheuermann's disease, a condition in which the vertebrae grow unevenly, creating a curvature of the back. Lucic's slouched posture on the ice has been evident throughout his career.

Lucic played junior hockey in the VMHA and considered quitting after he was not selected in the 2003 Western Hockey League draft. He persevered, ascending to the WHL with the Vancouver Giants. He helped the team to a Memorial Cup in 2007 and was named tournament MVP. Years later, fans named him the greatest Giants player of all time. He was honored in February of 2011 on "Milan Lucic Night."

Selected by the Bruins in the second round of the 2006 Entry Draft, Lucic formed a strong bond with executive Cam Neely. Both were from Vancouver and Lucic greatly admired Neely's physical two-way play—a style that gave rise to the term "power forward." Additionally, the two men were linked through an intricate series of transactions spanning two decades.

Under Neely's tutelage, Lucic became one of the hardest-hitting power forwards in the NHL. Though he wasn't as prolific a scorer as his mentor, he had some very productive seasons. While skating for the Bruins, Lucic netted at least 20 goals on three occasions, reaching a high of 30 during Boston's Stanley Cup run in 2010-'11. He had 20 or more assists in six of his eight seasons with the B's. But in spite of his offensive contributions, he was known more for his physicality.

Explaining his game philosophy to a writer, he once said: "When we play physical and bring that presence, we're playing our type of game. It's a system that benefits my style of play. It's something I've worked hard at in creating my space. I need to bring that physical edge to the rink every day because I won't get one thing without the other."[34]

As Lucic hammered away at opponents, he made plenty of enemies around the league. According to the popular website Hockeyfights.com, the ferocious left-winger had 72 brawls to his credit by October of 2019—55 of them occurring while wearing a Bruins jersey. He developed an ongoing feud with defenseman

Dalton Prout in the wake of a clash between the Bruins and Blue Jackets in November of 2014. After the siren sounded, Prout threw a sucker-punch that knocked Lucic to his knees. Lucic refused to let the incident go, calling Prout's actions "gutless" during a subsequent interview.[35] When the two met again more than a month later, Lucic went after him and appeared to get the upper hand. The two rivals—both standing 6-foot-3 and weighing over 220 pounds—squared off yet again in 2017 when Lucic was with the L.A. Kings. It was the third bout between the two. Prout wasn't Lucic's only regular sparring partner. He had three fights apiece with heavyweights Brandon Prust, Deryk Engelland and Jared Boll, landing his share of punches each time.

Interestingly, it was Lucic who was referred to as cowardly early into the 2011-'12 season. During a game against the Sabres, Lucic skated hard into goaltender Ryan Miller, who had ventured out of the crease to handle a puck. Miller fell heavily to the ice, sustaining a concussion. In post-game comments, the embittered net-minder called Lucic a "gutless piece of shit."[36] Lucic was not suspended for that incident, but a few weeks later, he was forced to sit out one game in the wake of an illegal hit on Flyers winger Zac Rinaldo.

In spite of his bad boy image, Lucic is said to be highly intelligent. In particular, he has a remarkable ability to recall numbers, stats and intricate details pertaining to a variety of topics. His fury on the ice has led to a number of injuries over the years, including a broken finger, broken toe, sprained ankle and multiple shoulder maladies. His hard work did not go unnoticed in Boston as he captured the Bruins' Seventh Player Award in 2008. He received the Eddie Shore Award—given in recognition of "hustle and determination"—twice.

In June of 2015, Lucic was traded to L.A. for two players and first round draft pick Jakub Zboril, who had yet to earn a roster spot in Boston as of the 2019-'20 campaign. As for Lucic, he wound up in Edmonton after one season with the Kings. He was later traded to the Calgary Flames. Though his offensive production has dropped off over the years, he continues to hit hard and make his presence known.

BRAD MARCHAND
(2009–PRESENT)

Marchand is known in many ways to many people. Agitator, trash-talker, relentless pest—each of these terms accurately describes him. When the Bruins were invited to the White House to celebrate their 2011 Stanley Cup victory, President Barack Obama referred to the diminutive Boston winger as "the little ball of hate"—a term originally given to former Devils star Pat Verbeek and later recycled for use on Marchand (who stands just 5-foot-9). A hero to some and a villain to others, Marchand is at the very least a necessary evil on a Boston team that made three appearances in the Stanley Cup finals between 2011 and 2019.

Born in Halifax, Nova Scotia, Marchand grew up in the Hammonds Plains area. He played junior hockey in the QMHJL, skating for three teams before turning pro with the Providence Bruins. Marveling at Marchand's persistence, Moncton Wildcats coach Ted Nolan remarked: "I've never seen a guy more determined to get a puck in all the years I've coached junior hockey."[37] Boston GM Peter Chiarelli felt the same way, surrendering a pair of early-round picks to the Islanders in order to acquire Marchand in the 2006 NHL Entry Draft.

Marchand became a regular in Boston during the 2010-'11 season, finishing in the running for the Calder Trophy. In an amusing sidebar, he ended up being excluded from the Bruins commemorative 2011 Stanley Cup DVD. As the story goes, he was so intoxicated during the after-party that teammates refused to allow him to be interviewed, fearing he might make some outrageous comments or embarrass himself.

In spite of the team's efforts to protect him, Marchand has repeatedly engaged in outrageous behavior on the ice. His most reprehensible acts include a low-bridge hit on Sami Salo of the Canucks that left the Vancouver defenseman with a concussion and a spearing penalty incurred for deliberately hitting Tampa Bay blue-liner Jake Dotchin in the crotch with his stick. Entering the 2019-'20 campaign, Marchand had half a dozen suspensions to his credit in addition to multiple fines.

At times, Marchand's behavior has bordered on the bizarre. In February of 2016, he attempted to kiss Dallas winger Patrick Eaves, who responded by roughly shoving Marchand away. In November of the following year, Marchand was at it again, planting a kiss on the cheek of Leafs center Leo Komarov. Komarov took it in stride, joking after the game: "I kind of liked it."[38] But he was less amused when Marchand licked him (quite literally) after the two traded blows in April of 2018. Demonstrating his cheeky sense of humor, Marchand told a reporter: "I thought he wanted to cuddle. I just wanted to get close to him. He keeps trying to get close to me. I don't know if he's got a thing for me or what. He's cute."[39] NHL officials felt obligated to intervene less than a month later when Marchand inexplicably licked Tampa Bay winger

Suspended and fined multiple times for various infractions, Brad Marchand has earned a reputation as an agitator. Most Bruins fans can overlook his indiscretions given his ability to put the puck in the net at opportune moments. As of 2020, he was the B's all-time leader in short-handed goals. Courtesy tsyp9 on VisualHunt.com/CC BY-SA.

Ryan Callahan during a confrontation. The league's deputy commissioner, Bill Daly, told an ESPN reporter that he would be speaking with Bruins team officials about the incident.

In spite of his incorrigible antics, Marchand has been an indispensible member of the Bruins top scoring line, which also features David Pastrnak and Patrice Bergeron. The trio, which has been dubbed "The Perfection Line" by sportswriters, averaged well over 200 points per year between 2016-'17 and 2019-'20. Marchand was the team's top point producer in three of those seasons. Not only does he score goals in bunches, but he scores them in timely fashion. In November of 2019, he set a franchise record with his 26th short-handed goal. And by January of 2020, he had attained a rank of number 6 among the Bruins all-time leaders in game-winning goals. His efforts earned him a pair of Seventh Player Awards in 2011 and 2016. But outside of Boston, he is largely viewed as a criminal.

Asked about his tarnished professional image, Marchand told a reporter: "It's tough. I've tried for awhile now to get away from that role and I just can't seem to escape it. I think obviously if you look back on the last few years, I've turned into a decent player and it's tough to be branded with that name consistently. Obviously, it's from my own doing but it's tough to escape it. Devil's advocate there, it's what I had to do to get into the league so I'll never say that I wouldn't go back and play the same way."[40]

Marchand may never escape the negative stigma he now carries. And it's a shame because he is among the league's elite in many respects. Writing for the popular Bruins blog *Stanley Cup of Chowder*, correspondent Shawn Ferris remarked: "The greatest strength in Marchand's game is his ability to create offense. Between his illusive skating, stick-handling skills and play-making skills, he has no problem creating extra shots for the Bruins."[41] Many of those shots have led to victories as Marchand's two-way play has kept the B's in contention throughout his career.

4

Defensemen

LIONEL HITCHMAN
(1925–1934)

Hitchman was content to carry out his defensive responsibilities while leaving the scoring to others. Because of that fact, he has been overlooked for the Hall of Fame and largely forgotten over time. He never collected more than 11 points in any season. Yet it's doubtful that the Bruins would have captured the 1929 Stanley Cup (the first in franchise history) without him.

Hitchman's father was a renowned journalist who wrote extensively about the sport of cricket. Born in Toronto, young Lionel played junior hockey with the city's Aura Lee Club. After his family relocated to Ottawa, he became a member of the Royal Canadian Mounted Police and continued his hockey career with the Ottawa New Edinburghs of the OCHL.

Signed by the Ottawa Senators in 1923, Hitchman joined the team late in the season and helped pave the way to a championship. In his first playoff appearance, he was crosschecked in the face by Hall of Famer Sprague Kleghorn. Hitchman was knocked unconscious on the play and Kleghorn received a game misconduct. When the ruling was announced, the crowd was incited to a near riot. Hitchman skated with a plaster cast over his nose for the rest of the playoffs as the Senators defeated the Montreal Canadiens, Vancouver Maroons and Edmonton Eskimos on their way to a Stanley Cup title.

Durability and perseverance were two of Hitchman's strongest qualities. He led the NHL in games played during four seasons and skated with a variety of maladies over the years, including shattered teeth and a broken jaw. One modern writer remarked that "there may not have been a sweater on any team that soaked more blood and sweat than the one Hitchman wore throughout his career."[1]

Hitchman was a dependable, aggressive, defense-oriented blue-liner. He often skated with Eddie Shore, a pairing that was undoubtedly among the greatest in NHL history. Though Shore has received far more acclaim, many have insisted that Hitchman was superior in some respects. Former teammate Frank Fredrickson said: "To me, Shore was a country boy who made good. He was a good skater and puck carrier, but wasn't an exceptional defensive player like his teammate Lionel Hitchman. Hitch was better because he could get them coming and going."[2] A columnist of the era added that "Shore may be the dynamo of the Boston club, but Hitchman is the balancing wheel."[3]

With Hitchman keeping watch over the defensive zone, Shore was free to join the offensive attack—a highly uncommon practice for the era. When things got hectic for Boston goaltenders, Hitchman and Shore would pool their efforts to eliminate scoring threats. Hitchman's job was far from glamorous, but it earned him the respect of anyone who had a more than superficial understanding of the game. *Windsor Star* journalist Vern DeGeer remarked: "You can count on the fingers of one hand the number of times Hitchman goes rushing up the ice. The average cash customer, itching for the thrills of flying skates and neatly executed goals, usually overlooks Hitchman in the excitement. Yet he's the type of defenseman that keeps a job year after year."[4]

True to that statement, Hitchman was a regular in Boston for portions of 10 seasons. He was named team captain before the '27-'28 campaign. And his number 3 was the first to be retired by the Bruins. During a ceremony at the Boston Garden honoring Hitchman, Bruins executive Art Ross referred to him as the "cornerstone of the franchise."[5]

After his retirement as a player, Hitchman served as head coach of the Boston Cubs then accepted a position as Bruins assistant coach under Art Ross. He later coached part of a season with the Springfield Indians. After leaving hockey behind, he continued his job with the Royal Canadian Mounted Police, ascending to the rank of sergeant. He died in Glens Falls, New York, at the age of 67.

EDDIE SHORE
(1926–1939)

Born near the turn of the 20th century, Shore grew up on a horse ranch in Cupar, Saskatchewan—a small community near the North Dakota border. Years of breaking horses, herding animals and lugging heavy bags of grain prepared him for a rough lifestyle on the ice. But Shore wasn't interested in hockey early on. In fact, he preferred baseball and soccer to the sport that eventually made him famous. While Shore was studying at Manitoba Agricultural College, his brother, Aubrey, told him he would never make it as a hockey player. Determined to disprove that statement, Shore joined the Saskatchewan-based Melville Millionaires in 1923. By 1926, he was skating for the Bruins.

Many words have been used to describe Shore over the years. Historian Stan Fischler wrote that the dynamic defenseman was "absurdly fearless, totally talented and dedicated to his profession like nobody before or since."[6] *Boston Globe* columnist Bob Ryan remarked that Shore was a "madman on skates."[7] And *Sport* magazine editor Ed Fitzgerald pointed out that Shore's "chilling disregard for personal safety enabled him to maintain peak speed to the point well beyond the limit dared by lesser men. The result was that he came up consistently with plays that other stars were lucky to duplicate once in a lifetime."[8]

Shore's unparalleled skating ability and remarkable puck handling skills allowed him to reinvent the position of defenseman. Before his arrival in the NHL, most blue-liners were content to hang back and guard the defensive zone. But Shore emerged as legitimate offensive presence, putting up double-digit assist totals in nine

Eddie Shore was among the game's first offensive defensemen. He won four Hart Trophies and came to be known as "the Ty Cobb of hockey" because of his ferocity on the ice. Courtesy Boston Public Library, Leslie Jones Collection.

seasons. Additionally, he scored 10 or more goals five times and was designated an All-Star on eight occasions. He won four Hart Trophies during his career.

Shore has been referred to by multiple sources as "the Ty Cobb of hockey" on account of his vicious play and insatiable need to prove himself to others. He demonstrated his ferocity during his first training camp in 1926. In the wake of a hard collision with fellow defenseman Billy Coutu (which put Coutu out of action for a week), Shore's ear was nearly torn off. He asked the attending doctor to snip off a part that was hanging by a thread, but the physician was able to repair the damage while Shore calmly watched the procedure using a hand mirror.

Opponents knew that Shore was a key ingredient to the Bruins' success and relentlessly hacked away at him during every match. There was no bigger drawing card during the '20s and '30s and many fans (especially those who rooted for opposing teams) attended games in the hope of watching him get run over. Shore absorbed an unimaginable amount of punishment and kept on skating. Over the course of his career, he had his nose broken more than a dozen times, his jaw broken five times and all of his teeth knocked out. He also received close to a thousand stitches.

Shore's brutality was on full display in a 1933 meeting against the Toronto Maple Leafs. The game had already been marred by multiple brawls when Shore went racing up the ice with a two-man advantage. On his way to the attacking zone, he collided with an opponent and slammed into the boards at full speed. Momentarily knocked senseless, he lumbered to his feet and attacked the player nearest to him, which happened to be winger Ace Bailey. Shore hit Bailey from behind, flipping him onto his head and fracturing his skull. A hush fell over the arena as Leafs defenseman Red Horner confronted Shore. "Why the hell did you do that, Eddie?" Horner snarled.[9] When Shore responded with a smile, Horner threw a punch that left the Bruins star flat on his back in a pool of his own blood. Shore received 16 stitches and returned to action not long afterward. Bailey, on the other hand, lay on the verge of death for nearly two weeks. Though he recovered from the injury, he never played hockey again. Three months later, the NHL arranged an All-Star game in Toronto to benefit Bailey and his family. Putting their differences aside, Bailey and Shore shook hands at center ice.

Shore's stellar and at times violent play led the Bruins to a pair of Stanley Cup titles in 1929 and 1939. Traded to the New York midway through the '39-'40 campaign, he appeared in 10 games with the Americans, helping them reach the playoffs. He made his last NHL appearance in a series-ending loss to the Red Wings.

Realizing he was nearing the end of his career, Shore purchased the Springfield Indians in 1939. During World War II, the U.S. Army took over the Springfield Coliseum, forcing the Indians out of action. Shore became head coach the Buffalo Bisons, leading them to a pair of Calder Cup championships. When the Indians were reactivated in 1946, he resumed his duties in Springfield.

Shore's coaching style was highly unorthodox. He advised the wives of players not to have sex with their spouses and forced the team to execute ballet steps during practice. He was also known to tape the hands of players to their sticks or bind their legs together with rope. In spite of multiple near-fatal heart attacks, he skated with players in practice and was said to be faster than some. Adhering to a stringent budget, he developed a habit of benching his top point producers when they got close to reaching the scoring bonuses in their contracts. "Most of us are a little crazy one way or another," he told a journalist. "Some of us admit it. As for me, I'm not sorry about anything I've done in my life. As long as I can be close to hockey, I'm happy to be alive."[10]

Shore kept a controlling interest in the Indians until 1976, when he sold the club. By then, he had three AHL championships and a dozen playoff appearances to his credit. While visiting his son in Springfield during the winter of 1985, he began coughing up blood. Transported to the hospital, he died the next day. It was later determined that he was suffering from liver cancer. He was 82 years old at the time of his passing.

FLASH HOLLETT
(1936–1944)

While playing for Boston, Hollett set scoring records even the great Eddie Shore could not surpass. His cocky, abrasive nature drew comparisons to Hall of Fame pitcher Dizzy Dean. Since he reached the pinnacle of his offensive prowess during World War II (when the NHL was depleted of talent), he has been excluded from the Hall of Fame. Yet many would argue that he is deserving of the honor.

Flash Hollett's single-season record for goals by a defenseman (20) stood until 1969, when it was broken by Bobby Orr. Hollett's cocky attitude drew comparisons to Hall of Fame pitcher Dizzy Dean. Courtesy Boston Public Library, Leslie Jones Collection.

Frank William Hollett was born in North Sydney, Nova Scotia—an Atlantic port community providing ferry service to Newfoundland. In addition to hockey, Hollett also played lacrosse. He was offered professional tryouts in both sports before signing with the Maple Leafs. He spent the '32-'33 season skating with Toronto's minor league affiliate—the Syracuse Stars. Upon arriving, he boldly told coach Mickey Roach: "I'm just the guy you're looking for to complete your squad."[11] Called to Toronto the following year, Hollett appeared in four games before he was loaned to the Ottawa Senators. He played a full season with the Leafs in '34-'35, gathering 10 goals and 16 assists—remarkable totals for a defenseman at the time.

Hollett could be quite difficult when it came to negotiating contracts and accepting his on-ice responsibilities. Toronto owner Conn Smythe eventually grew weary of his budding star and traded him to the Bruins in 1936 for a reported sum of $16,000 (a significant figure in those days). Hollett soon developed a prickly relationship with Bruins coach Art Ross.

Upon arriving in Boston, Hollett was encouraged by Eddie Shore and Dit Clapper to carry the puck more often. His superior stick-handling abilities and extraordinary speed (from which his nickname was derived) allowed him to continually set up scoring opportunities for teammates. But Hollett became unhappy with Ross's practice of using him as a substitute forward when regulars were injured. He also disliked serving up front on penalty kills—another one of Ross's common strategies. The two squabbled over the issue and Ross considered burying the outspoken defenseman in the Bruins' farm system. But in the end, Hollett was simply too valuable to the club and his demands were met.

During his time in Boston, Hollett tied a record for defenseman with 19 goals in consecutive seasons. He also finished with double-digit assist totals in six straight campaigns. During the Bruins championship years of '39 and '41, Hollett gathered 11 points in postseason action. His nine assists in the '43 playoffs were tops in the NHL.

When the Bruins got off to a mediocre start in '43-'44, Ross traded Hollett to the Red Wings for blue-liner Pat Egan. Though Egan would have a few decent seasons in Boston, Hollett would reach the peak of his offensive potential in Detroit. His 20 goals during the '44-'45 campaign were a record for defensemen that stood until 1969, when it was broken by none other than Bobby Orr.

Hollett's contributions helped guide the Red Wings to the 1945 Stanley Cup finals against Toronto. Though the Wings were shut out by goaltender Frank McCool in the first three games, Hollett's inspired play allowed Detroit to tie the series. He collected two goals and a pair of assists in the last four games, but the Wings ultimately came up short in the finale.

Battling injuries in '45-'46, Hollett got into a salary dispute with Detroit GM Jack Adams. He was subsequently traded to the Rangers, but refused to report, later remarking: "I had a young family and the prospect of apartment living in Manhattan didn't appeal to me or my wife."[12] He was suspended for his actions and never played in another NHL game. When he announced his retirement, Adams vowed to personally keep him out of the Hall of Fame.

Hollett finished his career in Ontario with the Kitchener Dutchmen and Toronto Marlboros. When he left the game for good, he was the highest scoring defenseman in NHL history. He died in 1999 at the age of 87 and, as of 2020, had yet to gain entry into the Hall of Fame.

MURRAY HENDERSON
(1945–1952)

Henderson is a member of hockey's so-called "royal family." His uncles Charlie, Lionel and Roy Conacher all had stellar careers that landed them in the Hall of Fame. His cousins Brian and Pete also had successful runs in the NHL. Born and raised in Toronto, Henderson had no intention of following in the footsteps of his famous uncles. He played junior hockey with the Toronto Young Rangers, but wasn't a standout. "I wasn't good enough to put it bluntly," he told a writer. "There were a lot of good hockey players around and I didn't show enough for anyone to be really interested in me. I guess I was a late-bloomer."[13]

During his amateur years, Henderson worked in the purchasing department of the Ontario hydro-electric power commission and believed he might make a career out of it. With the outbreak of World War II, he joined the Royal Canadian Air Force, aspiring to a pilot's rank. He flew air missions off the Pacific Coast and also played for the RCAF hockey team. He was discharged from the service following the death of his father.

Henderson's uncle Charlie helped initiate a contract offer from the Bruins through scout Harold "Baldy" Cotton. At the time, Henderson had played only sparsely over the previous year and was out of shape. The Bruins assigned him to the Boston Olympics of the Eastern Amateur Hockey League for conditioning. When Toronto Maple Leafs owner Conn Smythe got wind of the deal, he filed a protest with the NHL, claiming that Henderson had been signed prior to his military discharge (which would have been a violation of league rules). The issue was resolved amicably and Henderson ended up spending his entire career with the Bruins.

Murray joined the B's for five regular season games in 1945 and appeared in all seven playoff games against the Red Wings that year. He remained a full-time player in Boston for the next seven seasons. Murray's cousin, Pete, described his playing style as follows: "[He was] a typical stay-at-home defenseman ... not prone to a lot of unnecessary penalties, but could handle himself when he had to."[14] Murray more or less agreed with that assessment, remarking blandly: "I figure my job is to try to stop the other team from scoring and I try to do whatever I can."[15]

Murray may not have had a lot of flair, but he was a reliable defensive player who consistently helped keep the puck out of the Bruins' net. His hard work earned him the title of alternate captain in '46-'47. The honor also won the respect of Boston fans, who were notoriously hard on under-achievers. "They were a tough crowd," Henderson recalled years later. "They had an outfit up there called the Gallery Gods. They got rid of a lot of players. It was a tough place to play if the crowd got on you."[16] Murray's humility, dependability and workman-like attitude kept fans on his side throughout his career.

Though many players before and after him complained bitterly about the frugality of Art Ross, Henderson never had any contract issues. And though he never won a Stanley Cup, the Bruins missed the playoffs just once during his Beantown tenure (in 1950). Since he focused primarily on defense, his offensive numbers were modest. He reached personal high marks of 6 goals in '47-'48 and 12 assists in '46-'47. He played crisp, clean hockey, averaging just 38 penalty minutes per year.

After his final NHL season, the Bruins offered Henderson a position with the Hershey Bears as a player-coach. He served four years in that capacity, working with young prospects such as Don McKenney and Don Cherry. When he announced his retirement, he was offered a job as a scout, but turned it down.

With his professional hockey days behind him, Henderson returned to Toronto and worked in the beverage industry for Seagram's and the William Mara Company. He continued to skate with former NHL players (among them his cousin Pete) in exhibition games held for charity. He died in 2013 at the ripe age of 91.

FERN FLAMAN
(1945–1950/1954–1961)

Born in Dysart, Saskatchewan, Flaman grew up in Regina—the capital of the province. He learned the fundamentals of the game on outdoor rinks, accepting advice from just about anyone willing to offer it. During his youth hockey days, kids were in the habit of wearing the numbers of players they most admired. Flaman skated with Hall of Famer Babe Pratt's number on his sweater. In an interesting turn of events, he later replaced Pratt on the Bruins roster.

At the age of 17, Flaman joined the Boston Olympics of the Eastern Amateur Hockey League. Within a couple of seasons, he was promoted to the Hershey Bears. The war had drained the NHL of talent and Flaman was summoned to Boston for single-game appearances during the '44-'45 and '45-'46 campaigns. He became a full-timer the following season.

Hoping to make an impression, Flaman played with grit and determination. He became so adept at blocking shots that teammates came to think of him almost as a second goalie. He was also known for his bone-crunching hits. Gordie Howe once referred to Flaman as the toughest player in the NHL while Montreal icons Jean Beliveau and Henri Richard both regarded the Boston blue-liner as an incorrigible pest. "He's always got his stick between my legs," Richard complained. "When I go near that fellow, believe me, I look over my shoulder," Beliveau said.[17]

Describing Flaman's effect on opponents, writer Jim Proudfoot pointed out: "It is not a question of fear, for Flaman is not a vicious player, but a question of knowing that Flaman can deal a devastating body check, that he is among the most competent defensemen in the business, and that, if aroused, he is one of the most capable fisticuffers in the league."[18] Though Flaman had competed in boxing during his teen years, he was not particularly enamored with his designation as a bruiser. "I've got a wife and daughter to support," he told a journalist. "I can't have everybody in the league after me, which is what happens to players with that reputation."[19]

In spite of Flaman's obvious talent, he was traded to Toronto in November of 1950. By then, he had spent a majority of his career in New England and did not relish the idea of being uprooted. Bruins executives regretted the move soon afterward as Flaman's Leafs trampled Boston in the playoffs that season on their way to a Stanley Cup title. It was the only Cup Flaman won during his career.

Looking to bolster the defensive corps, Bruins GM Lynn Patrick re-acquired Flaman from Toronto in 1954. During his second stint with the Bruins, Flaman received three All-Star selections and was a candidate for the Norris trophy on five occasions. He reached a personal-high of 31 points (six goals/25 assists) during the '56-'57 campaign. A perennial fan favorite—especially among the Garden's Gallery Gods—he was honored with a car and numerous other gifts on "Fern Flaman Night" in 1959. He made his last NHL appearance during the '60-'61 campaign. He was among the all-time leaders in penalty minutes when he retired.

Flaman was trained as an electrician, but opted to continue his hockey career in a administrative capacity. He coached and managed in the AHL with the Providence Reds. He later moved on to coaching positions in the Western and Central hockey leagues. In 1970, he took over the Northeastern University team, becoming the longest tenured coach in the school's history. In 1982, he was named college coach of the year.

Flaman is a member of multiple halls of fame. During his lifetime, he was inducted into the Rhode Island Hockey Hall of Fame, the Northeastern University

Hall of Fame and the Hockey Hall of Fame in Toronto. Following his death in 2012, he was elected to the Saskatchewan Hockey Hall of Fame.

Bill Quackenbush
(1949–1956)

Since a defenseman's job is a very physical one, penalties seem to come with the territory. But Bill Quackenbush found a way around that, using his extraordinary hockey intellect to become the cleanest blue-liner in NHL history. Over portions of 14 seasons, he averaged just seven minutes of penalty time per year. With eight All-Star appearances to his credit, he proved that brains can prevail over brawn on any given night.

Born and raised in Toronto, Quackenbush was among the top Canadian athletes as a teenager. In addition to his primary sport, he was a standout with the prestigious Toronto Scottish soccer club. He could have played professionally, but the allure of the ice was stronger.

Quackenbush moved rapidly through the junior hockey ranks with the Toronto Native Sons and Brantford Lions. While skating for the latter team under future Red Wings coach Tommy Ivan, he got noticed by Detroit's chief scout, Carson Cooper. During a call-up in '42-'43, he broke his wrist and was sent to the AHL to rehab. He returned the following year to claim a full-time roster spot.

During Quackenbush's tenure in Detroit, the Wings made three appearances in the Stanley Cup finals, losing each time to the Maple Leafs. Looking to shake things up, GM Jack Adams sent Quackenbush to Boston along with winger Pete Horeck in exchange for four players. Quackenbush joined the Bruins during a period of financial hardship, but he made the best of it, becoming one of the club's top defensemen.

Quackenbush knew precisely where to position himself in the defensive zone. He was a clean, solid checker and skilled stick handler. One of his greatest assets was his remarkable ability to gather loose pucks around the net. He had plenty of speed on offensive rushes and developed a reputation as a play-maker in the mold of Eddie Shore. During the '50-'51 campaign, he collected a personal high of 24 assists—outstanding for a defenseman of the era. Over the course of his career, he incurred just one major penalty, which came in the wake of a brief tussle with winger Gaye Stewart.

The Bruins weren't an especially brilliant team in Quackenbush's day, missing the playoffs more than once. But in 1953, they made it all the way to the Stanley Cup finals. Quackenbush stuck around until the end of the '55-'56 campaign, retiring at season's end. Upon hanging up his skates, he went back to school, obtaining an engineering degree from Northeastern University.

Not content to leave the sport behind, Quackenbush returned to hockey as assistant coach at Northeastern. He later became head coach of the Princeton men's hockey team. When a women's team was added, he took over the program. He also coached varsity golf. In 1976, he was inducted into the Hockey Hall of Fame. In later years, he settled in Lawrenceville, New Jersey. He died in 1999 from pneumonia and complications of Alzheimer's. He was 77 years old.

DOUG MOHNS
(1953–1964)

Few players in Bruins history have demonstrated the versatility of Doug Mohns. When he wasn't frustrating opponents with his diligent defensive work, he was creating scoring opportunities as a substitute left-winger. He accepted his dual role without complaint, drawing high praise from coach Milt Schmidt, who remarked: "Doug could switch at a moment's notice and still give you a solid effort."[20]

Mohns grew up in Capreol, Ontario—the northern-most community in Greater Sudbury, which is located on the Vermillion River. His path to the NHL began with the Capreol Caps of the Northern Ontario Junior Hockey League. He later joined the Barrie Flyers, helping the club to a pair of Memorial Cup championships. He was added to the Bruins roster without any minor league experience—somewhat rare for the era.

Mohns began his career as a winger, exhibiting an unusual shooting style in which he leaned dramatically forward on his stick before releasing the puck. On occasion, this awkward posture caused him to tumble onto the ice. But it also gave his shots more power and velocity. In fact, he was known to knock the sticks right out of the hands of goaltenders.

At the start of the '56-'57 campaign, the Bruins decided they needed a defenseman who could handle himself at both ends of the ice. Mohns was called upon to make the switch. Defensive partner Fern Flaman gave Mohns a crash course in the art of minimizing scoring chances in the Bruins zone. An apt pupil, Mohns became one of the great blue-liners of the era.

Sturdily built at 6-foot, 185 pounds, Mohns was an excellent skater with above average speed. A phenomenal breakout passer, he delivered accurate, timely relays to teammates. On defense, he wasn't afraid to get a little dirty at times. One of his favorite tricks was to knock the sticks right out of opponents' hands. During a game against the Blackhawks, he sent Ian Cushenan's stick clear across the ice. Cushenan became so angry he attacked Mohns, breaking his jaw and landing him on the injured list for several weeks. Since Mohns was the instigator, Cushenan received a light fine and a game misconduct.

Mohns would appear at left wing sporadically for the remainder of his Bruins career. He once said that the thrill of stopping a shot was just as rewarding as scoring a goal. In '57-'58, he collected 13 points in 12 playoff games as a defenseman. In '59-'60, he tied Flash Hollett's record for blue-liners with 20 goals. He barely made it, lighting the lamp twice in the regular season finale. Unfortunately, the NHL discounted the feat since he had played in seven games as a winger. He was named Bruins alternate team captain the following year.

The B's slumped mightily near the end of Mohns's Beantown tenure. Though he was known for his enthusiasm and energy, he later admitted it was difficult to get motivated for games at times. Traded to the Blackhawks before the 1964 campaign, he returned to his wing position. With Stan Mikita and Kenny Wharram skating beside him, he averaged 23 goals and 28 assists per year between 1965 and 1969. The trio was dubbed "The Scooter Line" by sportswriters.

"Mohns could really skate," said Mikita. "He could move the puck and he had a terrific shot. After the three of us became a line during the '64-'65 season—Kenny on the wing and me at center—all of us thrived. For the next four years, each of us had at least 20 goals. I don't believe there were any other NHL lines that could match that."[21] Thanks to their collective efforts, the Blackhawks finished first in '66-'67, breaking the dreaded "Curse of Muldoon"—an alleged jinx placed on the club by head coach Pete Muldoon, who was fired after the '26-'27 campaign. Prior to '67, the Hawks had finished second or lower in every season following Muldoon's dismissal.

The versatile Mohns made three more stops before retiring as a player, appearing with the North Stars, Flames and Capitals. He was designated team captain in Washington before the '74-'75 season, which was his last. In spite of his sterling two-way play, he has yet to be added to the Hall of Fame.

In the years following his NHL departure, Mohns became heavily involved in various charities, including a food pantry and health center. He settled in Braintree, Massachusetts, and later moved to Bedford. He died in 2014 from complications of MDS—a group of cancers effecting immature blood cells in the bone marrow. He was 80 years old at the time of his passing.

LEO BOIVIN
(1954–1966)

Born in Prescott, Ontario, Boivin recalled being on skates from the time he could walk. He learned the basics of hockey playing on numerous outdoor rinks and on the St. Lawrence River, which froze over every winter. During his Bantam and Midget years, he gravitated to a defenseman's position because (in his own words) "they stayed on the ice longer."[22]

Boivin started his junior hockey career with the Inkerman Rockets. During a pre-season tournament against a Kingston team, he was spotted by a B's scout and promoted to the Port Arthur Bruins. His contract was eventually sold to the Maple Leafs, who elevated him to the AHL with the Pittsburgh Hornets. In 1951, the Leafs found themselves scrambling to fill a hole vacated by the death of hard-hitting defenseman Bill Barilko, who disappeared while on a fishing trip to Northern Quebec that summer (an unfortunate incident later commemorated in a popular song by the Canadian alternative rock band The Tragically Hip). Boivin was invited to Toronto near season's end. He was a regular there for two full campaigns, finishing third in voting for the Calder Trophy during his rookie year. Long after his retirement, he fondly remembered the thrill of playing against some of his boyhood heroes.

In November of '54, Boivin was reunited with the team that originally signed him. The Bruins weren't stellar in those days, but Boivin helped solidify the defensive corps. Primarily a positional blue-liner, Boivin was small yet sturdily built at 5-foot-7, 180-plus pounds. His low center of gravity helped him gain a reputation as a devastating checker. He frequently sent opponents sprawling across the open ice. Though he wasn't particularly dirty, he drew a fair amount of penalties, spending at least 70 minutes in the box during eight seasons. Recognized for his grinding defensive work, he finished in the running for the Norris Trophy twice.

The B's made a pair of Stanley Cup finals appearances with Boivin in '57 and

'58. They missed the playoffs several times as well and Boivin's plus-minus numbers slumped as a result. Looking to add some punch to the offense during the '62-'63 season, coach Milt Schmidt asked Boivin to skate at the left-wing position. He ended up with 10 goals that year—the highest mark of his career. He finished with double digit assist totals in seven consecutive seasons with the Bruins.

During his later years in Boston, Boivin served as team captain, helping in the development of future stars such as Gary Doak and Ed Westfall. Traded to the Red Wings in 1966, he missed the arrival of Bobby Orr by just a few months. Though he relished his time in Boston, he didn't brood over the trade. "It was quite a feeling to go in there because they had guys like [Gordie] Howe and [Alex] Delvecchio that I had hit hard through the years. But they welcomed me with open arms. I really enjoyed playing there," he said.[23]

The Wings went to the finals in '66, but lost to the powerful Canadiens. When the NHL added six teams 1967, Boivin was claimed by the Penguins in the Expansion Draft. He played portions of two seasons with Pittsburgh then finished his career with the Minnesota North Stars.

The defensive-minded Boivin had two stints as head coach of the St. Louis Blues in '75-'76 then again in '77-'78. He was fired during the latter season when the club got off to a poor start. He served as a scout with the Blues and Whalers until the early '90s. He was inducted into the Hockey Hall of Fame in 1986.

Reflecting on his career, Boivin said he had few if any regrets. "My dream was to win the Stanley Cup, but I never did win it. It's just the way it goes. I think the biggest thrill of my career was being inducted into the Hockey Hall of Fame.... That, to me, was even better than winning the Stanley Cup."[24]

A community center in Prescott, Ontario, now bears Boivin's name. He has remained active in local youth hockey. At the time of this writing, he was still alive and well in his late 80s.

DALLAS SMITH
(1959–1961/1965–1977)

For some players, it's a long, winding road to the NHL. Smith was definitely in that category. Born in Hamiota, Manitoba, he inked a deal with the B's as a teenager. Assigned to the Estevan Bruins, he played two seasons with the club before receiving a summons to Boston at the end of the '59-'60 campaign. He appeared to be on his way to stardom the following year, when he led the NHL with 70 appearances. But the Bruins were dreadful that season under coach Milt Schmidt, finishing in last place with a 15–42–13 record. Smith was sent to the minors, where he languished for the next several years.

After making an All-Star appearance with the Oklahoma City Blazers in '66, Smith found his way back to Boston and began the most productive stretch of his career. Being paired with Bobby Orr was a blessing and curse at the same time. On one hand, it was easy to be overlooked playing alongside the greatest defenseman of the era. But by the same token, Orr helped pad Smith's numbers for several years. When the NHL introduced the plus/minus statistic in 1967, Smith immediately reaped the benefits, recording a league-high plus-33 mark. In 1971, when Orr set the all-time single-season record with a plus-124, Smith posted the second highest total at plus-94 (a number eventually surpassed by Larry Robinson and Wayne Gretzky). Smith finished his Bruins career at plus-331 and currently holds a rank of number 3 among the all-time franchise leaders.

In 2013, a correspondent from the popular sports website, Bleacher Report, rated Orr and Smith as the top defensive pairing in franchise history. Owing much to Orr's offensive prowess, Smith collected 20 or more assists during nine seasons, averaging 24 per year from 1967 to 1977. He skated in four All-Star games during his time with the Bruins.

Smith got the nickname "Half-Ton" because he was constantly in search of half-ton trucks to purchase for use on his farm in Manitoba. Solidly proportioned at 5-foot-11, 180 pounds, the agricultural work helped build his muscles. According to one source, he was "freakishly strong."[25] On a Bruins team loaded with tough guys, he fit the mold, drawing close to 20 fighting majors during his career. He spent at least 70 minutes in the box during seven seasons and ran up more than a hundred penalty minutes three times.

Dissatisfied with the contract offer he received prior to the '76-'77 slate, Smith held out for more money and made himself available to various other clubs. There were no takers, so he ended up settling with the Bruins the day before the season began. He fell into a prolonged scoring slump and announced in March that he would be sitting out for the remainder of the year. "This is the last time I'm ever going to go through this kind of contract negotiation," he griped to a UPI reporter.[26]

Before the '77-'78 campaign, former teammate Phil Esposito, who was equally disillusioned with the way the Bruins conducted business, talked Smith into signing with the Rangers. In addition to Esposito, Smith was reunited with two other members of the B's '72 Stanley Cup squad—Don Awrey and Carol Vadnais. When the transaction was announced, Rangers coach Jean-Guy Talbot joked: "All we need is Bobby Orr now."[27]

Smith appeared in 29 games with the Rangers during the '77-'78 season before retiring for good. He continued to work on his Manitoba farm after his days on the ice were finished. He later purchased a large plot of land in Oregon and moved there with his wife.

TED GREEN
(1961–1972)

Some players make an impression with dazzling stick-work. Others get by on hustle and determination. Members of a third class become known for their nastiness. In the case of "Terrible Ted" Green, the latter grouping was inescapable.

Green grew up in St. Boniface, Manitoba and skated for the Winnipeg Braves—1959 Memorial Cup champions. Originally signed by the Canadiens, the Bruins acquired him in the summer of 1960, assigning him to their Kingston affiliate. He became a full-time player in Boston the following year.

Upon arriving in the NHL, Green was mentored by Hall of Famer Leo Boivin, who taught him how to deliver effective body checks and intimidate opponents. Green carried the intimidation factor to an extreme, becoming one of the roughest players in franchise history. "I had one philosophy and that was this—the corners are mine," he told one writer. "Any man who tried to take a corner away from me was stealing from me. I get mad when a man tries to steal from me."[28]

Justifying Green's hardcore style, GM Harry Sinden remarked: "In those days, the six NHL teams had to have someone who always had your back and he was our guy. He was a tremendous leader and a great Bruin."[29] Many opponents had less favorable opinions. Rangers president William Jennings once proposed that a bounty should be put on Green's head. And left-winger Wayne Maki became so infuriated by Green's antics, he fractured the defenseman's skull with his stick. It was one of the ugliest incidents in NHL history.

During a preseason game on September 21, 1969, Maki and Green engaged in a stick fight that landed Green in the hospital. Green temporarily lost the ability to speak and underwent multiple surgeries to repair the trauma to his brain. Out for the entire '69 campaign, he rehabbed with trainer Gene Berde, who had worked with Red Sox great Carl Yastrzemski. When Green returned to action in 1970, he was wearing a helmet. There was much speculation as to how effective he might be, but he defied the odds with one of his best offensive efforts (five goals/37 assists). "Teddy was the epitome of determination and toughness both physically and mentally," said teammate Ed Westfall. "There are few people I know or have ever met who could have survived what he did."[30] Maki and Green were both charged with assault then subsequently acquitted.

Though Green embraced an enforcer's role early in his career, he moved quickly away from it after the Maki incident. During his final season in Boston ('71-'72), he accrued just 21 penalty minutes in 55 games. He had averaged well over a hundred minutes per year prior to his remarkable 1970 comeback.

Remembered largely for his scrappy play, Green developed some valuable skills over time. He was an excellent passer and shot-blocker. This made him extremely useful on penalty kills. In fact, he sometimes served as a forward in short-handed situations. He collected at least 30 assists in three seasons with the B's, expending his finest offensive effort in '68-'69, when he gathered 46 points and made an All-Star appearance. In '64-'65, he received the Elizabeth C. Defresne Trophy for his outstanding performances in home games. He was a three-time Norris Trophy candidate.

In 1972, Green joined the New England Whalers of the World Hockey Association. He spent portions of seven seasons with the Whalers and Winnipeg Jets, winning three Avco World Trophies (the WHA equivalent to the Stanley Cup). Though Green didn't play during the Bruins championship season of 1970, his name was engraved on the Cup. He was around for Boston's title run in '72.

When his playing days were finished, Green became assistant coach of the Edmonton Oilers. He later served as a head coach for two full seasons and part of another. He also worked as an assistant to the Oilers' team president. By the time he left Edmonton, he had played a role in five of the Oilers' Stanley Cup titles. He was inducted into the Manitoba Sports Hall of Fame in 2003. He was a member of the of the inaugural WHA Hall of Fame class in 2010. He passed away in 2019.

GARY DOAK
(1966–1970/1973–1981)

Doak's statistics don't exactly leap off the page. In fact, he scored just 20 goals over portions of 14 seasons with the Bruins and never collected more than 13 assists in any single campaign. But a player's worth can't always be measured in numbers. Doak maintained a roster spot year after year on account of his high energy level, loyalty to the team and utter fearlessness on the ice. Among the greatest shot-blockers in Bruins history, he put himself in harm's way during every game, sacrificing his body for the good of the club. As a result, he missed significant portions of time with injuries in all but one of his seasons in Boston.

Doak grew up in Goderich, Ontario—a picturesque town situated on the eastern shore of Lake Huron. His father was a dock worker and Doak labored beside him when school was out. Originally signed by Detroit, he spent his junior years with the Hamilton Red Wings. At the age of 17, he was called to the AHL with the Pittsburgh Hornets. He became a full-timer in Pittsburgh during the '65-'66 campaign. After making his NHL debut with Detroit, the Bruins acquired him in a transaction involving six players, including Hall of Famer Leo Boivin.

Before training camp in '66, Doak suffered an unfortunate accident, breaking his leg while roller skating with friends in Goderich. The season was already underway by the time he was able to skate again and the Bruins sent him to their Oklahoma City affiliate to get back in shape. He made 30 appearances in Boston that year and became a permanent member of the B's in '67-'68. His sterling play inspired coach Harry Sinden to remark: "He doesn't rush like Orr, but defensively he takes a back seat to nobody on our squad."[31]

Doak's injury in '66 was not the first nor would it be the last. Over the course of his career, he suffered multiple leg breaks and a collarbone break along with various other maladies. He also dealt with chronic pain in his back, which required regular cortisone shots. There was hardly a part of Doak's body that wasn't affected and he contemplated early retirement more than once. In '77-'78, he was checked hard into the boards by Dennis Hextall of the Red Wings. He sustained broken cheekbones and received 13 stitches. Demonstrating the resilience that would come to characterize him over the years, he dove headfirst into a Bill Barber shot to save an empty net goal shortly after his return to action.

A member of the Bruins 1970 Stanley Cup squad, he left the team in '70-'71 to play for Vancouver. From there, he ended up in New York and Detroit before returning to "The Hub" near the end of the '72-'73 campaign. He won the Bruins Seventh Player Award in '76-'77 and finished his career in Boston with a plus-110 rating.

With his playing days behind him, Doak served as Bruins assistant coach for several seasons. He also coached at the University of Massachusetts. He remained active in Bruins alumni affairs for many years, helping raise money for various charities. He also held a supervisory position with the Massachusetts Department of Conservation and Recreation. When he died of cancer in 2017, many former Bruins equated it to losing a family member. Team president Cam Neely said: "He did so much with the organization after he retired. He hung around, he was always available for charity events, for the alumni. [It's] a sad day."[32] General Manager Don Sweeney added: ""You couldn't find a more charitable guy who loved the Boston Bruins and loved everything about the fabric and the family environment of the team."[33] Doak was survived by a wife, two children and several grandkids.

BOBBY ORR
(1966–1976)

Orr's father, Doug, was a top hockey prospect who turned down an invitation to play professionally, opting instead to join the Royal Canadian Navy during World War II. Upon his return from the service, he settled in Parry Sound—a community on the shores of beautiful Georgian Bay, Ontario. Bobby was born in 1948 and grew up with four siblings. He began skating at the age of four on the Seguin River, gravitating toward an informal version of hockey known as "shinny." Before long, he had established himself as the most talented player in his neighborhood.

Orr got his start in organized hockey at the age of five. His father wanted him to be a forward and he played at that position until his Pee Wee coach, Bucko McDonald (a prominent NHL blue-liner during the '30s and '40s), switched him to defense. At the age of 14, Orr's size seemed to be the only thing holding him back. In spite of

Considered by many to be the greatest defenseman in NHL history, Bobby Orr became a cultural icon. The Orr statue outside TD Garden is a popular tourist attraction. Courtesy pauljohnson414 on VisualHunt/CC BY.

his diminutive frame (5-foot-6, 135 pounds), the Bruins arranged for him to join the Oshawa Generals of the Metro Junior A League.

In '63-'64, the Metro League folded and the Generals became affiliated with the Ontario Hockey Association. Orr moved to Oshawa and attended R.S. McLaughlin High School. He set a new record for OHA defensemen with 29 goals that year. His offensive production increased every season, peaking at 94 points in '65-'66—his final year of junior hockey. By then, his size was no longer an issue as he had grown to 6-foot, 200 pounds.

During his 1966 Bruins debut, Orr endeared himself to the Beantown faithful with his abundant two-way skills. He didn't shy away from the physical side of the game and his remarkable speed allowed him to cover both ends of the ice proficiently. Unfortunately, he proved to be a bit too fearless on rushes at times. Injured in a collision with Toronto defenseman Marcel Provonost, he missed several games. It was the beginning of recurring knee problems that would ultimately lead to his premature retirement. Interestingly, Orr did not wear his iconic number 4 when he first arrived in Boston. He skated with the number 27 during the '66 preseason before choosing the digit he came to be known by.

Orr did not invent the archetype of the offensive defenseman, but he elevated it to a new level. A masterful skater with unparalleled acceleration, he knew where the puck was at all times and could almost always be found carrying it, pursuing it or redirecting it. Teammate Phil Esposito recalled a game in which the B's were on a penalty kill against the Oakland Seals. Orr took the puck behind the Bruins net and lost a glove in a scuffle with an opponent. Retaining possession of the puck, he skated over the blue line then back into the Bruins zone, where he picked up his glove and killed off a full minute of the penalty. Concluding one of the most astounding sequences Esposito had ever seen, Orr glided into the offensive zone and scored a short-handed goal.

Though Orr's detractors claimed that he was soft on defense, others begged to differ. B's goalie Eddie Johnston, who played with Orr for several seasons, remarked: "They say Bobby doesn't play defense. Heck, he makes a forty-minute hockey game for us. He's got the puck twenty minutes by himself. What better defense is there?"[34] On a similar note, coach Harry Sinden crowed: "You can have all the Bobby Clarkes of the world. I'll take one game from Orr. He'll make thirty moves no one has seen before."[35]

Orr established himself as a cultural icon in the same manner as Joe DiMaggio. More than just a player—he became a hero to the New England masses and a legend to hockey fans outside his primary fan base. His greatest seasons were packed into a relatively short span, but his star burned brightly long after he retired as a player. To the present day, he receives resounding ovations at every public event he takes part in. Interestingly, Orr never basked in the spotlight during his playing days. After Bruins victories, he would often hide in the trainer's room and avoid reporters so that his teammates could receive credit.

Due to the cumulative effect of multiple knee injuries, Orr played in just 36 games during his final three NHL seasons. When his contract expired before the '76-'77 campaign, he allowed his agent, Alan Eagleson, to negotiate for him. Describing the climate in Boston before the season began, historian Stan Fischler wrote: "As far as any Bruins fan was concerned, Orr was as much a fixture in Boston as Bunker

Hill. Anyone who would suggest that Orr would play for any of the other seventeen NHL teams at the time would be laughed off."[36] But Orr's contract negotiations were no laughing matter as Eagleson, who was a close friend of Chicago owner Bill Wirtz, turned down a generous offer from the Bruins. Kept in the dark about the specifics of the deal, Orr assumed the B's were looking to get rid of him. When Eagleson falsely reported to Orr that the Blackhawks had made a higher bid, Orr reluctantly signed with Chicago. He finished his career there, though he later admitted that he never felt entirely comfortable with the move. He retired with an impressive array of trophies—eight Norris, three Hart, two Ross and two Stanley Cups (among other accolades).

In spite of being the highest-paid player of his generation, Orr was facing bankruptcy at the time of his retirement. He worked as an assistant coach for the Blackhawks and also served as a consultant to the NHL and Hartford Whalers. He later formed a company known as Can-Am Enterprises, building a sizable group of clients seeking endorsements. Orr's clientele included Baybank of Boston and the Toronto-based food giant, Standard Brands.

When Orr eventually learned of Eagleson's deceit, he vowed never to speak with him again. In response to charges made by Orr and several others, Eagleson was convicted of fraud, embezzlement and racketeering in 1998. Orr was one of over a dozen players who threatened to resign from the Hall of Fame if Eagleson (who was enshrined as a builder) remained. Eagleson resigned of his own accord before he could be removed.

In 1996, Orr became an agent representing hockey players. In 2002, his business was incorporated into a conglomerate known as the Orr Hockey Group. Some of the group's highest profile clients currently include Connor McDavid, Auston Mathews and Eric Staal. In 2013, Orr finally released his autobiography, titled simply *Orr: My Story*. It was well-received by readers, peaking at number 8 on the New York Times Bestseller List.

In his retirement, Orr has been involved in a vast assortment of charitable activities. Fully embracing his status as a role model, he once said: "We're professional athletes. People know who we are, and if there's some way we can help with a friend or someone in need, that's a responsibility we have. I strongly believe that."[37] In an era of rising salaries and self-absorbed athletes, those words are highly refreshing.

RICK SMITH
(1968–1972/1976–1980)

Smith's NHL career has been referred to by some as a series of accidents since he had no intention of pursuing hockey as a vocation. Growing up in Kingston, Ontario, he was a painfully shy kid who had difficulty making personal connections. His mother enrolled him in the Church Athletic League hoping he would make some new friends. Overwhelmed by the social experience, he quit on two separate occasions. The second time, he was visited at home by his coach, Bob Senior, who convinced him to continue playing. He ended up being chosen for an All-Star team coached by future Bruins scout Garry Young. That connection proved to be the key to Smith's future.

During a tournament in Trenton, Michigan, Smith was scouted and signed by the Red Wings organization. He was assigned to their OHL affiliate in Hamilton. The transition triggered his social anxiety and he hitch-hiked back to Kingston (which is located on the opposite end of Lake Ontario) one weekend. This time, it was coach Rudy Pilous who talked him into sticking with hockey. While playing for the Hamilton Red Wings, Smith enrolled in courses at McMaster University with the intention of eventually studying dentistry at the University of Toronto. His plans changed when Garry Young convinced the Bruins to select him in the second round of the 1966 Entry Draft.

Smith was nervous and ambivalent about joining the Bruins until Wayne Cashman—also from Kingston—reached out to him personally. Cashman, who became one of Boston's brightest stars during the 1970s, drove Smith to training camp in London and helped him get comfortable around his new teammates. Smith spent some time in the minors and on the Bruins bench before an opening surfaced in 1968. He appeared in 48 games with the B's that season, helping the squad to a semi-finals loss against the Canadiens.

Coach Don Cherry once referred to Smith as a "defenseman's defenseman."[38] Fitting well into the Bruins lunch-pail philosophy, he was known for expending maximum effort on every shift. In addition to being an excellent shot-blocker, he gradually established an offensive presence, taking plenty of shots and setting up opportunities for teammates. Smith seemed to raise his game to another level in the playoffs. He went to the Stanley Cup finals with the Bruins three times, coming away with a plus-20 postseason rating in those campaigns. In the deciding game of the 1970 finale, his first period goal put the Bruins up, 1–0. He later assisted on a goal that sent the game into overtime and set the stage for Bobby Orr's famous series-clincher. "That moment has been spread across my entire lifetime," he commented years later. "As time has gone on, you appreciate it even more."[39]

Smith missed out on a second Stanley Cup when he was traded to the California Golden Seals in February of 1972. The transaction came without prior warning and he described his time with the Seals as the low point of his career. "That's the only place I wasn't happy," he said. "Charlie Finley ran the team in Oakland then, but I don't think his interests were in the best interests of the team. We were in turmoil all the time."[40]

Smith left the NHL to play for the World Hockey Association with the Minnesota Fighting Saints in 1973. He reached the most productive phase of his career away from Boston, collecting no fewer than 24 assists in four consecutive seasons. His elevated play inspired the Bruins to reacquire him in December of 1976. He gelled extremely well with linemates, retiring with a plus-241 rating during his Bruins career, which spanned portions of eight seasons. His nine assists in the '77 playoffs were third on the team to Jean Ratelle and Brad Park.

Studying in the offseason, Smith eventually got a Bachelor's Degree from Queen's University in Kingston. He played his final NHL season with the Washington Capitals in '80-'81 then obtained his Master's Degree in computer science. He bought a large plot of land on Buck Lake in Ontario and worked at Queen's University teaching computer skills to faculty. Over the years, he has participated in multiple alumni events with the Bruins.

BRAD PARK
(1975–1983)

Brad Park wasn't always popular in Boston. In fact, he had to work very hard to win over fans. A superstar with the Rangers for several years, his 1971 autobiography, *Play the Man,* caused a major stir for its scathing commentary on the Bruins and their fans. In it, Park referred to the Beantown faithful as "maniacal" and the Boston Garden as "downright grubby." Even worse, he commented that the players were "a bunch of bloodthirsty animals."[41] Traded to Boston during the '75-'76 campaign, he had a long way to go to gain acceptance. But as the years wore on, he filled enough highlight reels to win the respect of players and fans in "The Hub."

Born and raised in Toronto, Park attended Neil McNeil Catholic High School. The school's hockey program supplied the Toronto Marlboros (a Maple Leafs affiliate) with top prospects every year. In 1965, Park was invited to try out for the Marlboros with several teammates. He failed the audition, but when the Red Wings extended an invitation to their own junior training camp, the Maple Leafs placed him on a protected list. He joined the Marlboros partway into the '65 campaign and was selected by the Rangers in the 1966 NHL Amateur Draft.

A bit under-sized in his early teen years, Park matured into a 6-foot, 200-pounder. He played three seasons with the Marlboros before making the jump to the AHL in '68-'69. After 17 games with the Buffalo Bisons, the Rangers felt he was ready for the big time. He made 54 appearances in his NHL debut, finishing third in voting for the Calder Trophy.

Park's official Hall of Fame biography page states that he would have been considered the best defenseman of his generation in any other era. Unfortunately, he played at a time when Bobby Orr and Denis Potvin absorbed most of the headlines. Park admitted that Orr was the best he had ever seen and, in spite of frequent comparisons, became a sensational player in his own right. Known for his "submarine checks" that upended opposing players, Park was a smooth skater, accurate shooter and quintessential play-maker. He could also play the role of a bruiser when necessary. "He was tough as nails and could body check with the best," said Don Cherry.[42] Flyers Hall of Famer Bobby Clarke agreed, commenting: "[Park] was a big, real thick man. If he hit you, he hurt you."[43]

Park became a team leader in New York, guiding the Rangers to seven straight playoff appearances ('69-'75). Shortly after the release of his controversial autobiography, Park's Blueshirts made it all the way to the Stanley Cup finals against the Bruins. To this day, many believe that Park's harsh commentary gave the B's an edge. Four of the games were decided by a single goal as Boston won its second championship in three years.

When the Rangers got off to a poor start in '75-'76, the management decided to make some moves. The New York media had turned on Park by then anyway, claiming that he was overweight and that his skills were in decline. On November 7, Park was traded to Boston with veteran sniper Jean Ratelle. The duo became the galvanizing force behind Boston's consecutive finals appearances in '77 and '78.

Though Park had been expected to play the role of enforcer in New York, coach Don Cherry felt there were plenty of tough guys on his roster already. He encouraged

Park to focus solely on his two-way play. The results were dramatic as the veteran blue-liner gathered at least 50 assists in three campaigns with the B's, averaging 40 per year during his time in Boston. His best all around season came in '77-'78, when he piled up 79 points in 80 games. In the playoffs that year, he led the team with nine goals and 11 assists while compiling a remarkable 28.1 shooting percentage.

If Park had one thing over Orr, it was durability. The two skated together only briefly due to Orr's deteriorating knees. While Orr was driven into early retirement, Park kept right on going despite his own knee problems. He even had a sense of humor about it. Limited to 32 games with the Bruins in '79 due to major knee surgery, the outspoken defenseman jokingly referred to the medical procedure as "just another stop at the garage ... the man says: 'What's the model number and the part?' and starts looking for it."[44]

When Park's contract expired before the 1983 campaign, he signed with the Red Wings. His 53 assists helped steer the club to a playoff appearance that year. Recognized for his resilience at season's end, he received the prestigious Bill Masterton Trophy. He retired at the end of the '84-'85 campaign.

Finished as a player, Park took a shot at coaching the Red Wings in '85-'86. The club tried out five different goaltenders that year and started the season with an eight-game losing streak. Park took over on December 31, inheriting the job from Harry Neale, who was fired with 45 games still remaining. Unable to save the club from a last place finish, he stepped aside before the '86-'87 campaign.

Elected to the Hockey Hall of Fame in 1998, Park has been cited by multiple sources as one of the top 100 players of all time. Though he never won it, he was a runner-up for the Norris Trophy on six occasions. He has lived comfortably on the North Shore of Massachusetts and Sebago Lake area of Maine for several decades. He has five kids and many grandchildren.

MIKE MILBURY
(1976–1987)

Milbury wore many hats during his time with the Bruins. Over the course of two decades, he served as a player, head coach and assistant to the GM. He also worked in the B's minor league system. In spite of all his service to the organization, he is largely remembered for one regrettable incident.

It happened on December 23, 1979, at Madison Square Garden. The Bruins had just scored three goals in the third period to complete an inspiring come-from-behind victory over the Rangers. In the last five seconds of regulation, goalie Gerry Cheevers denied Phil Esposito on a breakaway, preserving the win. Espo broke his stick in frustration as Rangers goalie John Davidson got into an argument with B's left-winger Al Secord. Things began to escalate when a disgruntled fan tossed food at Boston players. Another fan hit Stan Jonathan in the face with a rolled-up program, drawing blood. Milbury—playing in his fourth full season with the Bruins—accompanied Cheevers to the dressing room after the siren, but soon noticed that none of his teammates had followed. When he heard the roar of the crowd, he knew there was trouble. He returned to the ice and found several of his teammates heading into the stands to tangle with fans. In an epic lapse of judgment, Milbury joined the fray, removing an unruly fan's shoe and striking him with it. Several fans were arrested and charged with disorderly conduct. Bruins players needed more than half a dozen mounted police and several NYPD cruisers to leave the scene safely. The incident would follow Milbury for the remainder of his career, which was otherwise fairly remarkable.

Born in the Brighton section of Boston, Milbury came of age in Walpole, which is about 13 miles south of the downtown area. Not only was he an excellent student, but he played four different sports in high school. A star football player, he was recruited by Colgate University. When Colgate's hockey coach, Ron Ryan, saw Milbury's credentials, he invited him to participate in some scrimmages. Milbury secured a roster spot and was eventually named captain. Though he never won any ECAC honors, he distinguished himself as the most penalized player on the team.

Signed by the Bruins during the '74-'75 campaign, Milbury spent two seasons with the Rochester Americans before earning a full-time spot in Boston. Primarily a stay-at-home defenseman, Milbury won the respect of Bruins coach Don Cherry, who admired his strength and intelligence. His game-winning goal against the Flyers in the semi-final round of the '77 playoffs earned him a reputation as a big-game player.

Milbury was far from flashy. His klunky style sometimes invited criticism from writers. One scribe compared him to an ugly yet reliable old car. Year after year, Milbury did whatever was asked of him to help out the team. And he did it with maximum intensity. He treated every game like the playoffs and was known to channel his rage inappropriately at times, breaking sticks and brawling with opponents. He served more than a hundred penalty minutes in eight seasons, offering apologies to no one.

Milbury spent his entire career in Boston, putting up double digit assist totals in nine straight seasons. He reached a personal high of 34 assists in '78-'79. Limited to just 22 appearances due to an injury in 1985, he still managed to accrue over a hundred penalty minutes, averaging 4.6 minutes per game. During his final season as a player, the Bruins struggled in the first half, getting off to a 19–19–5 start. Though the squad ultimately made the playoffs, Milbury's declining skills prompted boos from fair-weathered fans. He retired before the start of the '87-'88 campaign.

With his playing days behind him, Milbury coached for the Maine Mariners and spent two seasons at the Bruins helm. In '89-'90, he led the club to a President's Trophy and a berth in the Stanley Cup finals. Named head coach at Boston College in 1994, he butted heads with the school's athletic department and vacated his post before the season began. He joined the Islanders organization as a GM and head coach in 1995. He was elected to the U.S. Hockey Hall of Fame in 2006.

In recent years, Milbury has worked as a studio analyst for multiple sports networks. He is known for making brash, argumentative statements and has repeatedly clashed with other commentators on the air—particularly Hall of Famer Jeremy Roenick.

RAY BOURQUE
(1979–2000)

Whenever discussions are raised regarding the greatest Bruins defensemen of all time, Bourque is invariably mentioned in the same breath as Bobby Orr. While

Orr experienced a meteoric rise to stardom and a relatively brief reign as the game's premier blue-liner, Bourque's period of productivity was much longer. Because of his remarkable durability, he surpassed Orr in nearly every statistical category. And though he may not technically have been the greatest, he had a lot more time to leave a lasting impression on fans and insiders.

Born in the Saint-Laurent borough of Montreal, Bourque had a somewhat difficult childhood, losing his mother to cancer when he was 12 years old. He attended a French school and became bilingual. His road to the NHL began in the Quebec Major Junior Hockey League with the Trois-Rivieres Draveurs. During his rookie season, he was traded to the Sorel Blackhawks and stayed with the team when it moved to Verdun.

When Bourque was drafted in 1979, the Bruins were actually considering Keith Brown. They had traded goalie Ron Grahame to the Kings in exchange for a first-round pick. When the Blackhawks selected Brown first, the B's took Bourque. It turned out to be one of the best acquisitions in franchise history.

Bourque wore the number 29 during his first training camp. Before the season got underway, he was assigned Phil Esposito's old number, which was still active at the time. Bourque proved his worth to the Bruins on his very first shift, recording an assist. He netted his first goal later in the game, finishing the season with 65 points— good enough to claim the Calder Trophy. Years later, when Esposito's number was retired, Bourque honored the former superstar by removing his number 7 jersey during the ceremony and handing it over. He was wearing the number 77 underneath.

Designated an All-Star in 17 consecutive seasons, Bourque always felt that defense should be his primary focus. Coach Brian Sutter offered lavish praise for the versatile blue-liner, commenting: "In my opinion, [Bourque] was the greatest defenseman since the greatest-ever defenseman, Bobby Orr. He just did everything—and as good or better than anyone else. He was solid defensively, ran the power play—a guy that was always better in his own side of the rink—[he] played 30–35 minutes a night every night."[45] The Hockey Writers Association strongly agreed with that assessment, awarding Bourque the Norris Trophy five times.

Bourque served as team captain for 15 seasons. He had a positive effect on young players, offering guidance and support. His unwavering focus and exceptional puck-handling ability made him a valuable asset on special teams. Over the course of his Bruins career, he recorded 164 goals and 553 assists with a man-advantage. He added 14 short-handed goals along with 28 helpers in penalty-killing situations.

A man of routines, Bourque had a peculiar pre-game custom of touching the goalie's pads with his stick in a particular order. The ritual ended with a little spin and a final tap. As Bourque's fan base grew to epic proportions, the Bruins ordered two dozen sticks for him before every game. He chose four to use and donated the rest to be auctioned off for charity or given to fans as souvenirs.

Though many believed he would spend his entire career with the Bruins, Bourque was traded to Colorado in March of 2000. Asked about the deal, he said: "Why now? Well, two reasons: I asked to be traded because I want to win the Cup. It's the one thing I haven't accomplished in my career. And two: At this point in time, I needed a change. I want to find out what's left to Ray Bourque."[46] Bourque had plenty left to offer, gathering 92 points for the Avalanche in 128 games (including the playoffs). Skating alongside Hall of Famers Joe Sakic, Peter Forsberg and Patrick Roy, he won the Cup in his final season, retiring as a champion. He was elected to the Hockey Hall of Fame in 2004 and his number was retired in two cities (Boston and Colorado). He holds the record for most career goals (410), assists (1,169) and points (1,579) by a defenseman.

Bourque settled in the Boston area after his retirement. At the time of this writing, he was co-owner of a restaurant called Tresca in the city's North End. He has served as a Bruins team consultant and remains active in multiple charities. In 2017, he started the Bourque Family Foundation, which supports a wide array of charitable causes and educational endeavors. Two of Bourque's sons played hockey professionally.

GLEN WESLEY
(1987–1994)

Wesley grew up in Red Deer, Alberta—a populous city located halfway between Calgary and Edmonton. He got started in junior hockey with the Red Deer Rustlers and quickly ascended to the Western Hockey League. While skating for the Portland Winter Hawks, he was named WHL Defenseman of the Year in two consecutive campaigns.

During the summer of 1986, the Bruins traded Barry Pederson to the Canucks in exchange for Cam Neely and a first-round pick. The pick was used to grab Wesley in the '87 Entry Draft. Instead of sending him to the AHL for conditioning, the B's added him to their roster straight out of junior hockey.

The 19-year-old Wesley joined a young Bruins team on the rise. Playing alongside fellow rookies Craig Janney and Bob Sweeney, he collected 37 points, helping the Bruins reach the Stanley Cup finals against the Edmonton Oilers. He scored a pair of goals in the ill-fated Game 4, which ended in a 3–3 tie due to a power failure at the Boston Garden. His efforts that season earned him a berth on the NHL All-Rookie Team. He also finished fourth in voting for the Calder Trophy, which ultimately went to Joe Nieuwendyk of the Calgary Flames.

Early in his career, Wesley was asked to play a significant offensive role, appearing on the Bruins power play unit beside Ray Bourque. An excellent skater and breakout passer, he had a hard, accurate shot and was not shy about putting pucks on net. Though his numbers were likely skewed by the presence of Bourque, he gathered 30 or more assists during five of his seasons with the Bruins. His lowest total was 25 in '92-'93—a year in which he missed 20 games. Wesley reached the peak of his offensive prowess in '93-'94, collecting 58 points (14 goals/44 assists). In spite of his contributions, the B's finished second in their division and lost to the Devils in the semi-final round. Team executives began planning for the future at that point, trading Wesley to the Hartford Whalers in exchange for successive first round picks in '95, '96 and '97.

The departure of Wesley marked the beginning of a downward spiral for Boston. "There was a lot more to that trade than probably just the player," former Hartford general manager Jim Rutherford recalled.[47] At the time, Boston and Hartford were bitter New England rivals. Fearing the Whalers had given up too much to acquire Wesley, Connecticut governor Lowell Weicker approached Rutherford and said: "We are going to find out if that old, experienced guy in Boston is going to teach you a lesson."[48] Weicker was referring to Bruins GM Harry Sinden. In spite of the governor's vexing statement, Rutherford was confident his team had made the right decision. "We knew we were getting a true professional, a good player—on the ice and off the ice—with character, who we expected to have a long time, which we did."[49] The Bruins used their draft picks to acquire standouts Kyle McLaren and Sergei Samsonov, but the team ended up missing the playoffs three times in a five-year span.

Meanwhile, Wesley enjoyed a prosperous career with the Whalers, hanging around after the team moved to Carolina and began playing as the Hurricanes. No longer expected to be a major offensive presence, he became a top-notch defender and a mentor to young players. He had good instincts, knowing precisely where to position himself to slow down opponents. He avoided excess penalties and kept his mistakes to a minimum.

With the Hurricanes sitting in last place near the end of the 2002-'03 campaign, Wesley (playing in his 16th NHL season then) left the team to join the Maple Leafs, who were in contention for the Cup. Wesley missed out again as Toronto bowed to Philadelphia in the first round. He returned to Carolina the following year and helped the club to a championship in 2006. It was his fourth trip to the Stanley Cup finals. He made his last appearance as a player two seasons later.

During his days with the Bruins, Wesley lived in Danvers, Massachusetts. He moved to Avon, Connecticut, after he joined the Whalers and later migrated to Cary, North Carolina, when the team relocated. He officially became a United States citizen in 2005. His number was retired by the Hurricanes in 2009. Wesley's brother, Blake, was also an NHL defenseman. His son, Josh, was drafted by the Hurricanes in 2014. At the time of this writing, Wesley was working as director of defensive development for the St. Louis Blues.

DON SWEENEY
(1988–2003)

Sweeney was raised in St. Stephen, New Brunswick, which is situated on the St. Croix River near the U.S.-Canadian Border. The town—with a population of less than 5,000—is home to the Ganong chocolate company, Canada's oldest candy manufacturer. Sweeney is among a minority of professionals who never played junior hockey. He skated for a prestigious prep school in Concord, New Hampshire, known as St. Paul's. An excellent student, Sweeney was among a small body of undergraduates selected from all over the world.

In '83-'84, Sweeney scored 59 points in 22 games for St. Paul's, grabbing the attention of the Bruins. Drafted in the eighth round, he postponed his NHL career to attend Harvard University. While working on a degree in economics, he played four seasons with the Harvard Crimson, earning All-Star and All-American honors in his senior year. Upon graduating, he threw himself into professional hockey full time.

Sweeney spent portions of three seasons in the American Hockey League before securing a permanent roster spot in Boston. In '89-'90, he helped the Bruins reach the Stanley Cup finals against the Edmonton Oilers. The series ended in a disappointing four-games-to-one loss, but Sweeney contributed six points during the playoffs—the highest postseason total of his career. He never reached the final round again, but he did aid the Bruins to a total of 10 playoff appearances.

A defensive-minded blue-liner, Sweeney didn't contribute much to the Bruins' offense. Because defensive statistics such as hits, blocks and takeaways weren't officially recorded during his career, it's difficult to gauge his value to the club in a statistical sense. But his 1,052 appearances with a team known to place extremely high demands on its players are a testament to Sweeney's overall worth. As of 2020, only two other defenseman had skated in over a thousand games with Boston—Ray Bourque and Zdeno Chara. To say Sweeney is in elite company in that respect is a vast understatement.

Sweeney wasn't terribly large at 5-foot-10, 185 pounds, but he played hard. "I've always felt like I've been up against the wall—I don't want to say an overachiever— in terms of finding a way to battle despite my size and such," he once said.[50] Whatever he lacked in physicality, he made up for with his wide range and superior hockey intellect. Soft-spoken and modest, he was content to fly under the radar throughout his career. "It's my character to be quiet and try to be unassuming. I just go about my business," he explained.[51]

In spite of his attempt to avoid the spotlight, Sweeney collected a personal high of 34 points (7 goals/27 assists) in '92-'93 while accruing a plus-34 rating. Fans were duly impressed with his performance, giving him enough votes to claim the Seventh Player Award. Sweeney was a valuable asset to every unit he played on throughout his career, finishing with a positive plus/minus rating during nine seasons.

After spending portions of 15 campaigns with the Bruins, Sweeney joined the Dallas Stars in 2003. He retired at season's end. He worked as a broadcaster briefly before returning to Boston as director of player development in 2006. By 2009, he had aspired to the position of assistant GM. After the firing of Peter Chiarelli in May of 2015, Sweeney took over as GM—a post he still occupied as of 2020. At the time of this writing, the team was stacked with young talent and the future was looking bright.

KYLE McLAREN
(1995–2002)

McLaren is among an unfortunate group of former Bruins stars who have been stigmatized for their roles in regrettable on-ice incidents. McLaren's day of infamy occurred during Game 4 of the 2002 Eastern Conference quarter-finals. In the waning minutes of a 5–2 Bruins victory over the Canadiens, McLaren elbowed Montreal winger Richard Zednik in the face, knocking him senseless. Fans littered the ice with debris as Zednik lay semi-conscious for several minutes. McLaren received a match penalty and three-game suspension for his actions. Zednik was carted off the ice on a stretcher and ended up spending two days in the hospital. Though McLaren later expressed regret over the episode, it would follow him for the remainder of his career.

McLaren was born in Humboldt, Saskatchewan. He later attended high school in Alberta and played midget hockey with the Lethbridge Y's Men Titans. During the '92-'93 campaign, he netted 28 goals and added 28 assists, earning a promotion to the Western Hockey League. He was the third-highest scoring defenseman on the Tacoma Rockets squad in '94-'95, helping the team to a second-place finish in the Western Division. Enamored with his size and strength, the Bruins chose him in the first round of the '95 Entry Draft.

McLaren made his Bruins debut without any minor league experience. Though he was the youngest player in the NHL during the '95-'96 campaign, he was by no means the smallest. At 6-foot-4, 235 pounds, he was the most physically imposing skater on the Bruins roster. He had a solid rookie season, earning a selection to the NHL All-Rookie Team and finishing eighth in voting for the Calder Trophy. Fans in Boston took an immediate liking to him, handing him enough votes for the Seventh Player Award.

McLaren became known for his punishing hip checks and gritty style of play. Though he often served as an enforcer, he was not particularly spiteful or dirty, never accruing more than 84 minutes of penalty time in any season. "I play a physical game," he once said, "but I don't intentionally go out and try to hurt anybody."[52] The relentless grind of throwing his body around led to multiple injuries during his career—particularly between 2000 and 2002, when he missed more than 60 games with the Bruins.

McLaren's spirited play also resulted in plenty of altercations. During his 12 seasons in the NHL, he was involved in more than two dozen fights, frequently getting the upper hand. But he was not entirely one-dimensional. He reached a personal high of eight goals in '99–2000 and finished with double digit assist totals in eight campaigns.

During the summer of 2002, McLaren got into a contract dispute with Bruins GM Mike O'Connell, who offered him a two-way deal that included a significant pay cut if he was demoted to the minors. Those types of proposals are somewhat unusual for veterans and McLaren admitted to being insulted. "I've been in the league for seven years and it hurt," he said. "It's the fact that I was offered it that stung."[53] He held out for four months while waiting for the Bruins to decide what to do with him. At one point, he was skating with a junior team to stay in shape. In the end, the San Jose Sharks traded top prospect Jeff Jillson and veteran goaltender Jeff Hackett in exchange for McLaren. Upon leaving Boston, McLaren tried to clear the air. "It has nothing to do with the players on the team or the coaching staff or money," he commented.[54]

McLaren spent five seasons with San Jose, steering the club to four playoff appearances. This included a trip to the conference finals against the Flames in 2003-'04. He was hit in the face with a slapshot during the regular season that year, sitting out for two weeks. He played with a visor on his helmet from that point forward. In 2008, the Sharks put him on waivers due to salary cap issues. He ended up playing for the club's AHL affiliate in Worcester. Traded to the Flyers in March of 2009, he failed a physical and was released. The Rangers and Thrashers both invited him to their training camps in subsequent years, but he didn't make the cut.

Finished as a player, McLaren retired to the Sacramento area. At the time of this writing, he was still busy coaching junior hockey for the Sharks. He was also working as a broadcaster.

HAL GILL
(1997–2006)

Gill's story is one of a local New England boy who made good. Born in Concord, Massachusetts, he came of age in nearby Bolton. He grew up watching Bruins games on TV and was an avid fan of Ray Bourque. A multi-sport star at Nashoba Regional High School, he ultimately chose hockey over football and baseball. In his senior year, he collected 50 points (25 goals/25 assists) in just 20 games. He later received a call from the Bruins informing him that he had been drafted in the eighth round.

Gill spent four seasons honing his hockey skills with the Providence College Friars. He was invited to a tryout with the Bruins after his graduation. A big man at 6-foot-7, 250 pounds, he remembered nearly everyone wanting a piece of him during his first training camp. "I felt like I was getting into a scrap every day," he said. "I met my mother for dinner one night during camp and she saw the black eye and the bloody knuckles—it was a new experience for both of us."[55] He got through it with flying colors and fondly recalled Ray Bourque serenading him to the tune of Barry Manilow's "Looks Like We Made It" when it was over.

After a brief appearance with the Providence Bruins, Gill found a permanent roster spot in Boston. For eight seasons, he was one of the B's most durable defensemen, missing just a handful of games. Though he didn't figure heavily into the team's offensive scheme, he was a top-notch defender. His style of play changed as the NHL began to crack down on old school tactics. "It used to be that you'd grab a guy and hold him, hook him, pin him into the boards and wrestle and push," he said bluntly. "When the NHL returned after the lockout [in 2005], the rules changed. No more holding, no more hooking, there was more slashing and hitting. You'd have to try to whack a guy's hands.... Now they're taking that away. Defensively now, you just have to be fast and recover your position."[56]

Gill spent a fair amount of time in the penalty box before adjusting to the league-wide crackdown. He averaged over a hundred minutes of penalties per year between 2003-'04 and 2006-'07. His time in the box decreased exponentially after that. Because of his daunting size, he was expected to stand up for smaller teammates—a responsibility he willingly accepted. He is among a select group of players who have tangled with Zdeno Chara (then with the Senators) twice. The 6-foot-9 Chara gave Gill all he could handle both times.

In July of 2006, Gill signed as a free agent with the Maple Leafs. He spent portions of eight more seasons in the NHL with a number of teams, finally winning the Stanley Cup as a member of the Penguins in 2009. He served as alternate team captain during his tenure in Montreal, which spanned the better part of three campaigns. A practical joker, Gill and his Montreal teammates once stacked boxes in front of Brian Gionta's locker so the vertically challenged winger (at 5-foot-7) could stand on them during interviews.

Though he donned five other uniforms during his NHL career, Gill still holds fond memories of his time in Boston. He told one reporter that he loved being part of the Bruins-Canadiens rivalry and felt that it elevated his game. He also appreciated the passion and honesty of Boston fans, remarking that they were not shy about expressing their opinions—especially if he had turned in a poor performance.

Injured by a slapshot in 2012, Gill was limited to 32 games that season. He played with a steel plate and screws in his ankle afterward. He made his last NHL appearance with the Flyers in 2013-'14 and retired with more than 1,100 games under his belt. He also skated with the U.S. National Hockey Team in several World Cups, helping the squad to a Bronze Medal in 2004.

With his playing days behind him, Gill served as manager of player development for the Florida Panthers. He coached the Lincoln-Sudbury regional boys hockey team to a Division 2 North title in 2016. After making sporadic appearances for the NESN network as an analyst, he joined the Nashville Predators radio broadcasting team in 2017.

ZDENO CHARA
(2006–PRESENT)

The first thing that comes to mind when most people talk about Zdeno Chara is his size. At 6-foot-9, he is the tallest player in the NHL. The second topic most often discussed is his durability. As of 2020, Chara was in his 22nd NHL season and still averaging over 20 minutes of ice time per game.

Pretty remarkable for a 43-year-old.

Born in Trencin, Slovakia (formerly known as Czechoslovakia), Chara grew up in the same community as NHL standouts Marian Gaborik and Marian Hossa. Chara's father was an exceptional Greco-Roman wrestler who competed in the 1976 Summer Olympics in Montreal. Following his dad's example, Chara became preoccupied with physical conditioning while growing up. His earliest memory of North American hockey dates back to 1991, when a neighbor with a satellite dish invited him to watch the Stanley Cup final between the Pittsburgh Penguins and Minnesota North Stars. Chara maintained a keen interest in the NHL from that point forward.

Prior to being drafted, Chara's coaches tried to talk him into switching to basketball. He kept his sights set on hockey instead, playing in multiple European leagues before the Islanders made him their third-round pick in 1996. Assigned to the Western Hockey League that year, he made the jump to the AHL the following season, splitting time with the Islanders and the Kentucky Thoroughblades. He played his first full campaign with New York in 1999. In one of the biggest trades of the early 2000s, he was sent to Ottawa in exchange for veteran sniper Alexei Yashin and a first-round draft pick. Making the most of the deal, the Senators used their pick to acquire center Jason Spezza, who would average a point per game in more than a decade of play in Ottawa.

Chara skated with the Senators for four seasons, helping the club reach the playoffs every year. In 2003, the team narrowly missed a berth in the Stanley Cup finals. Down three games to one against the Devils in the Eastern Conference playoff, the Sens rallied to force a Game 7. The finale was tied at two in the third period before New Jersey winger Jeff Friesen beat goalie Patrick Lalime with less than three minutes remaining in regulation. The Devils moved on to an NHL title, beating Anaheim in seven games.

Chara remained with the Senators until July of 2006, when he jumped at a $37.5

Few opponents choose to tangle with the 6-foot-9, 250-pound Zdeno Chara. In this photograph, the brave challenger is Georges Laroque of the Penguins. Courtesy Dan4th on VisualHunt.com/CC BY.

million contract offer from the Bruins. He was designated team captain, filling an opening left by the departure of Joe Thornton. He was the third Slovakian captain in NHL history, following in the footsteps of Stan Mikita (Chicago Blackhawks) and Peter Stastny (Quebec Nordiques).

During his long stint with Boston, Chara has established himself as one of the game's elite defensemen. A lumbering skater, he makes up for his lack of speed with incredible range. Because of his extreme height, the NHL allows him to use sticks two inches longer than regulation. With his arm and stick fully extended, he has a reach of over 10 feet. When he can't sweep the puck away from opponents, he uses his hulking frame to deliver crushing body checks. His mere presence on the ice makes opposing players think twice about misbehaving. Among the most formidable pugilists of the modern era, Chara has engaged in more than 70 fights over the years, winning most of them. In lieu of dropping the gloves, he has also been known to shove, slash and spear opponents who irritate him. Though he accrued more than a hundred penalty minutes in seven consecutive seasons, he has mellowed a bit with age. His regular season penalty totals have not exceeded 80 minutes since the 2011-'12 campaign.

During the All-Star Skills Competition in 2012, Chara's slapshot was clocked at 108.8 miles per hour—an NHL record. Only Shea Weber has come close to matching the feat with speeds of 108.5 and 108.1. Chara's massive shots make him a valuable member of Boston's power play unit. Nearly 50 percent of his lifetime goals have come with a man-advantage. He has added no fewer than 23 assists on 11 occasions.

Chara's toughness is legendary. Since blocked shots became an official statistic in 2007, he has been plugged over a hundred times in eight campaigns. The one that hurt the most came in Game 4 of the 2019 Stanley Cup finals, when he took a slapshot to the face, resulting in multiple jaw fractures. Instead of sitting out the rest of the postseason, he returned to action in Game 5, wearing a full shield on his helmet. The Boston crowd gave him a rousing ovation and chanted his name before the National Anthem. His goal in Game 6 made him the oldest defenseman to score in the finals. His appearance in the series finale established a new record for most Game 7 starts (13). He has posted the highest plus/minus rating among postseason skaters twice during his career.

Chara speaks seven languages fluently, an impressive skill considering that a majority of folks in the United States aren't even bilingual. After tearing a ligament in his left knee during the 2014 campaign, he obtained his real estate license, explaining to a reporter: "I like to keep as many doors open as possible for the future."[57] As of 2020, his career was winding down, but his post-retirement prospects were looking bright given his considerable earnings over the years.

In 2018-'19, Chara received the John P. Bucyk Trophy for charitable and community endeavors. Over the years, he has been involved in multiple charities, including the "Right to Play," an international non-profit organization that empowers vulnerable children to overcome the effects of war, poverty and disease. In 2008, Chara spent two weeks in Africa with the organization. Over the Thanksgiving holiday in 2019, he showed up in person to serve turkey to disadvantaged individuals at a Boston soup kitchen. He received the Messier Trophy in 2011, which is awarded for leadership on and off the ice.

Chara's name was dragged through the mud during the 2011 campaign after his hard check on Max Pacioretty sent the Canadiens forward sprawling into a stanchion at the end of the player's bench. Pacioretty lost consciousness and was taken off the ice on a stretcher. He was later diagnosed with a fractured vertebrae and severe concussion. Video of the hit was reviewed by NHL officials, who determined that Chara's game misconduct penalty was sufficient punishment. Montreal police opened a criminal investigation shortly afterward, but found no cause to press formal charges. After Chara offered an apology to Pacioretty by phone, the Montreal winger said that all was forgiven and that he respected Chara for making the call.

In spite of the incident, Chara has earned universal respect from teammates and opponents over the years. A Norris Trophy recipient in 2009, he was a runner-up on two other occasions. Life off the ice has been equally fulfilling for Chara as his wife gave birth to twin sons in 2016. He has made his home in Boston for many years.

Andrew Ference
(2007–2013)

Though Ference gained a reputation as a spirited brawler, he didn't really fit the mold. A humanitarian and environmental activist, he was decorated for his efforts to save the planet and foster a more equalitarian culture within the world of hockey. Those efforts have continued to the present day.

Born in Edmonton, Alberta, Ference idolized Hall of Fame defenseman Paul Coffey while growing up. A standout from an early age, he joined the Portland Winter Hawks of the Western Hockey League and ended up being selected by Pittsburgh in the eighth round of the '97 Entry Draft. Assigned to the team's minor league affiliate in Wilkes-Barre/Scranton, he made his first NHL appearance during the '99–2000 campaign.

After multiple call-ups and reassignments, Ference finally caught on with the Penguins in 2001-'02. His full-time status was short-lived as he ended up being traded to Calgary for a third round pick the following year. He missed a majority of the '02-'03 campaign with groin and ankle issues, but returned to help the Flames to a Stanley Cup finals appearance in 2004. During the lockout that followed, he signed with a Czech Republic team and played overseas.

Looking to strengthen their defensive corps, the Bruins acquired Ference along with winger Chuck Kobasew in February of 2007. Though he wasn't a particularly large man (5-foot-11, 182 pounds), Ference became known for his fiery style of play. In the words of one writer, he "played like a man five inches taller and fifty pound heavier his entire career. [He] was utterly fearless during his time in Boston and earned a reputation for being a player that would seek instant justice for any slights committed on the ice."[58] Ference engaged in more than two dozen brawls over the course of his career, providing assurance to teammates that they could count on him when there was ugliness afoot.

Ference wasn't a dominant offensive presence, but he did gather 115 points in 442 games as a Bruin (including the postseason). He also finished with a positive plus/minus rating. His plus-22 mark in 2010-'11 was third best among Bruins defensemen behind Zdeno Chara and Adam McQuaid. In Game 4 of the 2011 quarter-finals against the Canadiens, he stirred up controversy when he accidentally gave fans at the Bell Centre the finger while celebrating a goal. "I was pumping my fist," he explained after reviewing the video. "I think my glove got caught up.... It looks awful. I admit it and I completely apologize for how it looks."[59] He was fined $2,500 in spite of the apology.

Ference scored four goals in the 2011 postseason—one of which was a game-winner. He added six assists as the Bruins captured their first Stanley Cup since the Bobby Orr era. When the series was over, Ference arranged to have his personal tattoo artist set up shop in the Boston Garden. A majority of Bruins players received variations of the classic spoked-B design.

Ference spent portions of seven seasons with Boston, finishing his playing career in Edmonton, where he was named team captain. He was a commanding clubhouse presence wherever he went. In 1999, he was named Western Hockey League Humanitarian of the Year. And in 2014, he received the NHL's prestigious King Clancy Memorial Trophy, which is given to players who demonstrate leadership qualities and engage in significant humanitarian endeavors.

For years, Ference's teammates jokingly referred to him as a "tree-hugger" or a "hippie" because he drove an electric car, rode his bicycle everywhere and was an outspoken advocate of composting. He worked with the David Suzuki Foundation to kick-start the NHL green initiative—a carbon-neutral program that significantly reduces the negative environmental impact of NHL teams. He is also a strong supporter of LGBTQ equality in hockey.

Just six games into the 2015-'16 campaign, Ference underwent season-ending hip surgery. He was placed on long-term injured reserve before announcing his retirement. In 2018, he became the NHL's first director of social impact, growth and fan development. With a degree in corporate sustainability from Harvard, he is well suited for the job. Ference believes that the culture of hockey is changing and embraces it. "We have to be more inclusive," he said of the NHL's future. "When you look at the demographics of the United States, when you look at the immigration that's going to happen in the U.S and Canada for decades to come, you have no other choice than to reach beyond the traditional audience of middle-aged white dudes. You have to change if you want to stay relevant."[60]

Wise words from a very wise man.

JOHNNY BOYCHUK
(2009–2014)

Of Ukrainian descent, Boychuk was born and raised in Edmonton. He has pointed out that hockey was not really a choice for him since he came from a family of devoted fans who expected him to play. He was actually quite drawn to baseball while growing up, trying out every position except pitcher. In 1997, his Pee Wee Hockey squad won the city championship, earning a berth in the annual Quebec international tournament. He focused primarily on ice-related activities from that point forward, climbing to the junior level with the Calgary Hitmen of the Western Hockey League.

Boychuk's two-way abilities caught the eye of Colorado scouts and he ended up being chosen 61st overall in the 2002 Entry Draft. During his long, winding road to the NHL, he played in the American Hockey League with the Hershey Bears, Lowell Lock Monsters, Albany River Rats and Lake Erie Monsters. He skated with the Avalanche briefly during the 2007-'08 campaign but failed to secure a permanent roster spot.

Boychuk served as a part-time forward in the Colorado system—a role he found somewhat troublesome. "It's kind of a weird situation," he said. "I'd be playing defense for half a period. Then they'd say, 'Hey, come play forward.' So I'd say, 'OK' ... then with the last 5–10 minutes of a game, they'd move me back to defense and I'd play the last 10 minutes on defense if it was a close game."[61]

Acquired by the Bruins in June of 2008, he was sent to Providence, where he became a full-time member of the defensive corps. He was an overnight success, gathering 66 points and winning the Eddie Shore Award, which is given to the top AHL defenseman. Boychuk was caught off guard by his sudden offensive surge. "It was a surprise," he admitted. "My previous high was 32. I was going to shoot for 35 or 40."[62]

Boychuk made the Bruins roster out of training camp in 2009-'10, but was a healthy scratch during the first few months of the season. He was sent back to Providence for a tune-up, returning in time to make 51 appearances for Boston. He scored five goals and added 10 assists while averaging over 17 minutes of ice time per game. Working well with linemates, he finished the regular season with a plus-10 rating. In the playoffs, he continued to emerge as an offensive presence, gathering six points in 13 games as the Bruins lost to the Flyers in the conference semi-finals. At season's end, Boychuk was on the list of candidates for the Calder Trophy.

Boychuk's ice time increased significantly during the Bruins' championship run in 2010-'11. He scored three goals in the postseason that year, one of which was a game-winner. By then, he had firmly established himself as one of the Bruins' top blue-liners. "He was patient before he got in our lineup," said Boston GM Peter Chiarelli. "He learned our system. He's got a dimensional shot. He competes. He's got size.... We have a very good defensive system and Johnny has picked it up."[63] In the wake of the Bruins' Stanley Cup victory, Boychuk was rewarded with a three-year contract extension.

As of 2020, Boychuk had double-digit assist totals in nine campaigns. During his five full seasons in Boston, he accrued a plus/minus rating of (+) 108 (including playoff action). A fearless shot-blocker, he avoided penalties and kept his checks clean. Used on both power-plays and penalty-kills, he became known for his hard slapshots, which sometimes caught opposing goalies off guard.

In October of 2014, salary cap restraints prompted the Bruins to trade Boychuk to the Islanders for a pair of second round picks. He has matured into a team leader and prominent offensive force, peaking at nine goals and 26 assists in 2014-'15. The Isles, a young and emerging team, made three playoff appearances during Boychuk's first five seasons with the club. In March of 2020, Boychuk sustained a frightening injury when he took an Artturi Lehkonen skate to the face, opening a wound that required 90 stitches. The injury affected his visual acuity and forced him into voluntary retirement before the 2021 campaign.

ADAM MCQUAID
(2009–2018)

McQuaid was born in Charlottetown, which is located on Prince Edward Island—the smallest but most populous of three Canadian maritime provinces. He grew up in nearby Cornwall and became enamored with hockey at an early age. His boyhood idol was Hall of Famer Doug Gilmour—a forward who started out as a defenseman. McQuaid began his own journey to the NHL with a local junior team. From there, he ascended to the OHL with the Sudbury Wolves. He spent four seasons in Sudbury, helping the team to an appearance in the J. Ross Robertson Cup finals during his last campaign. Selected by the Columbus Blue Jackets in the second round of the 2005 Entry Draft, he was traded to Boston for a fifth-round pick in 2007. Assigned to Providence, his tremendous physical play caught the attention of Bruins executives, who summoned him to Boston near the end of the 2009-'10 campaign.

McQuaid spent eight full seasons with the Bruins, earning the title of alternate captain in 2011. Known for his board-rattling hits, he flattened opponents in virtually every NHL city. Well-proportioned at 6-foot-4, 210 pounds, he served as an enforcer and protector. A more than capable fighter, he had a habit of grabbing opponents by the sweater and keeping them at arm's length while shaking them violently. His powerful roundhouse punches sent many sprawling to the ice. In spite of his willingness to drop the gloves, he never accrued more than 100 penalty minutes in any NHL season.

McQuaid was a bit slow afoot and not a terribly smooth skater. But his slapshots had good velocity. Though he didn't light the lamp very often, he had a knack for scoring at opportune moments. Twenty-five percent of his goals with Boston were of the game-winning variety.

McQuaid's selfless play won the admiration of teammates, who greatly appreciated his willingness to consistently put himself in harm's way. He finished among the team leaders in hits during every season in which he was healthy. And he blocked more than a hundred shots in four campaigns. His best all-around season came in 2010-'11, when he scored 15 points (3 goals/12 assists) and finished with a plus-38 rating (including the postseason). He was rewarded for his efforts with a Stanley Cup.

McQuaid's rough style of play resulted in a wide assortment of injuries over the years. Among the most bizarre was a concussion sustained after he tripped over his own suitcase. During the 2017 slate, he suffered a broken leg in a game against the Canucks. Traded to the Rangers the following year, he never fully recovered. After sitting out more than 40 games with New York, he was traded to Columbus in September of 2019. Blue Jackets GM Julius Bergman had high hopes for the veteran blue-liner. "Adam McQuaid is a tough, physical defenseman with a Stanley Cup championship on his resume," Bergman said. "He is very respected and will bring great character and leadership to our club."[64] Unfortunately, McQuaid ended up playing just 14 games with Columbus before landing on the injured list.

Prior to the 2019-'20 season, there was talk in Boston of re-acquiring McQuaid. But it was not to be. Unable to skate without pain, McQuaid spent the season debating his retirement. He told a reporter in November of 2019: "Ultimately it's just all about long-term health and getting back to feeling good. Sometimes you have to take a step back and think outside of just hockey itself. So that's kind of where I'm at now."[65] He had no regrets about his rough style of play. "You could say it shortened my career," he said. "Or you could say that my career wouldn't even have been as long as it was if I didn't play the way I did."[66]

McQuaid still lives in Boston and treasures the memories of his time with the Bruins. As of 2021, his NHL future remained uncertain.

Dennis Seidenberg
(2010–2016)

Born in the German town of Villingen-Schwenningen, Seidenberg idolized defenseman Uwe Krupp while growing up. Krupp was the first German-born player to win a Stanley Cup. As a pre-teen, Seidenberg played hockey with a team from Baden-Wurttemberg, which is located in southwest Germany near the border of

France. He appeared in the '94 and '95 International Pee Wee Hockey Tournaments in Quebec.

Seidenberg moved up to the junior level in 1999 and was rather quickly promoted to the Adler Mannheim team—a professional squad affiliated with the Deutsche Eishockey Liga (which is Germany's highest level of play). Selected by the Flyers in the 2001 Entry Draft, he spent two seasons with the Philadelphia Phantoms, helping the club to a 2005 Calder Cup championship. He would likely have been a full-timer in the NHL sooner if not for the lockout in 2004-'05.

Seidenberg had difficulty finding a permanent home in the National Hockey League. In 2005-'06, the Flyers traded him to the Coyotes. He was dealt to the Hurricanes the following year. He spent two full seasons in Carolina before signing with the Panthers prior to the 2009-'10 campaign. When the trade deadline approached, he was transferred to Boston in a deal involving four other players. He soon entered the peak of his career.

Seidenberg was an essential piece of the Bruins championship puzzle in 2011. Paired with Zdeno Chara, he scored 11 points and accrued a plus-12 rating during the postseason that year. He averaged over 27 minutes of ice time as the Bruins ended a Stanley Cup drought that had lasted more than three decades. Joining his boyhood hero on a very short list, Seidenberg was just the second German-born player to hoist the Cup.

In the locker room, Seidenberg was humble and cheerful—often smiling and joking with teammates. On the ice, he was all business. Bruins Coach Claude Julien remarked of Seidenberg's work ethic: "Seids is one of those guys that just never seems to get tired. We're the ones having to pull him back because constantly, everyday, he wants to work a little harder."[67]

Seidenberg played a rough, but clean game, never serving more than 41 penalty minutes in any season. He frequently appeared among the team leaders in hits. With little regard for his personal well-being, he threw himself in front of shots constantly. In 2014-'15, he blocked 146 shots yet somehow managed to avoid injury, appearing in all 82 regular season games.

In addition to his blue-line skills, Seidenberg's offensive abilities were frequently on display. Bruins GM Peter Chiarelli proclaimed: "[Seidenberg] is strong, defensively sound, moves the puck well from a good defensive position. But I think you've also seen his ability to make a very good pass. He's got a very good one-timer, he sees the ice well, he pinches in the offensive zone.... We knew there were other facets to his game."[68]

Used on both power plays and penalty kills during his career, Seidenberg had his best offensive season with the Bruins in 2010-'11, gathering seven goals and 25 assists. He was not afraid to shoot the puck, averaging more than a hundred shots per year during his six full seasons in Boston. He scored seven game-winning goals for the B's.

In 2016, Seidenberg signed with the Islanders, playing the role of mentor to a very young team on the rise. He opened his home to rookie Mat Barzal, who won the Calder Trophy while living with Seidenberg and his family. Limited to just 28 games due to injuries in 2017-'18, Seidenberg remained out of action the following year. He announced his retirement in October of 2019. "Physically it just does not work anymore," he told reporters. "My shoulder and wrists are pretty much done after fifteen years in the NHL."[69] At the time of this writing, Seidenberg had not made public any future plans in hockey.

Torey Krug
(2012–Present)

A product of "Hockey Town," Krug grew up in the Detroit suburb of Livonia. As a boy, he was a loyal follower of the Red Wings and dreamed of playing for them someday. His favorite player was Pavel Datsyuk, who he admired for his multi-dimensional skills. Krug skated in the 2003 Quebec International Pee Wee Hockey Tournament with the Detroit Honeybaked club. He later played at the junior level with the Indiana Ice. In 2008-'09, he collected 47 points (a team record for Indiana defenseman) and led his squad to a USHL championship.

All three of Krug's brothers participated in college sports. Krug was no exception, joining the Michigan State University hockey program in the fall of 2009. Though he was only expected to be a third-line player, he became a central figure on the club, leading CCHA rookie defenseman with 21 points. Other accolades soon followed as he was elected team captain in his sophomore year. During the 2011-'12 campaign, he was a finalist for the Central Collegiate Hockey Association Player of the Year. He was also a candidate for the Hobey Baker Award, which is given annually to the best college player in the nation. By the time Krug left school to play for the Bruins, he was being courted by multiple teams.

Krug made his NHL debut in April of 2012. He spent most of the following season in Providence, getting an emergency call-up from the Bruins around playoff time. He scored his first NHL goal in the semi-final round against the Rangers and later became the first rookie defenseman in history to net four goals in his first five postseason appearances. He has been a regular in Boston ever since.

Defensively, Krug relies on good positioning and superb stick work to disrupt offensive rushes. Though he stands just 5-foot-9, he is capable of laying thunderous hits on opponents. His monstrous check on Robert Thomas of the Blues during Game 1 of the 2019 Stanley Cup final (delivered without a helmet) was one of the brightest highlights of the series for the Bruins, who were physically battered by St. Louis throughout. Krug had his helmet torn off by St. Louis winger David Perron shortly before the hit and admitted that he wasn't pleased about it. Thomas, who is much taller and little heavier, was flattened as Krug went airborne. After the game, Krug joked: "I'm just glad I got a haircut a few days ago."[70]

Krug has exceptional speed, acceleration and puck-carrying ability, which makes him well-suited to run the power play unit. An accurate passer, he reads the defense well and anticipates the moves of opponents—qualities that have led to five consecutive seasons with at least 40 assists.

With his contract set to expire in 2020, he told an ESPN reporter that he might be willing to take a pay cut to stay in Boston. "I love the situation I'm in," he said. "I'm pretty sure my teammates would love me to come back. My coach, I know for a fact, loves the way I play.... I feel like I'm just hitting my prime."[71] In spite of those words, he was traded to the Blues.

Since attaining full-time status with the B's in 2013, Torey Krug has been one of the Bruins top offensive performers. By the end of the 2019-'20 campaign, he had collected at least 40 assists in five straight seasons. Courtesy tsyp9 on VisualHunt.com/CC BY-SA.

Though the best may be yet to come, there have been plenty of highlights already. During his first six full seasons in Boston, Krug averaged 10 goals and 38 assists in addition to more than 20 minutes of ice time per game. His 16 assists in the 2019 playoffs were tops in the NHL. In the unlikely event that hockey doesn't work out for him, Krug has a degree in Political Science to fall back on. He completed his undergraduate work at Michigan State University in 2017.

5

Goalies

CECIL THOMPSON
(1928–1938)

Thompson was born in the mining town of Sandon, British Columbia. As a boy, he played both baseball and hockey. Though he wasn't particularly drawn to goaltending, he often agreed to take the position in order to participate in neighborhood games. He explained that his nickname of "Tiny" (which followed him throughout his career) came from the fact that most of the kids he played with were much bigger than he was.

As a teenager, Thompson worked his way up through the junior ranks with the Calgary Monarchs, Pacific Grain Seniors and Bellevue Bulldogs. He turned pro in 1926 with the Minneapolis Millers of the American Hockey Association. During his third season in Minneapolis, he recorded 12 shutouts in 40 games, earning a contract offer from the Bruins. In 1928, he replaced Hal Winkler as Boston's primary goaltender.

Thompson had a spectacular rookie season, posting a 1.15 GAA while leading the league with 26 regular season wins. In the playoffs, he was literally unbeatable, going 5–0 with three shutouts as the Bruins claimed the first Stanley Cup in franchise history. With the advent of forward passing in 1929, Thompson's goals against average rose to 2.19, but it was still good enough to claim the first of four Vezina Trophies.

Thompson was among the most durable goalies of the era, going six straight seasons without missing a single game. Though he never won another Stanley Cup after the '28-'29 campaign, he kept the Bruins in contention year after year with his stellar play. In fact, Boston finished in first place six times during his tenure.

Thompson was a stand-up goaltender for the most part, though photos do exist of him sprawling on the ice. His signature defensive move was drop to one knee with his stick protecting the five-hole and his glove extended to cover the left side of the net. He was among the first goalies to effectively use his glove to catch pucks. And he wasn't afraid to get in front of shots at close range with minimal padding.

Thompson set several precedents during his distinguished career. He was the first goalie to record an assist during the '35-'36 season (on a Babe Siebert goal). He was also the first to be pulled for an extra skater. It happened in the semi-final round of the 1931 playoffs against Montreal and became a common practice among coaches afterward. Thompson's 38 wins in '29-'30 were a team record that stood for over 50 years. No Boston goalie has surpassed that mark since Pete Peeters in '82-'83.

With Four Vezina Trophies to his credit, Tiny Thompson was a lock for the Hall of Fame when he retired. In his rookie season, he posted a 1.15 GAA and led the B's to their first Stanley Cup. Courtesy Boston Public Library, Leslie Jones Collection.

Thompson's defining moment came in the opening round of the 1933 playoffs against the Maple Leafs. The series was tied at two games apiece when Thompson and Lorne Chabot engaged in one of the most grueling goaltending duels in NHL history. After the match remained scoreless for over a hundred minutes, Boston coach Art Ross and Toronto owner Conn Smythe petitioned NHL president Frank Calder to suspend the game until the following day to give players a much-needed rest. The request was denied and the marathon stretched into a sixth overtime. Thompson was finally beaten on a breakaway, giving Toronto a berth in the Stanley Cup finals. The crowd at Maple Leaf Gardens gave Thompson a well-deserved standing ovation.

When the NHL season was extended to 48 games in 1931-'32, Thompson requested a brief leave of absence. The Bruins publicly announced that he was on the verge of a nervous breakdown and offered auditions to goalies Wilf Cude and Percy Jackson. In spite of his outstanding performances, Thompson remained at odds with management for the rest of his Bruins career. At the beginning of the '38-'39 campaign, Art Ross sent shockwaves through the New England sports community when he traded Thompson to Detroit. Thompson spent two years with the Red Wings, helping them to the playoffs in both campaigns.

During his 12 NHL seasons, Thompson led the league in wins five times and shutouts on four occasions. His 81 career shutouts are among the top totals of all time. Upon leaving the NHL, he served as head coach of the Buffalo Bisons for two seasons. He later played a handful of games with a Calgary-based Air Force team during World War II. He finished his hockey career as a scout for the Blackhawks, covering the western region of Canada. He was elected to the Hockey Hall of Fame in 1959. He passed away in 1981 at the age of 77.

Frank Brimsek
(1938–1949)

Brimsek became Boston's first-string goalie during an awkward juncture in Bruins history. Hall of Famer "Tiny" Thompson had been traded to the Red Wings and B's coach Art Ross was under fire for making the deal. Historian Kerry Keene wrote that the transaction "reigned as the biggest shock on the Boston sports scene since Babe Ruth was sold to the Yankees nearly two decades prior."[1] With unimaginable pressure on him to perform, Brimsek broke Thompson's franchise record for the longest shutout streak shortly after his arrival in Boston. Eight All-Star selections and two Stanley Cups later, he had forged his own path to the Hall of Fame.

Brimsek was born and raised in Eveleth, Minnesota, where hockey was immensely popular. Four other players from Eveleth made it to the NHL during Brimsek's era. One of them—Mike Karakas—played high school basketball with Brimsek. An opening on the Eveleth High School hockey team surfaced unexpectedly when Brimsek's brother, John (a second string-goalie), was switched to defense. Brimsek took his brother's place, shifting his primary focus to hockey from that point forward. Upon completing high school, he played for St. Cloud State Teachers College and earned a degree there.

In 1934, Brimsek was invited to try out for the Detroit Red Wings. After clashing with coach Jack Adams, he signed with the Pittsburgh Yellow Jackets. He led the EAHL with eight shutouts in '35-'36, prompting the Red Wings to pursue his services again. Brimsek rejected an offer to play for a Wings affiliate in Pontiac, Michigan, remaining with the Jackets instead. In October of 1937, he was sold to the Bruins and assigned to the Providence Reds of the International-American Hockey League.

Brimsek's first season with Providence was pretty spectacular as he accrued a 1.75 GAA with 25 wins and five shutouts. On the strength of that performance, the Reds skated to a Calder Cup championship. When "Tiny" Thompson developed an eye infection at the beginning of the '38-'39 campaign, Brimsek filled in briefly and was sent back to Providence. Convinced that Brimsek had the skills to serve as Boston's primary goaltender, Art Ross dealt Thompson to Detroit.

Brimsek began his Bruins career on the road. During his first appearance at the Boston Garden, fans were uncharacteristically quiet as he skated out wearing Thompson's number 1. Brimsek's clumsy footwork and bright red pants—a deviation from the standard Bruins uniform colors—made fans uncomfortable at first. But by the end of his historic shutout streak, which spanned portions of four games, they were cheering enthusiastically for him. On December 20, 1938, a writer from the *Boston Post* proclaimed: "The Bruins are hot and Frankie Brimsek is perhaps the hottest of them all. He's making fans forget about Tiny Thompson."[2]

Frank Brimsek received the nickname "Mr. Zero" for his ability to shut down opponents. He collected 10 shutouts in his rookie season of 1938-'39. Courtesy Boston Public Library, Leslie Jones Collection.

A stand-up goalie with supreme confidence, Brimsek was known to lean casually against his net on penalty shots as skaters approached. He was extremely active with his stick, sweeping the puck away from opponents and knocking would-be goal scorers off their feet if he felt they were violating his personal space. Known as "Mr. Zero" to the New England faithful, Brimsek spent nine seasons with the Bruins, leading the league twice in shutouts. A candidate for the Hart Trophy on five occasions, he claimed the Vezina Trophy twice. He won no fewer than 25 regular season games during five seasons, helping the Bruins to Stanley Cup titles in 1939 and 1941.

Brimsek joined the Coast Guard during World War II and kept in shape playing in the Eastern League with the Coast Guard Cutters. He also served on a patrol craft in the South Pacific. When he returned to the Bruins in time for the 1945 campaign, he was a shadow of his former self. He later admitted that the war experience had taken a great toll on him. Traded to the Blackhawks in 1949, he had his worst season ever, leading the NHL in goals allowed. The Blackhawks finished in last place and Brimsek retired at season's end. At the time, he held the record for most shutouts by an American-born goalie.

After leaving hockey behind, Brimsek settled in Virginia, Minnesota, which is located near Eveleth. He worked as an engineer for the Canadian National Railroad. A member of the 1966 Hockey Hall of Fame class, he was also among the first inductees into the United States Hockey Hall of Fame. He died in 1998 at the age of 83. That same year, he was listed among the top 100 goalies of all time by *The Hockey News*.

Jim Henry
(1951–1955)

Born in Winnipeg, Henry was nicknamed "Sugar Jim" for his love of the sweet substance, which he consumed in large quantities as a young boy. His warm personality and humble manner made him deserving of the moniker as an adult. By the time he joined the Bruins, he was 31 years old with well over a decade of organized hockey experience. Prior to his arrival, he almost died in a fire at his hunting cabin in Kenora, Ontario. Badly scarred in the blaze, he was told by doctors that he would never play again. He proved them wrong by appearing in over 200 consecutive games with the B's.

Henry got his earliest junior experience with the Winnipeg Lombards and Brandon Elks. Signed by the Rangers, he led the club's senior league affiliate to an Allan Cup championship in 1941. He made the jump to New York the following season, appearing in all 48 games and gathering a league-high 29 wins. The season ended with a disappointing loss to the Maple Leafs in the semi-final round.

With the onset of World War II, Henry joined the Canadian Armed Forces, serving in the Army and Navy. He played for various military teams, helping the Ottawa Commandos to an Allan Cup title in 1943. He returned to New York in '45, but the Rangers had installed Chuck Rayner in net while he was gone. Recognizing Henry's value to the club, coach Frank Boucher established the first two-goalie rotation in NHL history. Henry and Rayner were actually known to alternate on a shift to shift basis.

In 1948, Henry was traded to the Blackhawks. The club was dreadful and he couldn't do much to turn things around. In a desperation move, Hall of Famer Frank Brimsek (past his prime by then) was brought in and Henry was demoted to the minors. In 1950, Henry was traded to Detroit in a deal involving eight other players. But the Wings had Terry Sawchuk in goal and there was no future for Henry there. In September of '51, his contract was sold to the Bruins.

For three straight seasons in Boston, Henry made more appearances than any goalie in the NHL. He won 85 games in that span and allowed the second fewest goals each year. His elevated play helped carry the B's to four consecutive berths in the playoffs, where he enjoyed some of his finest moments.

In the 1952 semi-final round against the Canadiens, Henry faced a formidable lineup featuring eight Hall of Famers. Hit in the face with a puck during Game 6, his eyes were practically swollen shut before the start of the series finale. He played anyway and, by the end of the third period, his face was a mess. Even his padding was torn. After Montreal sniper Maurice Richard netted the game-winning goal late in regulation, an iconic photo was taken showing Henry shaking hands with a battered and bloody Richard. Commenting on the punishment he took in net over the course of his career, Henry joked: "When it came to goaltending, I always used to say 'you don't have to be crazy, but it helps.'"[3] In his prime, one reporter remarked that Henry had "the eyesight of an eagle, the dexterity of a young gazelle, and the grit of spinach salad."[4]

During his four years in Boston, Henry recorded 25 shutouts (including the postseason). He was a second team All-Star in 1952. Hampered by injuries in '54-'55, he made just 26 regular season appearances. He sustained a broken jaw in the playoffs that season and never skated in another NHL game. During the latter part of the 1950s, he played for the St. Paul Saints of the IHL. He also appeared in the senior leagues with the Warroad Lakers and Winnipeg Maroons.

When he finally hung up his skates, Henry retired to Manitoba, where he spent his free time hunting and fishing. He died in 2004—the same year he was inducted into the Manitoba Sports Hall of Fame. He was 83 years old at the time of his passing.

Don Simmons
(1956–1961)

Simmons was a victim of bad timing. He played during the so-called "Golden Age" of professional hockey when there were only six starting positions available to goaltenders in the NHL. Though he was considered to be among the world's finest at his position, he spent his career playing back-up to four different Hall of Famers. A quiet, unassuming man who went out of his way to maintain anonymity, the circumstances suited him just fine.

Simmons hailed from Port Colborne, which is located on Lake Erie in the Niagara Region of Southern Ontario. He started his junior career with the Galt Blackhawks in 1948, later joining the St. Catharines Teepees. He was saddled with the nickname of "Dippy Don" for his habit of dropping low to the ice to deflect incoming shots. He turned professional with the Springfield Indians and was designated a second-team All-Star during his first two seasons with the club.

In January of 1957, the Bruins found themselves in search of a replacement for Terry Sawchuk, who was said to be suffering from a case of nervous exhaustion. Simmons rose to the challenge, leading the B's to consecutive Stanley Cup finals appearances in '57 and '58. He faced more postseason shots than any of his NHL peers during that span while posting three shutouts—also a league-high mark. Though he won 11 playoff games in those two seasons, he had the misfortune of facing a legendary Montreal squad on its way to a five consecutive NHL titles (an all-time record). In spite of Simmons' commendable efforts, the Bruins bowed to the Canadiens in both meetings.

Simmons served as Boston's primary goaltender in '58-'59, guiding the club to a semi-finals appearance against the Maple Leafs. But the Bruins used him as a back-up for the next two seasons. In January of '61, he was traded to Toronto for Ed Chadwick, who was dreadful in four games with the B's that year. The Leafs were already working with three goalies and Simmons spent the remainder of the season in the AHL with the Rochester Americans. He was added to the Toronto roster in '61-'62 as an understudy to Johnny Bower. After Bower was injured by a Bobby Hull slap-shot in Game 4 of the '62 Stanley Cup finals, Simmons took the reins, guiding the Leafs to a series victory over the Blackhawks. It was Toronto's first Stanley Cup in over a decade and the first of three consecutive NHL championships.

In spite of his postseason heroism, Simmons was demoted to second-string status again in '62-'63. His 2.47 GAA was tops in the NHL. Left unprotected in the '65 Inter-League draft, he was picked up by the Rangers, who used him as a back-up to Ed Giacomin. Lamenting Simmons' fate, hockey historian Eric Zweig wrote: "He never really gets to be the guy in any place, does he? He was pretty heroic in place of Bower in '62, but they didn't keep him around."[5] Fellow historian Bob Duff added: "If expansion came ten years earlier, we would probably know a lot more about Don Simmons. I think he was the greatest back-up in the history of the NHL."[6] The Rangers used him as a sporadic substitute and he spent most of his three seasons with the Blueshirts in the minors. By the time he retired at the end of the '68-'69 campaign, he had played in five different minor leagues. He never publicly complained about any of his assignments.

After Hall of Famer Jacques Plante introduced the face mask in 1959, Simmons became the second NHL goaltender to wear one, using multiple variations, including the pretzel model. He later opened a "super store" in Fort Erie Ontario specializing in goalie equipment. The store, under new ownership but still bearing his name, moved to Buffalo in 2019. Simmons passed away in 2010 at the age of 79.

EDDIE JOHNSTON
(1962–1973)

Johnston came of age in a rough, English-speaking section of Montreal's West End. He picked up the nickname of "E.J." as a young man and it stuck with him. A capable fighter, he made money on the side by sparring with convicts from a local penitentiary. He played for the Montreal Junior Royals in 1953—a team that was captained by legendary coach Scotty Bowman. Johnston claimed that the ultra-intense Bowman "terrorized" him during their time together.[7]

Originally a product of the Canadiens system, Johnston turned pro with the Winnipeg Warriors in 1956. He became property of the Blackhawks before joining the Bruins in 1962. Taking over for goalie Bob Perrault (who was sent to the minors), Johnston played in 160 straight games. He did it without the benefit of a protective mask, though masks were available and in use at the time. Reminiscing about his decision not to wear one, he joked: "On my back was my I.Q. back then. I was Number 1."[8] During Johnston's 160-game streak, he broke his nose three times in a two-week span. And then, on Halloween night in 1968, he was hit by a Bobby Orr slapshot during pre-game warm-ups. He ended up in a coma, losing a total of 40 pounds. When he finally returned to action in 1969, he donned a mask.

The Bruins were a mediocre club when Johnston first arrived, missing the playoffs in five straight seasons. But by 1967, the team was on the rise with the addition of several key players. When Bobby Orr joined the B's in 1966, his father asked Johnston if he would be Orr's roommate. Johnston, who was known to teammates as "Downtown Eddie" because of his love of the nightlife, didn't think it was a good idea, but the elder Orr insisted. Johnston recalled the 18-year-old phenom chauffeuring him around Boston in a Cadillac. He even bought Orr a chauffer's cap, which the iconic defenseman actually wore. The two developed a close friendship.

During his time in Boston, Johnston supplemented his income as owner of a successful nightclub known as "E.J.'s." With the rise of Gerry Cheevers, who joined the Bruins in '65, Johnston saw less playing time, though he was still an integral part of the team's newfound success. During Boston's Stanley Cup run in 1972, Johnston appeared in 38 regular season games, notching a superb 27–8 record. His six wins, .936 save percentage and 1.86 GAA during the postseason were all top marks in the NHL that year.

With the departure of Cheevers to the World Hockey Association in '72-'73, Johnston was reinstated as Boston's first-string goalie. His mediocre performance prompted a trade to Toronto for Hall of Famer Jacques Plante. The Leafs dished him to St. Louis the following year and he spent portions of four seasons with the Blues before ending his career with Chicago in '77-'78. During his 16 years in the NHL, he recorded 32 shutouts. He finished near the top of NHL leaderboards in multiple other categories many times.

Though Johnston's days between the pipes were finished, his hockey career was far from over. He coached the New Brunswick Hawks of the AHL in '78-'79, then took over the Chicago Blackhawks the following season. In 1980, he began a long association with the Penguins, making two separate stints as head coach. He held multiple other titles as well, including GM and senior advisor.

The highlight of Johnston's career as an NHL executive came in June of 1984, when he selected Mario Lemieux first overall in the Entry Draft. It wasn't an easy deal to pull off. The Pens had lost 58 games in '83-'84 to get the first-round pick. And initial talks with Lemieux's agent Gus Badali went poorly. Making things even more complicated, Johnston received many tempting offers from other teams. The Minnesota North Stars were willing to exchange all of their picks that year to get Lemieux. The Quebec Nordiques offered all three Stastny brothers—Peter, Anton and Marion. When the Canadiens got wind of the proposal, they agreed to meet any of Johnston's demands. In the end, Johnston stood firm on his choice of Lemieux, who would lead the Pens to consecutive Stanley Cup titles in '91 and '92.

Johnston left the Penguins in 1989 to serve as GM of the Hartford Whalers, but returned to Pittsburgh as head coach in 1993. He went into semi-retirement after the Pens' Stanley Cup victory in 2009. He has maintained his friendship with Bobby Orr to the present day. Orr was the best man at Johnston's wedding and is Godfather to one of Johnston's children.

GERRY CHEEVERS
(1965–1972/1975–1980)

Cheevers was destined for a career on the ice. He grew up in the hockey hotbed of St. Catharines, where the Toronto Maple Leafs held their training camps. His father worked as an assistant manager of the Garden City Arena and a part-time scout for Toronto. As a teenager, Cheevers was recruited by the Leafs and assigned to the St. Michael's Majors of the Ontario Hockey League. He played only sporadically during his first three seasons, but became a regular in '59-'60. Cheevers was ambivalent about goaltending until his coach decided to teach him a lesson by starting him as a forward in several games. "I was never so happy to get back in goal," he said. "A lot of guys were trying to get even for wayward sticks in the crease. I could always skate. I was just missing the instinct of knowing what to do with the puck."[9]

Cheevers knew exactly how to handle himself between the pipes, turning pro with the Pittsburgh Hornets in 1961. He made his NHL debut that season as a replacement for Leafs starting goalie Johnny Bower. When Bower returned, Cheevers was sent back to the minors, spending portions of four seasons with the Rochester Americans. While stationed in Rochester, he was instructed by coach Rudy Migay to practice without a stick, using his body and pads to deflect incoming shots. He was not afraid to stray far from the net to cut down a shooter's angle. And he was extremely aggressive with his stick, using it to swat at players who were loitering in the crease.

In the 1965 Intra-League Draft, the Maple Leafs sought to retain three of their goalies—Bower, Cheevers and Terry Sawchuk. Realizing they were only permitted to protect two, Toronto executives attempted to hide Cheevers by listing him as a forward. League officials spotted the ruse and prohibited it. As a result, Cheevers ended up being drafted by the Bruins.

Cheevers played without a mask during his first two seasons in Boston, but finally broke down when he realized the dangers of leaving himself unprotected. Hit lightly in the mask with a shot during practice one day, he retreated to the dressing room. When B's coach Harry Sinden found Cheevers casually drinking a beer and smoking a cigarette, he ordered the malingering net-minder (who was never fond of practicing) back onto the ice. Trainer John "Frosty" Forristall drew a stitch-mark on the mask as a joke and it became a tradition. Cheevers added a mark every time he was struck by a shot. He later estimated that the mask had saved him from more than 150 stitches.

Nicknamed "Cheesie," Cheevers was rarely at a loss for words. Teammates compared him to insult-comic Don Rickles because of wry, cutting wit. Among the most intense competitors at his position, he refused to shake hands with opponents after playoff losses. He was even known to drop the gloves on occasion. According to the popular website Hockeyfights.com, Cheevers engaged in five fights during his career, including a 1969 playoff scrape with center Forbes Kennedy of the Maple Leafs. It came during a demoralizing 10–0 Toronto loss.

Cheevers' goals against average remained below the 3.00 mark in eight of his 12 seasons with the Bruins. He set an NHL record by remaining undefeated in 32 consecutive games during the '71-'72 campaign. During Boston's Stanley Cup years of '70 and '72, he posted an 18–3 postseason record. Following the latter Cup victory, he signed with the Cleveland Crusaders of the World Hockey Association. Explaining his motivation, he remarked: "I was struggling to make the money I thought I deserved in Boston."[10] He led the WHA in shutouts three times before returning to action with the B's on February 8, 1976. Celebrating his return, he shut out the Red Wings, 7–0, with U.S. secretary of state Henry Kissinger in attendance.

During his time in Boston, Cheevers won 279 games including the playoffs. At the time of this writing, he held a rank of number 6 among Bruins goalies in shutouts. A leader on the ice, his name is always mentioned in discussions of Boston's greatest players. In a 1978 *Boston Globe* interview, forward Wayne Cashman said of Cheevers:

"Next to Bobby Orr, he's the greatest player ever. He takes control of the game ... he does it with his handling of the puck and by talking all the time. He keeps reminding us where to go, and you do what he says because that gives him an outlet for the puck."[11]

Cheevers played his last season in '79-'80 and was named head coach the following year. He led the Bruins to a pair of first place finishes and two second place showings, but the team never got past the conference finals during his tenure. Off to a mediocre start in '84-'85, he was dismissed from his duties. He worked as a color commentator for the Hartford Whalers for a decade before joining the Bruins broadcasting staff in 1999. He also served as a Boston scout for several years. Away from the ice, he owned thoroughbred horses, joking that it was his attempt to recoup all the money he had lost at various racetracks over the years. After being inducted into the Hockey Hall of Fame in 1985 and the Rochester Americans Hall of Fame in '87, he became member of the 2010 inaugural World Hockey Association Hall of Fame class.

GILLES GILBERT
(1973–1980)

Many female supporters of the Bruins during the 1970s remember Gilbert for his matinee idol looks. Most fans of the opposite gender recall his acrobatic work around the net. Detractors often associate him with an epic fail against the Montreal Canadiens in the 1979 semi-finals. Either way, Gilbert's years in Boston were quite eventful.

Born in Saint-Esprit, which is located just outside Quebec City, Gilbert excelled at multiple sports, spending his winters on the ice and summers on the baseball diamond (serving primarily as a pitcher). By the time he turned 17, he had both MLB and NHL representatives vying for his services. In the end, hockey seemed to be the most attractive option as the Minnesota North Stars selected him in the third round of the 1969 Entry Draft. Assigned to the Ottawa Stars of the Central Professional Hockey League, Gilbert appeared in one game with Minnesota that year, surrendering six goals on 39 shots. He served primarily as a back-up goalie over the next few seasons while receiving instruction from Hall of Famer Gump Worsley.

When Gerry Cheevers joined the World Hockey Association in 1973, the Bruins found themselves scrambling for a replacement. Taking a major risk, they traded center Fred Stanfield, who had collected 78 points the previous season, to acquire the untested Gilbert. Gilbert's debut in Boston was an adventure as he got stuck on the Tobin Bridge and missed warm-ups. He arrived just in time to make the start. He gathered a career-high total of 34 wins that season, helping the B's to a Stanley Cup finals appearance against the Flyers.

Gilbert was a great puck-handler and effective poke-checker. Extremely quick out of the net, he had a tendency to wander far beyond the crease. He stood upright for routine shots, but also spent a great deal of time on the ice, flailing his arms and legs as if he were executing a gymnastics routine.

Gilbert was rakishly handsome, making him extremely popular with female fans.

His cat-like reflexes ingratiated him to all four of the Boston coaches he played for. He gave his best years to the Bruins, finishing with 155 regular season wins and 39 ties in seven years of service. His finest all-around performance came during the '75-'76 slate, when he won 17 consecutive decisions. He finished the year with a 33–8–10 record and a 2.90 GAA, which was sixth best in the league.

Though the Bruins earned three berths in the Stanley Cup finals during Gilbert's tenure in Boston, he is inextricably linked to a Game 7 meltdown against the Canadiens in the '79 semi-finals. Gilbert surrendered just one goal through two periods and the Bruins appeared to be on the verge of victory. But a costly too-many-men-on-the-ice violation with 2:34 remaining led to a Guy Lafleur goal, sending the game into overtime. "You want the buzzer to go. You want it to be over," Gilbert recalled painfully, "but it goes on ... and on ... and on."[12] Yvonne Lambert scored the game-winner less than 10 minutes into overtime, handing the Bruins yet another crushing postseason loss. Many people have forgotten that Gilbert put forth a heroic effort in that game, making 47 stops. He later admitted it was the toughest loss of his career.

In July of 1980, Gilbert was traded to Detroit for Hall of Famer Rogie Vachon. The Wings were woeful and so was Gilbert as the club missed the playoffs in all three of his seasons there. He made his last NHL appearance with Detroit in 1983.

With his playing days behind him, Gilbert served as an Islanders scout for several years. In 1996, he became a goaltending instructor for the Isles, later holding the title of organizational coach. He eventually left New York, joining Canadian Hockey Enterprises as an instructor of adult and youth hockey camps. The organization sponsors international tournaments in both Canada and the U.S. Reflecting on his hockey career, Gilbert remarked that his years in Boston were "the greatest years of [his] life."[13]

PETE PEETERS
(1982–1985)

Born in Edmonton, Alberta, Peeters is of Dutch ancestry. His primary focus while growing up was competitive swimming. At the age of 17, he ascended to the junior hockey level with the Edmonton Crusaders of the AJHL. He surrendered quite a few goals before turning professional, but faced a lot of shots playing for weak defensive teams. Scouts admired his coolness under sustained pressure.

Chosen by the Flyers in the '77 Amateur Draft, Peeters was assigned to Milwaukee of the International Hockey League. From there, he was sent to the AHL-affiliated Maine Mariners. In '78-'79, he won the "Hap" Holmes Memorial Award for best GAA and made an All-Star appearance. The Flyers felt he was ready for Broad Street and summoned him to Philly that season. He appeared in five games, compiling a mediocre save percentage of .853.

In '79-'80, Peeters was inserted into Philadelphia's regular rotation, sharing net time with veteran Phil Myre. The Flyers had a phenomenal club with a top line featuring Bobby Clarke, Bill Barber and Reggie Leach (who scored 50 goals that year). Rookie winger Brian Propp added 75 points of his own as the squad went 35 straight games without a loss. Peeters benefited greatly from the talent around him, compiling a 22–0–5 record before suffering his first defeat on February 19. The Flyers went all the way to the Stanley Cup finals, losing to the powerful Islanders in six games. Peeters was excellent in the playoffs, compiling a 2.79 GAA in 13 appearances.

Unable to match the level of success he had enjoyed in his rookie season, Peeters became increasingly unhappy. Teammates nicknamed him "Grumpy" because he was irritable during warm-ups and downright petulant after losses. He griped about the Flyers' strict adherence to a goaltending rotation and was often curt to reporters. During the '81-'82 season, he was accused of shoving a journalist during a road trip. His poor overall performance prompted a trade to the Bruins in June of '82.

Peeters was a stand-up goalie. He had a tendency to stray from the crease to handle pucks. This left him unprotected against the sticks of opponents. Though he became renowned for his bad temperament in Philadelphia, he matured in Boston. "I'm starting to learn how to handle the mental aspect of the game," he told one reporter.[14] The change of scenery suited him well as he had his best season ever in '82-'83, compiling a 40–12–9 record with eight shutouts and a 2.37 GAA (lowest NHL mark of the decade). At one point, he went 31 games without a loss, narrowly missing an NHL record set by Gerry Cheevers. Peeters' performance earned him a spot on the All-Star team. Additionally, he won the Vezina Trophy and finished second in voting for the Hart Trophy behind Wayne Gretzky.

Peeters' '83-'84 follow-up was not as spectacular, but he did win 29 games for the B's while finishing among the top 10 candidates for the Vezina. Explaining his value to the club, he told the press: "I don't look at myself as a money goaltender. I just want to be at a level where the team can depend on me to do my job. I'm going to be there every night. I don't want to be mediocre."[15] Unfortunately, Peeters did drift toward mediocrity in his fourth season with the Bruins, prompting a trade to the Capitals for goalie Pat Riggin.

During the '87-'88 campaign, Peeters experienced a career revival, leading the league with a 2.79 GAA. During the playoffs, he posted the highest save percentage in the NHL at .895. Facing the Devils in Game 4 of the Patrick Division finals, he experienced a scary moment when he was knocked unconscious by a Mark Johnson wrist shot. The puck hit him squarely in the forehead, knocking him flat on his back. He lay motionless in the crease for several minutes before being carted off on a stretcher. Remarkably, he returned to close out the series for the Caps, getting a big win in Game 6. The finale remained tied at two until John MacLean scored with 6:11 remaining in regulation, giving New Jersey a dramatic 3–2 victory. It marked the end of Peeters' last great season.

In 1989, the Capitals sent Peeters back to the city where he began his NHL career. Frankly speaking, he had an awful season with the Flyers, going 1–13–5 with a 3.79 GAA. Though he was much better the following year, allowing far fewer goals, he decided to call it quits at season's end. He finished his career with 281 wins including playoff action.

Peeters returned to his farm in Edmonton and, though his days in net were finished, he remained in the game as a goaltending coach for several teams. He was most recently active with the Anaheim Ducks. His son, Trevor, was a goalie for several teams in the Western Hockey League.

REGGIE LEMELIN
(1987–1993)

Lemelin played in a high-scoring era when goaltending was statistically sub-par. But in comparison to the net-minders around him, he was among the most competent. Prior to his arrival in Boston, the Bruins had not been to the Stanley Cup finals in 10 years. Working in tandem with Andy Moog, Lemelin helped put an end to a long string of Wales Conference failures. And though he never won a Cup while wearing the Black and Gold, he kept the B's in contention for six full seasons.

Rejean Lemelin was born in Quebec City during the heart of the baby-boom. As a kid, he helped his Orsainville hockey squad to three consecutive appearances in the annual Quebec International Pee Wee Tournament. He played at the junior level with the Sherbrooke Castors of the QMJHL. In 1974, he was selected in two different drafts by the Philadelphia Flyers and Chicago Cougars (a World Hockey Association franchise). Neither club would benefit from his services as he ultimately signed with the Atlanta Flames.

Lemelin spent three years shuffling back and forth from the minors to the NHL. He stuck with the Flames long after they relocated to Calgary. For six full seasons, he served as the club's primary goaltender or full-time back-up, sharing the net with the likes of Pat Riggin, Don Edwards and Mike Vernon. Describing his career, Lemelin classified himself as a late bloomer. "With goaltending, I didn't really master the craft until I had already been playing for four or five years," he said. "I never felt like a solid, number-one goaltender until I was twenty-nine or thirty years old. When I retired, I felt extremely confident that I was capable of playing at an elite level."[16]

A stand-up goalie in the classic style, Lemelin was great at playing angles and redirecting pucks into unoccupied corners. He had quick reflexes and was capable of making highlight-reel-quality stops. One of his favorite tactics was to stack his pads against shots in close-quarters—a strategy that has been virtually abandoned by goalies in the current era. With great balance and positioning, Lemelin had a knack for making difficult saves look routine.

Lemelin's best year with the Flames came in '83-'84, when he went unbeaten in 19 straight appearances and finished as a runner-up for the Vezina Trophy. He actually had a better statistical season the following year with 30 wins and a lower GAA but finished third in Vezina voting. In '85-'86, he played in 60 regular season games with Calgary, leading the team to a berth in the Stanley Cup finals. Coach Bob Johnson transferred primary duties to Mike Vernon during the playoffs, which ended with a five-game loss to the Canadiens. During his days at the Olympic Saddledome in Calgary, fans got into the habit of chanting Lemelin's first name during great performances.

Signed as a free agent by the Bruins in 1987, Lemelin reached the peak of his career. He arrived in Boston with a lifetime goals against average of 3.67. By the time he retired with the B's in 1993, he had lowered that mark considerably. The significance of playing in Boston was not lost on him. "I think going to an original six team has more meaning when you're a player," he told one reporter. "The history that comes with it and the legacy the team has left behind—there's an element of pride in there to keep it going and be a part of that successful history."[17]

Lemelin added plenty to the team's legacy, guiding the club to Stanley Cup finals appearances in '88 and '90. In the latter campaign, Lemelin and Moog captured the Jennings Trophy, which is awarded annually to the net-minder(s) from the team with the fewest goals allowed. Lemelin has always been reluctant to assume credit for that honor, telling a reporter in 2018: "It's always a team game when you win the Jennings Trophy. The goaltenders have something to do with it, but the team in front of you has something to do with it. We had a team that played defense and understood that concentrating on defense was the key to success."[18]

Lemelin is best remembered in Boston for two things—his signature fist-pump after Bruins victories (executed for the benefit of family members who were usually watching on TV) and an incredible play he made against New Jersey in the '88 postseason. Referred to simply as "The Save," the stop came in Game 7 of the Wales conference finals. After a shot by Neal Broten was kicked aside by Lemelin, the rebound caromed directly to winger Pat Verbeek, who attempted to slap it into a wide-open net. Recovering quickly, Lemelin dove across the crease and made a stupendous back-handed catch on Verbeek's shot. The Bruins ended up winning in a semi-blowout, 6–2, advancing to the finals against the Oilers. A characteristically humble Lemelin tried to downplay the significance of the play. "You make saves like that all the time," he said. "It's just the timing of it and the stage of it."[19]

Before he shelved his pads for good in 1993, Lemelin commented jokingly that he knew it was time to retire when teammates started asking for permission to date his daughter (actress Stephanie Lemelin). He finished his Bruins career with 104 wins, including the postseason. He served as a goalie coach in St. Louis during the '93-'94 season then joined the Flyers staff the following year. He held the job in Philadelphia for more than decade. During his days with the Bruins, he lived in Lynnfield, Massachusetts, and wintered in Cherry Hill, New Jersey. He later settled in Peabody, Massachusetts, which is in the North Shore region adjacent to Salem. At the time of this writing, he was working in the real estate.

ANDY MOOG
(1987–1993)

Only two goalies from Moog's era have been elected to the Hockey Hall of Fame—Patrick Roy and Grant Fuhr. Though Moog was not on the level of "Saint Patrick," his statistics are equivalent to Fuhr's (a former teammate). Underrated and overlooked, Moog remains on a very short list of goalies who have been excluded from the Hall in spite of having won three Stanley Cup titles.

Moog was born in Penticton, British Columbia, which is situated in the southern interior of the province between Lake Okanagan and Lake Skaha. His father was a talented goalie who led the Penticton Vees amateur squad to a world championship in 1955. Moog considered his father a major influence along with Hall of Famer Gump Worsley, whose picture hung in Moog's locker during his NHL years. Moog entered junior hockey in '76 and ended up being drafted by the Edmonton Oilers four years later. He had difficulty earning a top slot in Edmonton due to the presence of Fuhr, who joined the club shortly after Moog.

Though Fuhr was Edmonton's go-to guy during the regular season, Moog gained a reputation for being a clutch performer in the playoffs. After appearing in just seven games during his NHL debut, a series of injuries to Edmonton's primary stoppers forced Moog into a starting role in the Preliminary Round of the '81 postseason. He rose to the occasion, leading the Oilers to an efficient sweep of the Canadiens. It was Edmonton's first taste of NHL playoff success. In '83, Moog cemented his reputation as a postseason hero, compiling an 11–1 record before getting swept by the Islanders in the finals. When Grant Fuhr went down with an injury in Game 3 of the '84 finals, Moog stepped in and guided the Oilers to their first Stanley Cup.

A writer from *Sports Illustrated* described Moog like this: "[He] is short and dumpling-like and he looks like a choirboy. The way he plays is another matter, for he combines the butterfly style of Tony Esposito with the amazing hands and rebound control of a Ken Dryden."[20] Moog had excellent reflexes, which he used to steer incoming pucks away from attackers. He generally stayed near the crease, where he could often be found sprawled out on his side or belly.

Tired of serving as a back-up to Fuhr, Moog demanded a trade at the end of the '86-'87 campaign. He left the Oilers the following year to play for Team Canada. He went 4–0 at the '88 Winter Olympics in Calgary, joining the Bruins shortly afterward. He later insisted there was no animosity between him and Fuhr. "We tended to vent to each other when things were crummy," he told a reporter. "You had the same feelings and experiences. It was the most sympathetic ear in the room."[21]

Moog split time equally with Reggie Lemelin in '89-'90, but gradually became the Bruins' number one goaltender. In 1990, the duo combined to win the Jennings Trophy. Moog continued his postseason mastery, ending a long-running "curse" by knocking out the Canadiens in three consecutive playoff matchups. The Bruins reached the Stanley Cup finals twice during Moog's tenure in Boston, losing both times to the Oilers. Recalling his career experiences on hockey's grandest stage, he remarked: "The first Cup was the ultimate highlight. My least favorite was [Edmonton's] last cup, because I was in the other net at the time."[22]

Over portions of six seasons with the B's, Moog won 172 games including the postseason. He currently ranks among the Bruins' top 10 of all time in wins, ties, shots-against and saves. He became tremendously popular with fans in Boston, who considered him a "Habs Killer."

Moog spent four seasons with the Dallas Stars beginning in 1993. He seemed to get better as the years wore on, recording a 2.15 GAA at the age of 37. He made his last NHL appearance with the Canadiens in 1998. When he retired, he had the highest winning percentage among goalies who had played at least 10 seasons. He was the first of his era to win 300 games.

During his career, Moog served as vice president of the NHL Players Association, assuming the role of spokesman during the '92 players strike and the '94-'95 lockout. He donated generous amounts of money to the Hospice Society in his hometown of Penticton. In 1998, the Moog & Friends Hospice House was opened there. Moog worked as a goalie consultant for the Thrashers and Canucks. He was named assistant coach of the Dallas Stars in 2009, but his contract was not renewed at season's end. He later joined the Fox Sports Southwest team, providing analysis during Dallas Stars broadcasts.

Byron Dafoe
(1997–2002)

Dafoe is among a handful of former NHL players born in the United Kingdom. Less than 10 in that group have been goalies. Originally from Worthing—a borough of West Sussex—Dafoe moved to Comox, British Columbia, as a kid. He played junior hockey for the Portland Winter Hawks and ended up being selected by Washington in the second round of the '89 Entry Draft. It was a highly unusual choice as the Capitals had already taken another goalie in the first round.

Dafoe's development was rather slow. During his first three seasons in the Western Hockey League, he posted GAA's in excess of 5.00. But he eventually perfected the butterfly style. Gifted with sharp reflexes, he had an extremely dexterous glove hand, which was perhaps his biggest asset.

Dafoe made his NHL debut during the '92-'93 slate but couldn't secure a permanent roster spot in Washington. He ended up being traded to Los Angeles in 1995. He served as the primary stopper that year on a dreadful club that won just 24 games. In '96-'97, he split time with Stephan Fiset, turning in his best performance to that point. Looking for help in net, the Bruins signed Dafoe in August of '97.

Dafoe reached the peak of his career with the Bruins, making no fewer than 41 appearances per year during his five full seasons in Boston. He finished among the top 10 in voting for the Vezina Trophy three times in that span. His finest effort came in '98-'99, when he won 32 games and posted a 2.00 GAA. His 10 shutouts were tops in the NHL that year. He added two more shutouts in the playoffs while accruing a sterling .921 save percentage. Unfortunately, it wasn't enough as the Bruins beat the Hurricanes in the quarter-finals then lost to the Sabres in the following round.

During his 12 seasons in the NHL, Dafoe formed a lasting bond with fellow goalie Olaf Kolzig. The two became close during a "Friendship Tour" of Russia that took place near the end of the Cold War. They later played together in the minors and in Washington. Despite their amicable relationship, Dafoe and Kolzig got into a scuffle during a 1998 game between the Bruins and Capitals. With several other fights in progress, both players felt pressured to trade punches because the crowd was in an uproar. Footage of the scrape shows them laughing while swinging half-heartedly at one another. Dafoe was in no joking mood when he squared off against goalie Patrick Lalime of the Senators in 2002. During a massive brawl in Boston, Dafoe pulled Lalime's helmet off and landed several solid blows that drew blood. "Yeah, that was legit," Dafoe said years later. "I'm definitely going to take a knockout win on that one."[23]

Dafoe recorded 142 victories in goal with the Bruins including the postseason. In a 2018 interview, he said that there was far more pressure playing in Boston than anywhere else he had been. "If you're going to play in the NHL, you need to perform under pressure," he remarked. "I think it brought another element to my game that I hadn't had in L.A. or Washington. I loved it."[24]

Before the 2002 campaign, Dafoe signed as a free agent with the Atlanta Thrashers. He made his last NHL appearance during the '03-'04 slate. Together with Kolzig and winger Scott Mellanby, Dafoe founded the charity Athletes for Autism. All three former players have children that were diagnosed with the disorder.

With his professional hockey days now behind him, Dafoe lives in Kelowna,

British Columbia, where he runs a specialized home wiring business catering to affluent customers. He owns his own 13,000 square-foot mansion, which also serves as a
demo for potential clients. He has had several surgeries on his knee and avoids playing in Bruins alumni games. Asked to compare the goaltenders of his own era to the
ones who are currently active, he said: "I'm 5–11 and I was around average when I
played. I would hesitate to guess that the average is 6–2, 6–3 for the top thirty goaltenders in the league right now. They're just taking up more net, which helps, but
again I think it comes back to athleticism. They can cover four-by-six much better
than goalies of the past."[25]

TIM THOMAS
(2002–2012)

Thomas remains a controversial figure on account of his outspoken criticism of
the U.S. government. After the Bruins won the Stanley Cup in 2011, he opted to skip
the team's visit to the White House. In a prepared statement, he claimed that "the federal government has grown out of control, threatening the rights, liberties and prop-
erties of the people This is being done at the executive, legislative and judicial level.
This is in direct opposition to the Constitution and the founding fathers vision of the
federal government. Because I believe this, today I exercised my rights as a free citizen and did not visit the White House."[26]

While some people viewed Thomas's snub as an act of bravery, there were many
who saw things differently. *U.S. News and World Report* correspondent Susan Mulligan pointed out that presidential meet-and-greets with athletes are apolitical events
intended as nothing more than "gifts" to participants. In Mulligan's unbridled opinion, Thomas's actions "underscored a distressing trend in this country: people who
have lost the ability to distinguish between speaking truth to power and just being a
jerk."[27]

Born in Flint, Michigan, Thomas graduated from Davidson High School. As a
boy, he admired Michigan-born goalie John Vanbiesbrouck and sought to emulate his
style. Rather than immediately pursuing a career in the NHL, Thomas chose to attend
the University of Vermont. He was on the Catamounts' roster from 1993 through
1997. During his time at the school, he set UVM records for wins and saves while
helping the squad to a Frozen Four appearance in '96.

Selected by the Quebec Nordiques in the 1994 Entry Draft, Thomas's route to
Boston was a circuitous one. He had multiple stints in the AHL, IHL and Finnish
SM Liiga (Finland's top professional circuit) before joining the Bruins organization in
2001. Though he made his Beantown debut the following year, he would not become
the B's primary goalie until the 2005-'06 campaign. After spending two seasons
with Providence, he returned to Finland during the '04 lockout, winning the Lasse
Oksanen Trophy (given to the league's best player).

In 2007, Thomas began a yoga-based conditioning program designed to increase
his flexibility and strength. The results were dramatic although he drew ongoing criticism for his slow movement across the crease and reliance on acrobatic maneu-
vers to keep pucks out of the net. He got the job done regardless, becoming the first

Bruins goaltender to win the Seventh Player Award twice. In 2008-'09, he posted a league-best .933 save percentage along with a 2.10 GAA, capturing the Vezina Trophy. Proving he had not yet reached the summit of his career, he turned in another Vezina performance in 2011. During Boston's successful Stanley Cup run, he compiled a 16–9 record with four shutouts—numbers good enough to claim the Conn Smythe Trophy (for best playoff performance). He was the first goaltender since Bernie Parent (in '74-'75) to win the Stanley Cup, Vezina Trophy and Conn Smythe Trophy in the same year.

Over portions of eight seasons with the Bruins, Thomas won 196 regular season games and added 29 victories in the playoffs. His .921 save percentage is among the top marks in franchise history. Additionally, he ranks among the top five in shots-against, saves and shutouts. He participated in four All-Star Games while wearing the Black and Gold.

Thomas was conspicuously absent from training camp in 2012, later announcing that he would sit out the entire season. At 38 years of age, the Bruins figured he was nearing the end of his career and traded him to the Islanders for future considerations. He returned to the ice with the Panthers the following year, appearing in 40 games before a late-season trade landed him in Dallas. He made his last NHL start in April of 2014.

Shortly before his induction into the U.S. Hockey Hall of Fame in 2019, Thomas made headlines again when he revealed that he was suffering from traumatic brain damage sustained over the course of his NHL career. Doctors told him that two-thirds of his brain was receiving 5 percent blood flow while the rest was averaging about 50 percent. In a tearful statement to the press, he said: "I wake up every day and basically I have to reorder everything in my mind for the first couple hours of the day and then make a list and try to make some choices to get some stuff done."[28] He added that he has reached the point where he is capable of making meaningful decisions, but that it has taken him years to get there.

Tuukka Rask
(2007–Present)

Rask was born in Savonlinna, Finland, which is in the southeastern part of the country near Lake Saimaa. Rask's older brother, Joonas, is a professional hockey forward in Europe. Tuukka got his start with local youth teams in Savonlinna. By 2004, he was playing professionally with the Ilves Tampere of the SM Liiga (Finland's top hockey circuit). In the 2005 Entry Draft, Rask was considered the most promising European goaltending prospect. The Maple Leafs chose him 21st overall then traded him to the Bruins for Andrew Raycroft. It would prove to be a colossal miscalculation as Raycroft failed to demonstrate consistency in net. Rask, on the other hand, became one of Boston's all-time greatest stoppers.

Rask made brief appearances on the Bruins roster in 2007 and 2008 but would not attain official rookie status until 2009-'10. Demonstrating his readiness to play at hockey's highest level, he led the league with a .931 save percentage and 1.97 GAA. He finished fourth in voting for the Calder Trophy. His strong postseason performance

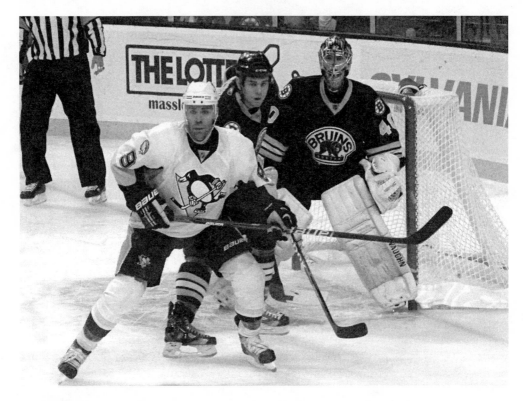

Tuukka Rask (#40, pictured here in action against the Penguins) helped the Bruins to three appearances in the Stanley Cup finals between 2011 and 2019. Also shown are Pascal Dupuis of the Penguins and Matt Bartkowski of the Bruins. Courtesy Dan4th on Visual hunt/CC BY.

helped the Bruins beat the Sabres in the quarter-finals and extend the semi-final showdown against Philadelphia to seven games. Five of those matches were decided by a single goal as the Flyers ultimately prevailed.

Over the next two seasons, Rask served a back-up role, playing competently behind Tim Thomas. In the wake of Thomas's 2012 departure, Rask became Boston's primary net-minder—a role he has maintained for nearly a decade. Rask is a great positional goalie. At 6-foot-3, he takes up a lot of space in the net. He sees very well through traffic and has an agile glove hand. Goaltending coach Eli Wilson described Rask's skill set in the following words: "Every save he makes [is] with a purpose, either keeping it or putting it where he wants it.... If you catch a goalie off balance or leaning one way, you can usually beat him the other way, but Tuukka always had the ability to make a save based on athleticism and it didn't really matter if he was set for a particular play."[29]

Early in his career, Rask gained a reputation for being temperamental, breaking sticks and throwing water bottles after tough losses. In recent years, he has kept his emotions in check for the most part. If there has been one complaint throughout his career, it is the fact that he loses focus from time to time, allowing "soft" goals in the wake of other mistakes. Like most net-minders, he has been known to fall into periodic "slumps." In spite of that, he remains tremendously popular with Boston fans, who chant his name after great saves. Because of the way his first name is pronounced, it sounds like he is being booed.

After missing out on the Vezina Trophy in his greatest statistical season (2009-'10), Rask claimed the prize in 2013-'14. He won 36 games that year and posted a .930 save percentage. As of 2020, he was the Bruins' all-time leader in wins, shots-against, and saves. He currently ranks second on the B's all-time list in shutouts.

In 2013, the Bruins rewarded Rask with an eight-year, $56 million contract. Considering his performance since then, it has turned out to be a pretty good deal for Boston. Early in the 2018-'19 season, Rask surprised team officials by taking a temporary leave of absence to clear up some personal matters. He returned in time for a 4–2 win over the Blackhawks in the Winter Classic. At the game's conclusion, he made a cryptic comment to the press. "This might be my last outdoor game, you never know," he told an NBC reporter. "It's a great experience to get the result. The next one, when it happens, maybe I'll be sitting up in the press box drinking beer, who knows."[30] Though many speculated that Rask might be considering retirement, he returned as Boston's number 1 goalie the following year. A concussion sustained in January of 2020—his third in a span of three seasons—put Rask out of action for an extended period and raised further doubts about his future. He left the club again during the 2020 playoffs due to coronavirus concerns. His 2.12 GAA was tops in the NHL.

6

Hall of Famers
Briefly with the Bruins

Sprague Cleghorn
(Defense, 1925–1928)

Before Eddie Shore and Bobby Orr, there was Sprague Cleghorn—one of the game's first offensive defensemen. A native of Montreal, he turned pro in the National Hockey Association during the 1910-'11 season. After the league folded, he joined the Ottawa Senators. Cleghorn was known for his durability, leading the NHL in games played three times.

A fierce competitor, Cleghorn resorted to outright brutality at times. He was charged with assault for his on-ice activities on two separate occasions. Universally hated and feared by opponents, efforts to ban him from the NHL produced no results.

Cleghorn was more than just a bully. He scored 16 goals (in 21 games) during the '19-'20 campaign then followed with 17 in '21-'22. He finished among the top 10 in assists four times. A clutch performer, he netted 14 game-winners during his NHL career. Three of those came during the playoffs.

By the time he joined the Bruins in 1925, Cleghorn was 35 years old and somewhat past his prime. But the team needed a seasoned veteran to assume a leadership role. Cleghorn served as captain during his first two seasons, yielding the title to Lionel Hitchman in '27-'28. He remained a dominant physical presence, averaging more than 50 penalty minutes per season during his three-year stint in Boston. The B's made it to the playoffs twice during his residency.

Cleghorn finished his playing career in the Can-Am League. He later coached a mediocre Montreal Maroons squad to a 19–22–7 record in '31-'32. He was inducted into the Hockey Hall of Fame in 1958.

Frank Fredrickson
(Center, 1927–1928)

Frederickson was born and raised in Winnipeg. His parents were native Icelanders and he didn't learn a word of English until he was six years old. In 1915, he led his senior hockey squad to a league championship, receiving the title of team captain.

With the outbreak of World War I, he joined the Royal Flying Air Corps. During a trip from Egypt to Italy, his transport ship was torpedoed. He and other crewmates were rescued in lifeboats.

Discharged from the military in 1919, Fredrickson returned to the Manitoba Hockey Association with the Winnipeg Falcons. He scored 28 points in 10 games, guiding the team to an Allan Cup title. After a Gold Medal performance at the 1920 Summer Olympics, Frederickson turned pro. He spent four seasons in the Pacific Coast Hockey Association and two more in the Western Hockey League, winning a Stanley Cup with the Victoria Cougars in 1925. When the WHL folded the following year, the Cougars were reassembled as an NHL franchise (later known as the Red Wings). Fredrickson spent part of the '26-'27 campaign with the Cougars before a January trade landed him in Boston.

In his Bruins debut, Frederickson led the club in assists while finishing third in goals. The B's advanced through two rounds of the playoffs without a loss before falling to the Ottawa Senators in the finals. Frederickson's performance earned him serious consideration for the Hart Trophy. He finished third in voting, less than four percentage points behind the winner—Canadiens defenseman Herb Gardiner.

Frederickson's point production dropped off sharply in '27-'28 as the Bruins made a first-round playoff exit. After 12 games with Boston in '28-'29, Fredrickson was traded to the Pittsburgh Pirates. In his absence, the Bruins won the Stanley Cup. Fredrickson finished his NHL career with the Detroit Falcons in '30-'31. He also appeared in the International Hockey League that season. He was elected to the Hockey Hall of Fame in 1958.

Duke Keats
(Center, 1926–1927)

Keats grew up in North Bay, Ontario. His given name was Gordon, but he received the nickname "Duke" from friends during his formative years. The moniker was in reference to a warship. As a boy, he gained a reputation for being a superb puck handler. By 1915, he had become one of the top scorers in the National Hockey Association.

Keats lost portions of three seasons to military service during World War I. Upon being discharged, he joined the Edmonton Eskimos of the Big 4 Western League. He led the circuit in scoring twice. After Edmonton joined the Western Canada Hockey League in 1921, Keats was named a 1st Team All-Star in five straight seasons. His game-winning goal on a penalty shot in the 1923 WCHL finals sent the Eskimos to a Stanley Cup showdown against the Ottawa Senators.

On the brink of financial collapse in 1926, the Eskimos sold Keats to the Boston Bruins with six other players for a reported sum of $50,000. Keats's career in Boston was remarkably brief, lasting from September of '26 until January of '27, when he was traded to Detroit. He was one of the few bright spots on an awful Cougars club that compiled the worst record in the NHL.

Keats began the '27-'28 season with Detroit but ended up being suspended for swinging his stick at a fan who was directing insults at him. He was traded to Chicago, where he led the team in scoring. Unfortunately, the Blackhawks finished in last place and Keats missed a playoff opportunity yet again.

After making three appearances with Chicago in '28-'29, Keats left the NHL for good, signing with the Tulsa Oilers of the American Hockey Association. He was the league's top scorer that season. He retired as a player after the '33-'34 campaign. He was inducted into the Hockey Hall of Fame in 1958.

MICKEY MacKay
(CENTER, 1928–1930)

Duncan "Mickey" MacKay was born in Chesley, Ontario, and grew up on a nearby farm. He joined the Canadian Army at the age of 14 but was discharged when it was discovered he was too young. Late to hockey, he didn't learn to skate until he was in his mid-teens. After two seasons at the senior level in Chesley, he joined the Edmonton Dominions of the Alberta Senior Hockey League. He paced the circuit with eight playoff goals in 1913.

MacKay turned pro with the Vancouver Millionaires in 1914, leading the Pacific Coast Hockey Association in points. On the strength of his performance, Vancouver won the PCHA title then defeated the Ottawa Senators to claim the Stanley Cup. Over the next several seasons, MacKay earned seven All-Star selections. He went to the Stanley Cup finals again with Vancouver in 1918, but in spite of his postseason-best five goals and five assists, the Millionaires were defeated by their NHL opponents— the Toronto Arenas.

The PCHA merged with the Western Canada Hockey League in 1924 and was renamed the following season (becoming the Western Hockey League). In spite of those changes, the circuit folded in 1926. MacKay joined the Chicago Blackhawks, finishing among the club's top scorers in two straight seasons. When the Hawks missed the playoffs in 1928, MacKay was dealt to the Pittsburgh Pirates. Off to a 1–7–4 record the following season, the Pirates traded MacKay to the Bruins for aging superstar Frank Fredrickson. MacKay made 31 appearances for Boston down the stretch, helping the club to its first Stanley Cup title.

Though the Bruins compiled an .875 points percentage in '29-'30 (highest in NHL history), the season ended with a disappointing loss to the Canadiens in the finals. MacKay announced his retirement shortly afterward. He settled in Grand Forks, British Columbia and began a career in the mining business. In 1940, he suffered a heart attack at the wheel of his car, struck a telephone pole and died. He was posthumously elected to the Hockey Hall of Fame in 1952.

CY DENNENY
(LEFT WING, 1928–1929)

Denneny was somewhat of a lumbering skater during his playing days. But he had a very accurate shot and was extremely clever. Among the first to use opposing defenseman as a screen, he helped pioneer the use of curved stick blades, which made his shots rise or sink unpredictably and flustered many goalies. He began his career as an enforcer but mellowed with age.

Born in Farran's Point, Ontario, Denneny spent a majority of his professional career with the Ottawa Senators, joining the club in 1916. When the National Hockey Association ceased operations the following year, the Senators moved to the NHL. Denneny arrived in the new league as a feisty scrapper, averaging four penalty minutes per game in his debut. After the '19-'20 campaign, he never spent more than 28 minutes in the box during any season.

Over the course of his NHL career, Denneny netted no fewer than 21 goals in seven seasons—an impressive figure considering that the NHL schedule consisted of 21 games when he arrived. He finished among the top 10 in goals on nine occasions and gathered 25 hat tricks. Seven of them came during his first NHL campaign—a record that stood until 1980-'81, when Mike Bossy of the Islanders collected nine.

In October of 1928, Denneny's contract was sold to the Bruins. He arrived in time to add a fifth Stanley Cup to his collection. He played a minor role with the Bruins that year, appearing in just 23 regular season games and two playoff games. It was his last year as a player.

In 1929, Denneny returned to the ice as a referee. He later coached the Ottawa Senators to a dreadful 11–27–10 record. Finished with hockey by 1934, he worked for the Canadian Federal Government. He retired from civil service in 1959—the same year he was inducted into the Hockey Hall of Fame.

BILLY BURCH
(FORWARD, 1932–1933)

Born in Yonkers, New York, Wilfred "Billy" Burch was big for the era at 6-foot, 200-plus pounds. Though he would have been well-suited to an enforcer's role, he was quite gentlemanly, averaging just 18 penalty minutes per year during his NHL tenure, which began in 1922. Extremely durable, he led the league in games played five times.

Burch finished with double-digit goal totals in six straight seasons, reaching the 20-goal mark in back-to-back campaigns. He won the Hart Trophy in '24-'25 with the Hamilton Tigers, aiding the club to a first-place finish. The season had been extended from 24 to 30 games and, seeking additional pay, Hamilton players went on strike before the playoffs. The entire team was suspended and the Montreal Canadiens were declared NHL champions after beating the Toronto St. Patricks in a two-game series.

In 1926, the Tigers moved to New York and became known as the Americans. Looking for a marketing ploy, they dubbed Burch: "Yonkers Billy—The Babe Ruth of Hockey." Though he was by no means on Ruth's level, he was definitely one of the few talented players on a perennially mediocre squad. The club made just one playoff appearance during Burch's seven seasons in the Big Apple.

Strapped for cash, the Americans sold Burch's contract to the Bruins in April of 1932. After 25 games, team officials became dissatisfied with his offensive production and traded him to the Blackhawks. He skated in 22 games with Chicago before ending his career.

With his hockey days behind him, Burch retired to Toronto. Sadly, he wasn't around for his induction into the Hockey Hall of Fame in 1974. He died shortly after celebrating his 50th birthday in November of 1950.

BABE SIEBERT
(LEFT WING/DEFENSE, 1933–1936)

Born in Plattsville, Ontario, Siebert grew up in nearby Zurich, which is located on the shores of Lake Huron. A standout at every level of play, he ascended to the NHL with the Montreal Maroons before the '25-'26 campaign. In Montreal, Siebert became part of the most respected line in hockey, teaming with Nels Stewart and Hooley Smith. Stewart was the sniper and Smith was the playmaker while Siebert used his size and strength to neutralize opponents. Dubbed the "S-Line" by sportswriters, the trio carried the Maroons to a Stanley Cup title in 1926.

Stewart's physical play frequently landed him in the penalty box. He averaged close to 100 minutes of penalties per year between 1925 and 1930—an alarming figure considering that the NHL season was much shorter back then. In 1927, he was suspended for assaulting Billy Boucher of the New York Americans with his stick.

Strapped for cash, the Maroons sold Siebert's contract to the Rangers before the '32-'33 campaign. He performed exceptionally well, helping the club to a Stanley Cup title. Off to a slow start the following year, the Rangers traded him to the Bruins. After Eddie Shore was suspended for a vicious assault on Ace Bailey, coach Art Ross moved Siebert from left wing to defense. Siebert adjusted well, finishing among the Bruins' top scorers in each of his two-plus seasons in Boston. Interestingly, Shore and Siebert strongly disliked one another due to an ongoing feud that began when they were opponents. Multiple sources reported that the tension between them was palpable whenever they skated together.

Bruins executives made a colossal miscalculation in September of 1936, trading Siebert to the Montreal Canadiens. Siebert responded by winning the Hart Trophy that season. He was equally impressive the following year, completing a run of three consecutive All-Star selections while finishing third in MVP voting. He made his last appearance as a player in 1939.

Named head coach of the Canadiens immediately following his retirement, Siebert never assumed the role. Prior to the '39-'40 campaign, he drowned in Lake Huron while swimming with his daughters. The NHL arranged a memorial game at the Montreal Forum for Siebert's wife, who had become paralyzed while giving birth to the couple's second child. Attendance at the event was fairly low, but a reported sum of $15,000 was raised. Siebert was posthumously elected to the Hockey Hall of Fame in 1964.

BUN COOK
(LEFT WING, 1936–1937)

The Cook brothers—Bill and Fred—hailed from Kingston, Ontario. They were quite close despite a dramatic age difference and skated together through most of their professional careers. When all was said and done, they were both inducted into the Hockey Hall of Fame.

Fred played for St. Mary's School prior to joining amateur clubs in Brantford and Sault Ste. Marie. In 1924, he guided his team to an Allan Cup championship. He was a major star in the Western Canada Hockey League before the circuit folded in 1926. The Rangers acquired both Cook brothers in the aftermath.

Fred was a swift skater and acquired his nickname, "Bun," from a writer who proclaimed that he was quick as a bunny. He has been credited as the innovator of the slap shot and drop pass, averaging 15 assists per year during his 10 seasons with the Rangers. A capable goal-scorer, he lit the lamp at least 13 times in nine straight campaigns. His six goals in the '32 playoffs were tops in the league.

In '35-'36, Cook sat out more than 20 games with an arthritic condition. Figuring his career was over, the Rangers sold his contract to the Bruins. Though he didn't reach the statistical heights of his prime years, he did make 44 appearances, helping the B's to a second-place finish. They lost to the Montreal Maroons in the quarter-finals. It was Cook's last NHL season.

Finished as a player, Cook embarked upon a long and prosperous coaching career in the IAHL and AHL. He led the Providence Reds and Cleveland Barons to a combined total of seven Calder Cup championships. After hockey, he settled in Kingston. He was 85 when he died, missing his induction into the Hockey Hall of Fame (in 1995) and AHL Hall of Fame (in 2007).

HOOLEY SMITH
(FORWARD, 1936–1937)

Among the most talented players of his era, Smith was also one of the nastiest. At 5-foot-10, 155 pounds, he defied his size by dishing out punishing hits and spending an inordinate amount of time in the penalty box.

Born Reginald Joseph, Smith's father gave him the nickname "Hooley" in reference to a popular comic strip character known as Happy Hooligan. Smith grew up in Toronto and dabbled at multiple sports, including rowing, rugby and boxing. After guiding the Toronto Granites to an Allan Cup championship and Gold Medal in the 1924 Olympics, Smith signed with the Ottawa Senators.

Capable of playing both center and left wing, Smith quickly established himself as one of the top scorers in the NHL. He also proved to be extremely volatile. In the 1927 Stanley Cup finals (won by the Senators), he attacked Bruins forward Harry Oliver, touching off a bloody brawl. League president Frank Calder suspended him for a month.

Strapped for cash before the '27-'28 campaign, the Senators sold Smith's contract to the Montreal Maroons for a record sum. Smith teamed with Nels Stewart and Babe Siebert to form the renowned "S-Line." In 1935, the trio carried the Maroons to a Stanley Cup title. But the Great Depression had taken a toll on hockey and, facing financial ruin, the Maroons traded Smith to the Bruins the following year for cash and future considerations.

Smith spent one full season in Boston, finishing among the top five in team scoring. In spite of carrying a dozen Hall of Famers on the roster at various points in the season, the Bruins lost to Smith's former team—the Maroons—in the first round of the playoffs. Sweeping changes were made before the '37-'38 campaign and Smith was sold to the New York Americans.

Smith's clashes with coach Red Dutton in New York were epic. Though he still proved to be a valuable asset on both offense and defense, he was suspended for insubordination during his final season. When he died in 1963, he was the last surviving member of the "S-Line." He became a member of the Hockey Hall of Fame in 1972.

SYLVIO MANTHA
(DEFENSE, 1937)

Born in Montreal, Mantha grew up in St. Henri—a blue collar neighborhood located near the old Montreal Forum. He began his hockey career at right wing. His size and considerable strength impressed Canadiens GM Leo Dandurand, who signed him before the '23-'24 slate. The Habs used Mantha as a winger only briefly, assigning him to defense shortly after his debut. In an era when most teams carried just three defensemen, Mantha demonstrated his durability by leading the league in games played six times.

Master of the hip-check, Mantha was a difficult man to skate around. He was fast, agile and fearless, dropping gloves with anyone who challenged him. His 108 penalty minutes in '29-'30 were third in the NHL. A two-time All-Star, he spent a total of 13 seasons with the Canadiens, guiding the team to three Stanley Cup titles (in '24, '30 and '31).

Mantha skated alongside his younger brother Georges for eight of his 14 NHL seasons. Georges—primarily a left-winger—enjoyed his peak offensive years after Sylvio left the club, but most historians would agree that the Manthas were among the top sibling duos in the NHL during their time together.

Sylvio was known for taking charge on the ice and, in 1935, he put those abilities to work as a player-coach. Unfortunately, he didn't have much talent to work with and the Canadiens missed the playoffs on his watch. He was dismissed from his duties at season's end. He contemplated retirement during the 1937 campaign, but when the Bruins got into a salary dispute with Eddie Shore, Mantha was added as a replacement. He lasted just four games before deciding he couldn't cut it at the NHL level anymore.

After hanging up his skates, Mantha worked as a linesman and referee in the AHL and NHL. He coached at the junior level through most of the 1940s. In 1960, he was inducted into the Hockey Hall of Fame. He was 81 years old when he died. Both Mantha brothers have arenas named after them in Montreal.

BUSHER JACKSON
(LEFT WING, 1941–1944)

Jackson is among hockey's most tragic figures. In his prime, he had it all—speed, finesse and matinee idol looks. A flashy dresser, he drove around in fancy cars and lived the life of a playboy. But his frivolous spending and hard drinking eventually drove him to ruin.

Born and raised in Toronto, Jackson learned the basics of the game on a local rink known as "Poverty Pond." As a teenager, he was recruited by Maple Leafs assistant GM Frank Selke, who assigned him to the Toronto Marlboros of the OHA. In 1929, Jackson led the club to a Memorial Cup championship, earning a promotion to the NHL. Born Ralph Henry, he got his nickname after making a brash remark to a Leafs trainer, who disparagingly referred to him as a "Busher."

Jackson teamed with winger Charlie Conacher and center Joe Primeau to form a high-scoring unit known as the "Kid Line." Their youth and enthusiasm helped rejuvenate the team. In '31–'32, Jackson became the youngest scoring champion in NHL history at 21 years and three months of age (a record that stood until Wayne Gretzky arrived). He added seven points in the postseason, carrying the Leafs to a Stanley Cup title. It was the only Cup he would win during his career.

Leafs owner Conn Smythe tried to talk Jackson into saving money and settling down, but the star winger was incorrigible. Traded to the New York Americans in '39, his scoring dropped off considerably. In '41, he got into a salary dispute with team manager Red Dutton. After a long holdout, his contract was sold to the Bruins.

In Boston, Jackson joined his younger brother, Art, who was one of the top forwards of the talent-depleted World War II era. In addition to his duties at left wing, Busher was used as a part-time defenseman to compensate for injuries and war-time enlistment. He had a career revival in '42–'43, posting his highest point total in several years. His overtime goal against the Canadiens at the Montreal Forum in the semi-finals was the last post-regulation goal scored by the B's in Montreal until 1992. The Bruins advanced to the Stanley Cup finals in '43 but ended up getting swept by the Red Wings. Jackson performed well the following season, scoring 32 points in 42 games for the Bruins, but opted for retirement at season's end.

Life after hockey was not kind to Jackson. Facing bankruptcy at the end of his playing days, he continued to drink heavily. In 1958, he broke his neck after falling down a flight of stairs. He later suffered from jaundice and epileptic seizures, dying relatively young at the age of 55. Because of his sad downfall, his entry into the Hockey Hall of Fame was delayed until 1971. He was five years in his grave by then.

BABE PRATT
(DEFENSE, 1946–1947)

Including his days in youth hockey, Pratt won more than a dozen championships during his long career. In his prime, he was one of the biggest players in the NHL at 6-foot-3, 212 pounds. But despite his imposing presence, he played relatively clean for the era.

Pratt was born in Stony Mountain, Manitoba, which is less than 10 miles from Winnipeg. A passionate fan of baseball while growing up, he was nicknamed after Yankee slugger Babe Ruth. He joined the Kenora Thistles at the age of 17 and carried the club to a Manitoba Junior Hockey League championship in 1934. He was the circuit's top scorer the following year.

Signed by the Rangers in 1935, Pratt spent part of the season in the Can-Am League with the Philadelphia Ramblers. Upon securing a permanent roster spot in New York, he spent six full seasons with the Rangers, helping the club to a Stanley Cup title in 1940. A superb sick-handler, Pratt worked hard throughout his career to keep the puck in the opponents' zone. He believed that this was the key to good defense.

Traded to the Maple Leafs in November of '42, Pratt reached the peak of his career offensively. He averaged 16 goals and 30 assists per season for Toronto between 1942 and 1945. His efforts paid great dividends as the Leafs won the Cup in '45. The following year, he was suspended for betting on games. He admitted his indiscretions but insisted that he had never wagered on his own team to lose. After vowing to clean up his act, he was reinstated.

In June of '46, Pratt was traded to the Bruins. He arrived as a 31-year-old veteran of 12 NHL seasons. The years had taken their toll on him, however, as he appeared in just 31 games, scoring eight points—his lowest total since his rookie campaign. Though he never appeared in another NHL game after '47, he continued in the AHL and PCHL with several clubs until his retirement in 1952. He later coached the New Westminster Royals in British Columbia. Pratt was inducted into the Hockey Hall of Fame in 1966. His son, Tracy, played 10 NHL seasons with six different teams.

TERRY SAWCHUK
(GOALIE, 1955–1957)

Born in the North End of Winnipeg, Sawchuk came of age in East Kildonan. One of his siblings died very young of scarlet fever. Sawchuk's oldest brother, a promising goalie who he idolized, succumbed to a fatal heart attack at the age of 17. When Sawchuk was 12, he dislocated his right elbow playing rugby. Fearing his parents would be unhappy with him, he hid the injury. It healed improperly, limiting his mobility and leaving him with one arm shorter than the other.

In spite of his handicap, Sawchuk was scouted by Detroit in his early teens and sent to play for a Wings affiliate in Galt, Ontario. Called to Detroit for seven appearances in '49-'50, he won the Calder Trophy the following season, gradually emerging as the NHL's premiere stopper.

A stand-up goaltender, Sawchuk developed a crouched stance to see through the legs of skaters. It left him with a permanent stoop in his posture, but that was the least of his problems. He played through unimaginable pain during his career, sustaining a plethora of injuries that included a broken foot, collapsed lung, severed tendons in his hand and ruptured discs in his back. It has been estimated that he received roughly 400 stitches to his face (some without the benefit of anesthetic) before he finally began wearing a mask.

Though it was never officially diagnosed, many believe that Sawchuk was suffering from bipolar disorder. His sulky moods were punctuated by epic temper tantrums, which alienated him from reporters and fans. His volatility led to a trade from Detroit to Boston.

Sawchuk was deeply hurt by the trade and had trouble adjusting to life with the

Bruins. He posted the highest GAA of his career to that point and lost an NHL-high 33 games during the '55-'56 campaign. He played better in his second season but came down with a case of mononucleosis. Upon returning to action, he fell into a slump and announced that he was retiring from hockey. Though he later denied the claim, Bruins coach Milt Schmidt allegedly questioned Sawchuk's dedication to the team. The Red wings reacquired Sawchuk by trading Johnny Bucyk, who became one of the B's all-time greats.

Sawchuk continued for seven more seasons with the Wings before a trade landed him in Toronto for the '64-'65 campaign. He won the Vezina Trophy that year (the fourth of his career) and led the Leafs to a Cup in '67 (also the fourth of his career). He spent his last NHL season with the Rangers.

While playing in Toronto, Sawchuk befriended winger Ron Stewart. The two ended up renting a house together on Long Island while playing for the Rangers during the '69-'70 slate. Sawchuk appeared in just eight games with New York that year and fell into a deep depression. During the offseason, he and Stewart got into an argument at a local bar that led to a violent altercation. Sawchuk was hospitalized afterward with a ruptured gallbladder and bleeding liver. He underwent separate operations for each condition and spent a month in the hospital before suffering a fatal pulmonary embolism. A jury investigated Stewart's role in the death, which was ultimately ruled an accident.

Sawchuk was elected to the Hockey Hall of Fame in 1971 and later became a member of three other Canadian Halls of Fame. The Red Wings retired his number in 1994. In 2019, a biopic film about his life was released, dramatizing his many problems on and off the ice.

ALLAN STANLEY
(DEFENSE, 1956–1958)

Stanley proved that you don't need speed to succeed in the NHL. He earned the nickname "Snowshoes" for his clumsy skating style. A classic stay-at-home defenseman, he played the angles exceptionally well, using his body to dish out big hits and throw attackers off course. By the time he retired, he had four Stanley Cup titles to his credit.

Born in Timmins, Ontario, Stanley was tutored on the finer points of the game by his Uncle Barney—a Hall of Fame winger. Originally a center, Stanley was switched to defense when his lack of speed became evident. He made his NHL debut with the Rangers in '48-'49, aspiring to the title of team captain in 1951. Fans never warmed to him, however, and he ended up being traded to the Blackhawks shortly into the '54-'55 campaign. He scored a personal-best 10 goals that year, but after a disappointing follow-up, he was sold to the Bruins.

Stanley spent two seasons in Boston and played solidly. He was the Bruins top-scoring defenseman in both campaigns. The B's made it to the finals in '57 and '58 but lost to the Canadiens by a combined total of 11 goals. Looking for answers to the Montreal "curse," changes were made. Stanley wound up being traded to Toronto, where he began the most productive stretch of his career.

In all, Stanley spent 10 full seasons with the Leafs, making three All-Star appearances while finishing in the running for the Norris Trophy twice. His presence helped guide Toronto to four NHL championships, including three in a row from 1962 through 1964. Stanley played past his 42nd birthday and retired with the Flyers after the '68-'69 campaign.

In 1981, Stanley was elected to the Hall of Fame. In 2009, he was ranked at number 60 among the Rangers all-time greatest players. He died in October of 2013 in Bobcaygeon, Ontario. He was 87 years old at the time of his passing.

WILLIE O'REE
(LEFT WING, 1958/1960–1961)

O'Ree has been labeled the "Jackie Robinson of Hockey" though the comparison is not entirely accurate. While Robinson spent 10 years in the majors, O'Ree was denied the opportunity to establish lasting tenure at hockey's highest level. Nevertheless, he was the first black player to reach the NHL, appearing in 45 games over portions of two seasons.

Born in Fredericton, New Brunswick, the precocious O'Ree was skating by the age of three and playing in organized youth leagues at five. A talented second baseman and shortstop, he was offered a contract by the Milwaukee Brewers (then a minor league team) during his teen years. His first love was hockey, however, and he chose to pursue a career on the ice instead.

O'Ree has pointed out in multiple interviews that he was not discriminated against in the youth leagues of New Brunswick. He said that a majority of the racism he encountered occurred during his days as a professional. Signed by the Bruins, he spent most of the '57-'58 campaign with the Quebec Aces. When one of the B's regular wingers fell prey to an injury that year, O'Ree made NHL history by appearing in two games alongside center Don McKenney and right-winger Jerry Tappanzzini.

Though O'Ree was welcomed and accepted by his Boston teammates, his arrival on the professional hockey scene was not warmly embraced by everyone. Fans spit on him and dumped beverages on him. Opponents picked unnecessary fights. Through it all, O'Ree persevered, retaining his dignity and pride.

O'Ree carried a secret throughout his professional career. While playing for the Kitchener Canucks in '55-'56, he was hit in the face with a puck. The injury led to permanent blindness in his right eye. With the odds already stacked against him, he hid the condition from teammates and coaches. In spite of his affliction, O'Ree played in more than a thousand professional games. He returned to Boston in 1960-'61, making 43 appearances and scoring 14 points. Out of the NHL for good after that, he continued to skate in multiple professional leagues for well over a decade. He won two scoring titles in the WHL, reaching the 30-goal mark five times between 1964 and 1974. He retired as a player after the '78-'79 campaign.

Since then, O'Ree has served a variety of roles for the NHL, establishing more than three dozen grass roots programs targeting economically disadvantaged youths of various ethnicities. He won the prestigious Lester Patrick Award for outstanding service to U.S. hockey in 2003. He was inducted into the Hockey Hall of Fame as a builder in 2018.

TOM JOHNSON
(DEFENSE, 1963–1965)

Born in Baldur, Manitoba, Johnson had the privilege of playing alongside a number of Montreal Canadiens legends, including Jean Beliveau, Jacques Plante and the Richard brothers. Though it led to a total of six Stanley Cups, Johnson was overshadowed and underrated for most of his career. He lasted 14 full seasons in Montreal, putting forth his finest effort in '58-'59, when he captured the Norris Trophy.

Lacking exceptional speed, Johnson was content to hang back while his teammates gathered most of the points. Rarely used with a man-advantage, his solid physical play made him a valuable asset on penalty kills. In an extremely rough era, he had a habit of hitting opponents from behind. He was also known to hang onto his stick during fights, using it to defend himself. Highly durable, he led the NHL in games played five times, battling through knee issues and two serious eye injuries.

After scoring just eight points in 42 games during the '62-'63 campaign, the Canadiens let Johnson go in the Waiver Draft. The Bruins were in a rebuilding phase and figured they could use a veteran to shore up their defensive corps. Johnson collected 21 assists during his first season in Boston—the highest mark among B's defensemen. He was having a decent follow-up campaign when disaster struck. In a game against the Blackhawks, he was slashed in the leg by the skate of winger Chico Maki. A nerve was severed, leaving him with a permanent limp.

Finished as a player, Johnson settled in the New England area and aspired to the position of Bruins head coach. Known for his laissez-faire attitude, he was well-liked by players. He led the team to a Stanley Cup title in his second year at the helm but ended up being replaced by Bep Guidolin with 26 games remaining in the '72-'73 campaign. In the wake of his firing, the Bruins made a first-round playoff exit. Johnson stayed with the organization, serving as an assistant to GM Harry Sinden for many years. He was inducted into the Hockey Hall of Fame in 1970. He died in 2007 at the age of 79.

BERNIE PARENT
(GOALIE, 1965–1967)

Had Bruins executives known how good Parent would be, they might not have given up on him so early in his career. Though he made his NHL debut with Boston, Parent had two of his worst seasons while wearing the Black and Gold. Feeling as if they had overestimated his talents, the Bruins let him go in the '67 Expansion Draft. A long, successful career with the Flyers followed.

Born and raised in Montreal, Parent didn't learn to skate until he was 11. He described himself as a loner growing up and considered goaltending an ideal position given its solitary nature. He idolized Hall of Famer Jacques Plante as a boy and tried to emulate his stand-up style.

After two seasons at the junior level, Parent was called to Boston and installed as the number 1 goaltender. It was a rocky debut as he accrued a 3.69 GAA in 39 appearances. Demoted to secondary status with the Bruins in '66-'67, improvement was barely evident. Over the next several seasons, Parent established himself as one of the top goalies in the NHL. After a brief stint in the short-lived World Hockey Association, he entered the prime of his career with the Flyers.

Parent gave his finest performances between 1973 and 1975, when he won back-to-back Vezina Trophies. He led the NHL in wins during both campaigns and helped Philly to consecutive Stanley Cup titles. Additionally, he was honored with a pair of Smythe Trophies (given to the NHL's playoff MVP).

Parent remained in goal with the Flyers until February of 1979, when he was hit in the face with a stick. For two weeks, he was completely blind in his right eye. Though his vision eventually returned, he lacked the acuity to continue as a player. He was only 34 when he retired.

As of 2020, Parent was the Flyers' all-time leader in shots-against, saves, and shutouts. Elected to the Hockey Hall of Fame in 1984, he had a long stint as a goaltending coach in Philly. He currently serves as the Flyers' ambassador of hockey.

JACQUES PLANTE
(GOALIE, 1973)

Born on a farm in Maurice, Quebec, Plante was a walk-on addition to his school's hockey team at the age of 12. He took over after another youngster was removed from net in the wake of an argument with the coach. Plante quickly became the club's number one goaltender. In his early teens, he was paid a salary to play in a local factory league. He got professional contract offers, but his parents encouraged him to finish high school first. He did. And by 1953, he was playing for a Montreal Canadiens.

Extremely active outside the crease, Plante was among the first to venture behind the net to play the puck—a practice that many of his coaches found worrisome. He was also the first to raise his hand to signal an icing. He had amazing analytical skills, allowing him to spot issues with his own mechanics and those of teammates.

During his illustrious playing career, spent primarily with the Canadiens, Plante won six Stanley Cups and seven Vezina Trophies. He was among an elite group of goaltenders to claim the Hart Trophy, winning it with Montreal in '61-'62. By the time Plante reached his mid–30s, he was plagued by recurring knee issues and asthma. Canadiens coach Toe Blake became unhappy with Plante's work ethic and traded him to the Rangers. Plante played portions of two seasons with New York before going into temporary retirement. He returned in 1968 with the St. Louis Blues and lasted for six more seasons.

In March of '73, the Bruins were gearing up for a playoff run and acquired Plante in a trade. In his mid–40s by then, he performed very well in eight regular season games, posting a .927 save percentage. He bombed in the postseason, however, allowing 10 goals in two appearances. He played one more pro season with the

WHA-affiliated Edmonton Oilers then retired for good. He was elected to the Hockey Hall of Fame in 1978. In the fall of '85, he was diagnosed with terminal stomach cancer. He died the following year at the age of 57.

ROGIE VACHON
(GOALIE, 1980–1982)

Born in Palmarolle, Quebec, Vachon grew up on a dairy farm with seven siblings. He got his first big break at the age of 14, when a local senior-level coach came looking for a last-minute replacement. Vachon had no idea at the time that he would be tending goal for the Canadiens several years later.

Vachon was called to Montreal in '66-'67 after an injury forced fellow Hall of Famer Gump Worsley out of action. When back-up goalie Charlie Hodge failed to get the job done, Vachon was asked to step in. His first NHL save came against Gordie Howe on a breakaway. He posted an 11–3–5 record that year, helping the Canadiens to a Stanley Cup finals appearance against the Maple Leafs.

Splitting time equally in net, Vachon and Worsley combined for a 2.23 GAA in '67-'68—the lowest mark in over a decade. The Canadiens won the Stanley Cup and their net-minding duo shared Vezina Trophy honors.

Short for a goaltender at 5-foot-8, Vachon was known for his great reflexes and quick glove hand. He never allowed a goal on a penalty shot during his entire career. In spite of his obvious talent, he lost his number 1 status to rookie phenom Ken Dryden in 1971. The Habs captured their third Cup in four years and Vachon ended up being traded to Los Angeles shortly into the following campaign. He was named team MVP in four consecutive seasons with the Kings. At the time of his retirement, he held franchise records for wins, shutouts and single-season GAA.

Traded to Detroit in 1978, Vachon put up disappointing numbers in back-to-back campaigns. In the summer of 1980, he was traded again—this time to the Bruins in exchange for goalie Gilles Gilbert. In Vachon's Boston debut, he performed slightly better than he had with the Wings. But he suffered a complete meltdown in the preliminary round of the playoffs against the Minnesota North Stars. After giving up five goals in the opening game, he yielded six in the second match. He ended up being pulled from the net. He returned for Game 3, but was equally ineffective, finishing the series with a disappointing 5.88 GAA.

Vachon's performance did not improve the following year in Boston and he retired at season's end. With his playing days behind him, he served as GM of the Los Angeles Kings from 1984 to 1992. He helped orchestrate the deal that brought Wayne Gretzky to the club.

GUY LAPOINTE
(DEFENSE, 1983–1984)

Most die-hard Boston fans had mixed feelings about the arrival of Lapointe in 1983. Not only had he been signed as a replacement for popular blue-liner Brad Park, but his former club had dominated the Bruins in playoff competition. At the very least, the Beantown faithful could take comfort in the fact that he wouldn't be on the opposing bench trying to beat them anymore.

Born and raised in Montreal, Lapointe grew up idolizing Canadiens great Jean Beliveau. A product of the Canadiens farm system, he made brief appearances with the Habs near the end of the 1960s. Team executives were worried about his consistency until he scored 15 goals in '70-'71—a franchise record for rookie defensemen.

A member of Montreal's "Big Three" defensive specialists (a trio that included Larry Robinson and Serge Savard), Lapointe helped the Canadiens to six Stanley Cups in a nine-year span. Standing 6-foot and weighing more than 200 pounds in his prime, he knew how to dish out crushing hits. His heavy slapshot made him a valuable resource on power plays. During his 14 full seasons in the NHL, he gathered 59 goals and 196 assists with a man-advantage.

A four-time All-Star, Lapointe set a Canadiens team record for defensemen with 28 goals in '74-'75. He followed with 21 and 25 (respectively) over the next two seasons, establishing himself as one of the franchise's greatest offensive-minded blue-liners. No other member of the Canadiens rear guard reached the 20-goal mark until 2006-'07, when Sheldon Souray lit the lamp 26 times.

Traded to the Blues in March of '82, Lapointe suffered a broken cheekbone and made limited appearances with the club down the stretch. He finished second among St. Louis defensemen in scoring the following year. Upon joining the Bruins in '83, he got to skate alongside an up-and-coming Boston legend—23-year-old Ray Bourque. By the time he retired at season's end, an entire dream-team roster could have been assembled from the Hall of Famers Lapointe played with.

Lapointe served as GM of the Longueuil Chevaliers of the QMJHL as well as assistant coach for the Quebec Nordiques. He later scouted for the Flames and Wild. The Habs retired his number 5 in 2014, more than a decade after his induction into the Hockey Hall of Fame.

JOE MULLEN
(RIGHT WING, 1995–1996)

Mullen's life could have turned out very differently. Born in New York City, he grew up in Hell's Kitchen—a violent neighborhood controlled by the infamous Gambino family. In multiple interviews, he has stated that many of his childhood acquaintances got involved with gangs and drugs. Mullen, whose father was a member of the Rangers ice crew at Madison Square Garden, turned to hockey instead.

A bit under-sized at 5-foot-9, Mullen was an excellent skater with slick moves. A Penguins announcer nicknamed him "Slippery Rock Joe" for his ability to maneuver around opponents. Known for his gentlemanly play, he was in the running for the Byng Trophy every year from 1984 through 1990. He won the award twice. An accurate shooter, he netted at least 18 percent of his shots during nine seasons. His lifetime mark is among the top 30 totals of all time.

Mullen enjoyed his finest offensive campaign with the Calgary Flames in '88-'89. He scored 51 goals and added 59 assists while accruing a stellar plus-51 rating (tops in the NHL). Aided tremendously by his league-leading 16 playoff goals, the Flames won the Stanley Cup.

Traded to Pittsburgh in 1990, Mullen helped the Penguins to consecutive NHL titles in '91 and '92. Though the Pens had Hall of Famers Mario Lemieux, Paul Coffey and Mark Recchi in residence prior to the '90-'91 campaign, the arrival of Mullen along with Jaromir Jagr helped push the team over the top.

By the time Mullen joined the Bruins in 1995, he was 38 years old with 14 seasons of NHL experience. The Bruins had a strong team that year with Adam Oates, Cam Neely and Ray Bourque driving the offense. Unfortunately, Mullen sat out three months with back and knee issues. He played one more season with the Penguins in '96-'97 then announced his retirement. Inducted into the U.S. Hockey Hall of Fame in 1998, he was enshrined at the Hall of Fame in Toronto two years later.

DAVE ANDREYCHUK
(LEFT WING, 1999–2000)

By his own admission, very few of Andreychuk's lifetime goals were of highlight reel quality. In fact, most of them fell into the "garbage" category. At 6-foot-4, 220 pounds, he made a habit of parking himself in front of the net and stuffing in his own rebounds. It was a practice that carried him all the way to the Hall of Fame.

Hailing from Hamilton, Ontario, Andreychuk established himself as one of the greatest players of his era. An accomplished playmaker, he collected close to 700 regular season assists during his career. He added 55 helpers in playoff action. A sniper on the power play, he lit the lamp 274 times with a man-advantage—the highest mark in NHL history. Because of his imposing size, he was very difficult to push around. He was charged with a fair amount of penalties, but also finished in the running for the Byng Trophy twice.

In the latter half of his career, Andreychuk became a gun for hire, spending portions of seven seasons in New Jersey and Toronto, where he became affectionately known to Leafs fans as "Uncle Dave." In July of 1999, he signed as a free agent with Boston. He added some punch to a mediocre offense, but when the Bruins fell out of playoff contention, team executives decided to shake things up. Andreychuk was dealt to Colorado along with Ray Bourque shortly before the trading deadline. The Hall of Fame duo helped the Avalanche reach the 2000 conference finals against Dallas.

Andreychuk continued in the NHL for five more seasons, finishing his career as captain of the Tampa Bay Lightning. In 2003-'04, he led his squad to the first Stanley Cup in franchise history. He played beyond his 42nd birthday and stayed with the Lightning organization after his retirement as a community representative. He was subsequently promoted to vice president of Corporate and Community Affairs. Elected to the Buffalo Sabres Hall of Fame in 2008, Andreychuk waited nine more years to get into the Hall in Toronto.

PAUL COFFEY
(DEFENSE, 2000)

Had Ray Bourque decided not to pursue a career in hockey, Coffey would be the highest-scoring defenseman in NHL history. Despite finishing behind Bourque on the all-time points list, Coffey managed to claim a number of records for himself. His 48 goals in '85-'86 are the most by any blue-liner in a single campaign. And his 11 seasons with at least 60 assists are also an NHL-high among defensemen. As of 2020, he held over a dozen more all-time marks.

Born in the Toronto neighborhood of Weston, Coffey was raised in Mississauga. During his third season in juniors, he was drafted by the Edmonton Oilers. The Oilers were a dominant offensive club in the early '80s with the presence of Wayne Gretzky, Mark Messier and Jari Kurri. The addition of Coffey propelled the team to three Stanley Cups in a four-year span. Coffey emerged as a prime-time player, gathering 103 points in 94 playoff games with Edmonton. He continued his postseason success with the Penguins, winning another Cup in '91. Coffey's 59 lifetime playoff goals are an NHL record for defensemen. Remarkably, not a single one went into an empty net.

An elegant skater, Coffey was smooth and fast on both sides of the puck. His remarkable on-ice vision allowed him to make precise passes to teammates. He had a high-velocity shot that intimidated opposing goalies and made him a legitimate scoring threat from anywhere in the attacking zone. On defense, he wasn't afraid to get his hands dirty, accruing more penalty minutes than any blue-liner with 1,000 career points.

After spending portions of five seasons with Pittsburgh, Coffey traveled extensively, playing for six different clubs before arriving in Boston for the 2000-'01 slate. At 39 years old, he was a shadow of his former self. The B's used him in just 18 games that season before releasing him.

Over the course of 21 NHL seasons, Coffey received eight All-Star selections and three Norris Trophies. He finished among the top five in Norris voting on eight other occasions. After hanging up his skates, he coached briefly at the Midget level. He is currently co-owner of the Pickering Panthers of the Ontario Junior Hockey League. Inducted into the Hockey Hall of Fame in 2004, the Oilers retired his number several years later.

BRIAN LEETCH
(DEFENSE, 2005–2006)

Leetch is a Rangers legend. He spent portions of 17 seasons with the club before defecting to Toronto in a deal involving three teams. In 1994, he helped the Blueshirts to their first Stanley Cup since 1940. Frankly speaking, they could not have done it without him. His 23 assists, 34 points and four game-winning goals during the playoffs (not to mention his plus-19 rating) were all tops in the NHL that year.

Leetch was born in Corpus Christi, Texas. His family moved to Cheshire, Connecticut, when he was an infant. He learned to skate proficiently at a local rink managed by his father. A pitcher of note, he led his high school team to a state championship and once struck out 19 batters in a game. He was even better at hockey, gathering 160 points in 54 games during his junior and senior years at Avon Old Farms boarding school. Upon graduating, he enrolled at Boston College and became an All-American defenseman.

It didn't take long for the scouts to come calling. After just one season with the B.C. Eagles, Leetch was recruited by the Rangers. He made his NHL debut during the '87-'88 campaign and then, after attaining official rookie status, won the Calder Trophy. His 23 goals were a record for rookie defensemen.

Leetch was a quiet, respectful player who finished among the top 10 in voting for the Byng Trophy four times. Among the greatest blue-liners in Rangers history, he is the franchise's all-time assists leader. He ranks second to winger Rod Gilbert in points. Additionally, he is the only non–Canadian to win the Calder, Norris and Conn Smythe Trophies during his career.

After the 2004 lockout, Leetch signed a one-year deal with the Bruins worth $4 million. He collected his 1,000th point and finished as the B's top scoring defenseman that year. Beyond that, highlights were sparse as the Bruins missed the playoffs. Leetch never played in another NHL game despite receiving multiple contract offers.

In 2007, Leetch received the Lester Patrick Trophy for outstanding contributions to hockey in the U.S. The Rangers retired his number the following year. More accolades would follow as he gained entry into the U.S. Ice Hockey Hall of Fame and the Hockey Hall of Fame in Toronto.

MARK RECCHI
(RIGHT WING, 2009–2011)

Born and raised in Kamloops, British Columbia, Recchi played junior hockey with a local outfit in the Western Hockey League. He left such an impact on the team that his number was retired after he left for the NHL. Drafted by the Penguins, he spent portions of two seasons with the Muskegon Lumberjacks before earning a permanent roster spot in Pittsburgh. Aided tremendously by his 100-point season in '90-'91 (the first of three), the Penguins captured a Stanley Cup.

Though he spent time with seven different clubs during his NHL tour, Recchi is perhaps best remembered as a member of the Flyers. In '92-'93, he set a franchise record for points in a single season, collecting 53 goals and 70 assists. The line he skated on, featuring center Eric Lindros and Left-winger Brent Fedyk, became known as the "Crazy Eights Line" for their physicality and jersey numbers. The trio wore the numbers 8, 88 and 18, respectively.

Recchi had excellent speed and an accurate wrist shot. He earned the nickname "Recch-ing Ball" for his no-holds-barred, aggressive style of play. Some have remarked that he was like a human pinball bouncing around the ice. He could take hits as well as dish them out and he was very creative with the puck—consistently generating scoring chances. During two separate stints with Philadelphia, Recchi attained an all-time rank of number 5 among the franchise leaders in assists and points per game. He currently appears among the top 10 in game-winning goals with 39. He had back-to-back 100-point seasons with the Flyers in '92-'93 and '93-'94.

Recchi's extensive travels brought him to Carolina in 2006, where he helped the club win a Stanley Cup title. After making stops in Pittsburgh, Atlanta and Tampa Bay, he was acquired by the Bruins near the 2009 trading deadline. He remained productive throughout his time in Boston, helping the club to three postseason appearances. He was especially effective in the 2011 Stanley Cup finals against Vancouver, averaging a point per game. One of his goals was a game-winner.

Though he could have played longer, Recchi opted for retirement at the end of the 2011 playoffs. Since then, he has served as a consultant for the Dallas Stars and a player development coach for the Penguins. He was promoted to assistant coach after the Pens won consecutive Stanley Cup titles in 2016 and '17. Inducted into the Hockey Hall of Fame in 2017, Recchi is part-owner of the Kamloop Blazers of the WHL.

Jaromir Jagr
(Right Wing, 2013)

Jagr was not officially a member of the Hockey Hall of Fame as of 2020, but he is a prime candidate. At the time of this writing, he held an NHL rank of number 2 in points (1,921) and number 3 in goals (766). His 1,155 lifetime assists are fifth on the all-time list. A five-time winner of the Art Ross Trophy and two-time Stanley Cup champion, there is nothing standing in the way of his induction.

Except maybe for his retirement.

As of 2019, he was still active in Europe at the age of 47.

Jagr grew up in Kladno, Czechoslovakia, which is located northwest of Prague—the capital city. He began skating at the age of three. At 15, he had reached the highest level of play in his country and, at 17, he became the youngest member of the Czech National Team.

Known for his trademark mullet, bright smile and lively personality, Jagr was a tough man to defend in his prime. At 6-foot-3, 230 pounds, opponents literally bounced off of him. He protected the puck exceptionally well, often carrying it on a meandering tour of the attacking zone. An accomplished playmaker, he frequently left opponents wondering exactly how he had beaten them.

Jagr spent 24 seasons with nine different NHL teams. He had his longest stint with the Penguins from 1990 through 2001. Over the course of his career, he won 12 Golden Hockey Sticks—an award given annually to the top Czech player. He gathered 30 or more goals in 15 consecutive seasons, reaching the 100-point mark on five occasions. A clean player, he kept his penalties to a minimum. He was a Byng Trophy candidate several times.

Jagr came to Boston in a late-season trade with Dallas during the 2012-'13 campaign. After skating in 11 regular season games, he helped the B's reach the finals against Chicago. The series ended in a disappointing four-games-to-two loss and Jagr's contract was not renewed. He left for New Jersey the following season, finishing his NHL career in 2018 with Calgary.

Jagr still has a handful of years to go in order to beat Gordie Howe's record of being the oldest player to appear in an NHL game (at age 52). But who knows? If he is willing to delay his entry into the Hockey Hall of Fame awhile longer, there may a team willing to sign him when the time comes.

JAROME IGINLA
(RIGHT WING, 2013–14)

In June of 2020, Iginla became the fourth black player to be inducted into the Hall of Fame, joining Grant Fuhr, Willie O'Ree, and women's hockey pioneer Angela James. The honor was well-deserved as Iginla collected 1,300 career points and helped three different clubs to playoff appearances.

Born in Edmonton, Iginla grew up in nearby St. Albert. In addition to hockey, he excelled at baseball, playing catcher for the Canadian national junior team. He began his youth hockey career as a goalie before moving to right wing permanently. In 1993, he ascended to the junior level with the Kamloops Blazers of the Western Hockey League. He was one of several standouts who guided the club to a pair of national championships. Drafted by the Dallas Stars in '95, he ended up being traded to the Calgary Flames in December of that year.

Iginla spent portions of 16 seasons with Calgary, serving as captain from 2003 to 2013. In March of 2009, he replaced Theo Fleury as the team's all-time points leader. Considered a power forward, his aggressive play was respected by teammates and opponents. In spite of his grinding style, he averaged just 50 penalty minutes per year during his 20 seasons in the NHL and received serious consideration for the Byng Trophy on several occasions.

A six-time All-Star, Iginla joined the Bruins in July of 2013. He tied with Patrice Bergeron for the team lead in goals that year. He netted eight game-winners during the regular season as the Bruins won the President's Trophy. In the playoffs, the B's took out the Red Wings in the first round but fell to the Canadiens in a hard-fought Atlantic Division showdown. Iginla signed with the Avalanche in the offseason.

After spending three seasons in Colorado, the Alberta-native finished his career with the L.A. Kings. He played beyond his 39th birthday. Though he never won a Stanley Cup, he made it to Game 7 of the finals with Calgary in 2004. The Flames held a three-games-to-two advantage, but couldn't finish off the Lightning in Game 6, which went to double overtime. Iginla led postseason skaters with 13 goals that season.

In 2007, Iginla bought a minority share of the Kamloops Blazers with three other former players. He has served as an ambassador for NHL Diversity programs. He has also been highly active in a number of charities over the years, including the Ronald McDonald House and Doctors Without Borders. In 2009, he won the Mark Messier Trophy for his outstanding leadership skills.

7

Coaches

ART ROSS

Ross began his career near the turn of the 20th century. Considered one of the premier defensemen of his era, he was among the first to skate the puck up ice rather than passing it to a forward. When his playing days ended in 1918, he got to experience the other side of the game as a referee. In 1924, he became the first head coach and GM of the Bruins. Using his Canadian connections to import a steady stream of talent, he led the B's to their first Stanley Cup title in 1929. The club's .875 points percentage the following season remains an NHL record. Ross had three separate coaching stints with Boston spanning 19 campaigns. He gathered 419 wins including the playoffs and captured two Stanley Cups—the second one coming in 1939. He was the first coach in history to pull his goaltender for an extra skater. Always seeking to improve the game, he modified nets so that they held onto pucks. In 1947, he gave the NHL a trophy to be awarded to the player with the most points. It still bears his name today.

CLAUDE JULIEN

Julien had a brief career in the NHL as a defenseman, appearing in 14 games with the Quebec Nordiques. He spent over a decade in the minor leagues learning the intricacies of the game. He began his coaching career in the Quebec Major Junior Hockey League, guiding the Hull Olympiques to a Memorial Cup championship in 1997. He ascended to the AHL with the Hamilton Bulldogs in 2000 and got his first NHL position with the Canadiens three years later. Fired by the Habs midway through the 2005-'06 slate, he took over the New Jersey Devils for one season before moving on to a long career with the Bruins. The team finished in first place during four of Julien's nine full campaigns in Boston and made it to the finals twice. Using an old-school approach with emphasis on defense and positional play, Julien delivered the team's first Stanley Cup since 1972. He won the Jack Adams Award as Coach of the Year in 2008-'09. After a pair of consecutive playoff misses and a lukewarm start in 2016-'17, Julien was dismissed from his duties. His lifetime total of 419 regular season wins are the most by any Bruins coach. He was still active with the Canadiens as of 2020.

DON CHERRY

Cherry had a long minor league career as a defenseman from 1954 to 1972, appearing in one NHL game with the Bruins during the '55 playoffs. After three seasons at the helm of the Rochester Americans, he was appointed head coach of the B's. He had a host of talented players at his disposal when he arrived, including superstars Bobby Orr and Phil Esposito. When the duo left Boston, Cherry filled his roster with grinders and enforcers, ushering in a new "lunch pail" philosophy. Cherry was old-school all the way, favoring a rugged style of smash-mouth hockey. The Bruins reached the Stanley Cup finals twice on Cherry's watch, eliminating the infamous "Broad Street Bullies" of Philadelphia both times. But after three consecutive playoff losses to Montreal, Cherry was fired by GM Harry Sinden. He coached the Colorado Rockies for one season then moved on to an extensive career in broadcasting. He became known for his eccentric personality (dramatically illustrated by his outlandish taste in fashion) and brash remarks, which often bordered on being inappropriate. In 2019, he was fired for making divisive comments about Canadian immigrants during a Hockey Night in Canada broadcast. He returned to the airwaves as host of his own podcast.

HARRY SINDEN

Sinden was a very promising defenseman in his prime. He played junior hockey for the Oshawa Generals from 1949 to 1953, scoring 46 points in his best offensive season. Ascending to the senior level with the Whitby Dunlops, he helped the club to an Allan Cup title and World Hockey Championship. Signed by the Bruins, he served as a player-coach for the Kingston Frontenacs. He made the EPHL All-Star team in '61-'62 but was never promoted to the NHL as a player. In 1966, he was appointed head coach in Boston. At 33, he was the youngest coach in the league. After missing the playoffs in his first season at the helm, he guided the B's to a quarter-finals appearance in '68. The Bruins came one step closer to the Cup the following season, eliminating the Maple Leafs in the opening round before falling to Montreal in the semi-finals. With the Habs out of the playoffs in 1970, the B's went all the way, claiming their first Stanley Cup since 1941. Sinden announced his retirement shortly afterward and, though he received multiple NHL contract offers, he turned them all down. In June of '72, he accepted an assignment as head coach for the eight-game Summit Series, which pitted Team Canada against the USSR. After a stirring come-from-behind victory over the powerful Soviets, Sinden was appointed general manager of the Bruins. He occupied that post for over 28 years, making brief stints as head coach in '79-'80 and '84-'85. He also served as team president for nearly two decades. He retired to a consulting role in 2006. He was inducted into the Hockey Hall of Fame as a Builder in 1983.

TOM JOHNSON

Johnson spent portions of 16 NHL seasons with the Canadiens and Bruins, winning six Stanley Cups and a Norris Trophy between 1952 and 1960. After finishing his playing career in Boston, he remained with the organization for over 30 years, serving a variety of important roles. In '70-'71, he took over as head coach and steered the club to the best record in the NHL. The season ended in typical fashion with a disappointing loss to Montreal. When the Habs were eliminated by the Rangers in the '72 quarter-finals, there was nothing standing in Boston's way. Johnson became the toast of the town as the Bruins captured their second Stanley Cup title in three years. Known for his snazzy bowties and laid-back personality, Johnson was very popular among players. But GM Harry Sinden felt that the Bruins needed a taskmaster and removed Johnson from his post with 26 games still remaining in the '72-'73 campaign. Johnson moved to the assistant GM position, where he remained for 16 years. Additionally, he served as vice president. In a statistical sense, he is the most successful Bruins coach of all time with a franchise-best .738 points percentage.

COONEY WEILAND

Known for his durability, Weiland missed only a handful of games during his Hall of Fame playing career. Though his stint as head coach in Boston was brief—lasting just two seasons—he attained a level of success matched by only three other Bruins coaches during the 20th century. Taking the reins in '39-'40, he guided the B's to a first-place finish. Though the club jumped out to a two-games-to-one lead over the Rangers in the semi-finals, the Bruins managed just one goal in the last three games against Vezina Trophy-winner Dave Kerr. Weiland and his crew (which featured seven Hall of Famers) got back to work the following year, finishing first again. They survived a grueling seven-game showdown against Toronto, in which the last four games were decided by a single goal, then breezed to a sweep of Detroit in the finals. When Weiland left Boston after the '40-'41 campaign, a long Stanley Cup drought followed. He later coached the Harvard Crimson to five consecutive Ivy League championships.

MIKE MILBURY

Milbury's stint as head coach in Boston was brief but very successful. After spending his entire playing career with the B's, he took over the AHL-affiliated Maine Mariners for two seasons. In 1989, he brought his old-school philosophy back to the Bruins bench. While additionally serving as assistant GM, he guided the team to a President's Trophy and a berth in the Stanley Cup finals. His squad proved to be no match for a dominant Oilers team that won five Cups in a seven-year span. During Milbury's second season in charge, the Bruins returned to the conference finals. The team jumped out to a 2–0 series lead over the Penguins before dropping the next four games by a combined total of 13 goals. With seven Hall of famers on the roster, the Pens went on to win the Cup that year. Milbury stepped down as coach but continued with his executive duties until 1994, when he voluntarily left to coach at Boston College. He vacated that post on account of philosophical differences with school officials, later accepting a position as GM of the Islanders. The team operated on a shoestring budget during his tenure and fared poorly in the standings. Milbury served as head coach in New York for one full season and three partial campaigns beginning in 1995. The Islanders never finished higher than fourth place on his watch. He later moved on to a career as a broadcaster, providing studio analysis for several networks. He was inducted into the U.S. Hockey Hall of Fame in 2006.

TERRY O'REILLY

A first-round draft pick in 1971, O'Reilly wore the Black and Gold throughout his playing career, earning a reputation as a scrapper and an on-ice leader. He put his skills to work as head coach from 1986 to 1989. With the B's off to a slow start under Butch Goring in '86, O'Reilly took the reins. The team fared much better after Goring's departure, collecting points in 10 of 11 games from November 22 through December 14. The season ended with a first-round playoff sweep at the hands of the Canadiens, but O'Reilly didn't let that discourage him. In 1988, he guided the club to a division finals victory over the Habs, breaking a string of 18 consecutive playoff losses to Montreal (dating back to 1946). It was among the most triumphant moments in Bruins history, but it was short-lived as Boston fell to the Oilers in the Stanley Cup finals. Recognizing his accomplishments, O'Reilly was named Coach of the Year by *Hockey Digest*. After a second-place finish in '88-'89, O'Reilly's Bruins failed to get past the Canadiens in a division finals rematch. The man known affectionately to Boston fans as "Taz" vacated his post at season's end to care for his son, who was seriously ill. O'Reilly has remained active in Bruins alumni affairs over the years.

GERRY CHEEVERS

Cheevers ended his goaltending career in '79-'80 and moved straight to a position as head coach. He later admitted that the transition was a very difficult one. In his first season at the Boston helm, he led the team to a second-place finish in the Adams Division. Though the B's were heavily favored to beat the North Stars in the preliminary round of the playoffs, the series ended in an astonishing Minnesota sweep. Prior to then, the North Stars had never won a game in the Boston Garden. Harry Sinden—notoriously impatient with coaches—kept Cheevers around anyway. "Cheesie" led the Bruins to a pair of first place showings and a second-place effort over the next three seasons, but the club never advanced to the Stanley Cup finals. Things might have turned out differently had the Bruins not faced the Islanders in the '83 conference finals. With a host of legendary players, including Mike Bossy, Bryan Trottier and Denis Potvin, the Isles won four consecutive Stanley Cups beginning in 1980. Cheevers was let go in 1985 with 204 regular season wins to his credit—fifth on the Bruins all-time list. He later worked in broadcasting and also served as a Bruins scout.

BRUCE CASSIDY

A high-scoring defenseman during his junior hockey days, Cassidy averaged more than 100 points in two full seasons with the Ottawa 67's. He made brief appearances in six different campaigns with the Chicago Blackhawks, including one playoff game in 1989. After hanging up his skates, he coached several teams at the minor league level before ascending to the NHL with the Washington Capitals. He led the team to the playoffs in 2003 but was released after a poor start the following season. A stint as assistant coach in Chicago preceded his tenure with the Providence Bruins. He worked under head coach Rob Murray for three years, taking charge of the club in 2011. The "Baby B's" made the playoffs in four of Cassidy's five seasons at the helm and, in 2016, Cassidy was recruited as an assistant to Claude Julien in Boston. He took over as head coach with the firing of Julien in February of 2017. As of 2020, Cassidy's points percentage was among the best in franchise history. Having coached in Providence, he gained a reputation for working well with the club's top prospects. It paid great dividends as several budding stars had breakout performances in Boston under Cassidy, including David Pastrnak, Charlie McAvoy and Jake DeBrusk. In 2018-'19, Cassidy led the Bruins to a showdown against St. Louis in the Stanley Cup finals. The Blues played a punishing style of hockey that resulted in two player suspensions. By Game 7, a number of Bruins personnel were battling serious injuries and the team folded in the finale. Cassidy was offered a multi-year contract extension in 2019. He made the most of it, keeping the Bruins in contention for the President's Trophy throughout the 2019-'20 campaign.

Appendix A: Lifetime Statistics of Featured Players (Through 2019-20)

Centers

	GP	G	A	PTS.	+/−	PIM	GWG
Cooney Weiland	509	173	162	335	N/A	149	38
Marty Barry	507	194	193	387	N/A	231	25
Frank Fredrickson	161	39	34	73	N/A	211	9
Duke Keats	82	29	19	48	N/A	114	6
Mickey MacKay	114	44	19	63	N/A	79	8
Hooley Smith	717	200	226	426	N/A	1056	43
Nels Stewart	650	324	191	515	N/A	950	70
Bill Cowley	549	195	354	549	N/A	143	34
Milt Schmidt	776	229	346	575	N/A	466	35
Don McKenney	798	237	345	582	−62	205	27
Bronco Horvath	434	141	185	326	−37	313	18
Derek Sanderson	598	202	250	452	141	911	21
Fred Stanfield	914	211	405	616	50	134	26
Phil Esposito	1282	717	873	1590	252	910	118
Gregg Sheppard	657	205	293	498	129	243	32
Jean Ratelle	1280	491	776	1267	236	276	68
Peter McNab	955	363	450	813	128	179	47
Barry Pederson	701	238	416	654	64	472	36
Steve Kasper	821	177	291	468	−57	554	21
Ken Linseman	860	256	551	807	221	1725	29
Craig Janney	760	188	563	751	−13	170	32
Adam Oates	1337	341	1079	1420	33	415	56
Joe Thornton	1636	420	1089	1509	186	1248	67
Brian Rolston	1256	342	419	761	65	472	72
Patrice Bergeron	1089	352	517	869	201	424	67

	GP	G	A	PTS.	+/-	PIM	GWG
Marc Savard	807	207	499	706	−54	737	36
David Krejci	911	207	479	686	127	323	40

Right-Wingers

	GP	G	A	PTS.	+/-	PIM	GWG
Harry Oliver	465	127	85	212	N/A	147	31
Dit Clapper	835	229	248	477	N/A	452	45
Bobby Bauer	327	123	136	259	N/A	38	21
Johnny Peirson	544	153	173	326	N/A	309	31
Leo Labine	643	128	193	321	N/A	728	19
Ed Westfall	1226	231	394	625	82	544	25
John McKenzie	692	206	268	474	26	923	33
Ken Hodge	880	328	472	800	260	777	57
Terry O'Reilly	891	204	402	606	222	2095	32
Bobby Schmautz	764	271	286	557	37	988	36
Rick Middleton	1005	448	540	988	175	157	59
Joe Mullen	1062	502	561	1063	167	241	73
Keith Crowder	662	223	271	494	131	1354	27
Cam Neely	726	395	299	694	83	1241	61
Mark Recchi	1652	577	956	1533	0	1033	91
Jaromir Jagr	1733	766	1155	1921	322	1167	135
Glen Murray	1009	337	314	651	14	679	55
Steve Heinze	694	178	158	336	−20	379	31
Jarome Iginla	1554	625	675	1300	30	1040	101
David Pastrnak	390	180	199	379	63	171	30

Left-Wingers

	GP	G	A	PTS.	+/-	PIM	GWG
Cy Denneny	329	247	89	336	N/A	296	50
Billy Burch	390	136	60	196	N/A	263	32
Babe Siebert	594	140	154	294	N/A	1002	24
Bun Cook	477	158	146	304	N/A	458	31
Woody Dumart	774	211	219	430	N/A	99	34
Red Beattie	329	62	85	147	N/A	135	11
Busher Jackson	634	241	234	476	N/A	450	38
Roy Conacher	490	226	201	427	N/A	88	40
Herb Cain	572	206	192	398	N/A	177	27

	GP	G	A	PTS.	+/−	PIM	GWG
Vic Stasiuk	745	183	254	437	−10	665	26
Willie O'Ree	45	4	10	14	−18	26	2
John Bucyk	1540	556	813	1369	−7	493	92
Wayne Cashman	1027	277	516	793	278	1039	37
Don Marcotte	868	230	254	484	191	317	30
Stan Jonathan	411	91	110	201	68	751	10
Randy Burridge	706	191	251	450	62	458	29
Dave Andreychuk	1639	640	698	1338	32	1177	77
Ted Donato	796	150	197	347	−2	396	22
Sergei Samsonov	888	235	336	571	11	103	38
P.J. Axelsson	797	103	184	287	−26	276	14
Milan Lucic	958	206	315	521	90	1126	36
Brad Marchand	751	290	356	646	221	756	56

Defensemen

	GP	G	A	PTS.	+/−	PIM	GWG
Lionel Hitchman	417	27	38	65	N/A	557	4
Eddie Shore	551	105	179	284	N/A	1099	22
Sprague Cleghorn	262	85	63	148	N/A	549	11
Sylvio Mantha	542	63	77	140	N/A	671	13
Babe Pratt	518	83	210	293	N/A	491	10
Flash Hollett	560	132	181	313	N/A	358	20
Murray Henderson	405	24	62	86	N/A	305	1
Fern Flaman	911	34	174	208	N/A	1372	6
Tom Johnson	978	51	213	264	56	960	10
Bill Quackenbush	775	62	223	285	N/A	95	11
Allan Stanley	1244	100	333	433	117	792	12
Doug Mohns	1391	248	462	710	−96	1261	40
Leo Boivin	1150	250	322	572	−212	1196	7
Dallas Smith	889	252	307	559	318	955	5
Ted Green	621	48	206	254	−47	1029	2
Gary Doak	790	23	107	130	124	908	5
Bobby Orr	657	270	645	915	582	953	26
Rick Smith		2	167	219	181	558	7
Guy Lapointe	884	171	451	622	329	893	22
Brad Park	1113	213	683	896	363	1429	28
Mike Milbury	754	49	189	238	175	1552	7
Ray Bourque	1612	410	1169	1579	527	1141	60

	GP	G	A	PTS.	+/−	PIM	GWG
Paul Coffey	1409	396	1135	1531	298	1802	43
Glen Wesley	1457	128	409	537	66	1045	15
Don Sweeney	1115	52	221	273	112	681	12
Brian Leetch	1205	247	781	1028	25	571	38
Kyle McLaren	719	46	161	207	27	671	5
Hal Gill	1108	36	148	184	44	962	4
Zdeno Chara	1553	205	451	656	288	1956	35
Andrew Ference	907	43	182	225	−33	753	4
Johnny Boychuk	725	54	152	206	123	331	12
Adam McQuaid	512	16	57	73	62	694	4
Dennis Seidenberg	859	44	207	251	39	359	8
Torey Krug	523	67	270	337	23	220	14

Goalies

	GP	W	L	T	SHO	SV%	GAA
Cecil Thompson	553	284	194	75	81	N/A	2.07
Frank Brimsek	514	252	182	80	40	N/A	2.70
Jim Henry	405	161	174	69	28	N/A	2.84
Terry Sawchuk	971	445	336	171	103	.907	2.50
Jacques Plante	837	437	246	145	82	.920	2.38
Don Simmons	249	100	102	41	20	.904	2.89
Eddie Johnston	592	236	256	78	32	.896	3.25
Gerry Cheevers	418	227	104	76	26	.901	2.89
Bernie Parent	608	271	198	119	54	.915	2.55
Rogie Vachon	795	353	293	123	51	.896	3.00
Gilles Gilbert	416	192	143	60	18	.883	3.27
Pete Peeters	489	246	156	51	21	.886	3.09
Reggie Lemelin	506	236	161	63	12	.884	3.46
Andy Moog	713	372	209	88	28	.891	3.14
Byron Dafoe	415	171	170	56	26	.904	2.69
Tim Thomas	426	214	145	49	31	.920	2.52
Tuukka Rask	536	291	158	64	50	.922	2.26

Appendix B: Bruins Playoff Appearances and Results

1926-'27
Coach: Art Ross
Lost Final to Ottawa Senators (0–2–2)
Appearances by Sprague Cleghorn, Frank Fredrickson, Lionel Hitchman, Harry Oliver, Eddie Shore

1927-'28
Coach: Art Ross
Lost Semi-Finals to New York Rangers (0–1–1)
Appearances by Dit Clapper, Sprague Cleghorn, Frank Fredrickson, Dutch Gainor, Harry Oliver, Eddie Shore

1928-'29
Coach: Art Ross
Won Stanley Cup Final over New York Rangers (2–0)
Appearances by Dit Clapper, Dutch Gainor, Mickey MacKay, Ernie Shore, Tiny Thompson, Cooney Weiland

1929-'30
Coach: Art Ross
Lost Stanley Cup Final to Montreal Canadiens (0–2)
Appearances by Dit Clapper, Eddie Shore, Harry Oliver, Cooney Weiland, Marty Barry, Lionel Hitchman, Mickey MacKay, Tiny Thompson

1930-'31
Coach: Art Ross
Lost Semi-Finals to Montreal Canadiens (2–3)
Appearances by Cooney Weiland, Dit Clapper, Eddie Shore, Marty Barry, Dutch Gainor, Red Beattie, Lionel Hitchman, Harry Oliver, Tiny Thompson

1932-'33
Coach: Art Ross
Lost Semi-Finals to Toronto Maple Leafs (2–3)
Appearances by Marty Barry, Nels Stewart, Dit Clapper, Eddie Shore, Lionel Hitchman, Harry Oliver, Tiny Thompson

1934-'35
Coach: Frank Patrick
Lost Semi-Finals to Toronto Maple Leafs (1–3)

Appearances by Red Beattie, Dit Clapper, Ernie Shore, Nels Stewart, Marty Barry, Tiny Thompson

1935-'36
Coach: Frank Patrick
Lost Quarter-Finals to Toronto Maple Leafs (1–1)
Appearances by Dit Clapper, Eddie Shore, Cooney Weiland, Red Beattie, Tiny Thompson

1936-'37
Coach: Art Ross
Lost Quarter-Finals to Montreal Maroons (1–2)
Appearances by Bill Cowley, Dit Clapper, Red Beattie, Bobby Bauer, Woody Dumart, Flash Hollett, Milt Schmidt, Cooney Weiland, Hooley Smith, Tiny Thompson

1937-'38
Coach: Art Ross
Lost Semi-Finals to Toronto Maple Leafs (0–3)
Appearances by Bill Cowley, Flash Hollett, Eddie Shore, Bobby Bauer, Dit Clapper, Woody Dumart, Milt Schmidt, Cooney Weiland, Tiny Thompson

1938-'39
Coach: Art Ross
Won Stanley Cup Final over Toronto Maple Leafs (4–1)
Appearances by Bobby Bauer, Frank Brimsek, Roy Conacher, Bill Cowley, Woody Dumart, Flash Hollett, Milt Schmidt, Eddie Shore, Tiny Thompson, Cooney Weiland

1939-'40
Coach: Cooney Weiland
Lost Semi-Finals to New York Rangers (2–4)
Appearances by Herb Cain, Roy Conacher, Flash Hollett, Dit Clapper, Bobby Bauer, Woody Dumart, Bill Cowley, Frank Brimsek

1940-'41
Coach: Cooney Weiland
Won Stanley Cup Final over Detroit Red Wings (4–0)
Appearances by Herb Cain, Milt Schmidt, Roy Conacher, Woody Dumart, Bobby Bauer, Flash Hollett, Dit Clapper, Frank Brimsek

1941-'42
Coach: Art Ross
Lost Semi-Finals to Detroit Red Wings (1–2)
Appearances by Herb Cain, Roy Conacher, Flash Hollett, Bill Cowley, Busher Jackson, Frank Brimsek

1942-'43
Coach: Art Ross
Lost Stanley Cup Final to Detroit Red Wings (0–4)
Appearances by Herb Cain, Bill Cowley, Flash Hollett, Dit Clapper, Busher Jackson, Frank Brimsek

1944-'45
Coach: Art Ross
Lost Semi-Finals to Detroit Red Wings (3–4)
Appearances by Herb Cain, Bill Cowley, Dit Clapper, Murray Henderson

1945-'46
Coach: Dit Clapper
Lost Stanley Cup Final to Montreal Canadiens (1–4)
Appearances by Bill Cowley, Milt Schmidt, Bobby Bauer, Woody Dumart, Herb Cain, Murray Henderson, Dit Clapper, Roy Conacher, Frank Brimsek

1946-'47
Coach: Dit Clapper
Lost Semi-Finals to Montreal Canadiens (1–4)
Appearances by Milt Schmidt, Bobby Bauer, Woody Dumart, Bill Cowley, Fern Flaman, Murray Henderson, Frank Brimsek

1947-'48
Coach: Dit Clapper
Lost Semi-Finals to Toronto Maple Leafs (1–4)
Appearances by Milt Schmidt, Johnny Peirson, Murray Henderson, Woody Dumart, Fern Flaman, Frank Brimsek

1948-'49
Coach: Dit Clapper
Lost Semi-Finals to Toronto Maple Leafs (1–4)
Appearances by Johnny Peirson, Woody Dumart, Milt Schmidt, Fern Flaman, Murray Henderson

1950-'51
Coach: Lynn Patrick
Lost Semi-Finals to Toronto Maple Leafs (1–4)
Appearances by Woody Dumart, Johnny Peirson, Bill Quackenbush, Milt Schmidt, Murray Henderson

1951-'52
Coach: Lynn Patrick
Lost Semi-Finals to Montreal Canadiens (3–4)
Appearances by Fleming Mackell, Milt Schmidt, Bill Quackenbush, Johnny Peirson, Woody Dumart, Leo Labine, Murray Henderson, Jim Henry

1952-'53
Coach: Lynn Patrick
Lost Stanley Cup Final to Montreal Canadiens (1–4)
Appearances by Fleming Mackell, Milt Schmidt, Leo Labine, Woody Dumart, Johnny Peirson, Bill Quackenbush, Jim Henry

1953-'54
Coach: Lynn Patrick
Lost Semi-Finals to Montreal Canadiens (0–4)
Appearances by Fleming Mackell, Milt Schmidt, Doug Mohns, Leo Labine, Woody Dumart, Johnny Peirson, Bill Quackenbush, Jim Henry

1954-'55
Coaches: Lynn Patrick, Milt Schmidt
Lost Semi-Finals to Montreal Canadiens (1–4)
Appearances by Don McKenney, Fern Flaman, Don Cherry, Doug Mohns, Fleming Mackell, Leo Labine, Bill Quackenbush, Jim Henry

1956-'57
Coach: Milt Schmidt
Lost Stanley Cup Final to Montreal Canadiens (1–4)
Appearances by Don McKenney, Fern Flaman, Fleming Mackell, Leo Labine, Leo Bovin, Doug Mohns, Johnny Peirson, Vic Stasiuk, Don Simmons

1957-'58
Coach: Milt Schmidt
Lost Stanley Cup Final to Montreal Canadiens (2–4)
Appearances by Don McKenney, Fleming Mackell, Bronco Horvath, Allan Stanley, Vic Stasiuk, Leo Labine, Doug Mohns, Leo Bovin, Fern Flaman, Johnny Bucyk, Johnny Peirson, Don Simmons

1958-'59
Coach: Milt Schmidt
Lost Semi-Finals to Toronto Maple Leafs (3–4)
Appearances by Doug McKenney, Fleming Mackell, Bronco Horvath, Vic Stasiuk, Leo Labine, Doug Mohns, Fern Flaman, Johnny Bucyk, Leo Boivin

1967-'68
Coach: Harry Sinden
Lost Quarter-Finals to Montreal Canadiens (0–4)
Appearances by Ken Hodge, Phil Esposito, Ed Westfall, Ted Green, John McKenzie, Bobby Orr, Johnny Bucyk, Derek Sanderson, Dallas Smith, Fred Stanfield, Wayne Cashman, Gary Doak, Gerry Cheevers

1968-'69
Coach: Harry Sinden
Lost Semi-Finals to Montreal Canadiens (2–4)
Appearances by Ken Hodge, Phil Esposito, Ed Westfall, Ted Green, John McKenzie, Bobby Orr, Johnny Bucyk, Derek Sanderson, Dallas Smith, Fred Stanfield, Wayne Cashman, Eddie Johnston, Rick Smith, Gerry Cheevers

1969-'70
Coach: Harry Sinden
Won Stanley Cup Final over St. Louis Blues (4–0)
Appearances by Ken Hodge, Phil Esposito, Ed Westfall, Ted Green, John McKenzie, Bobby Orr, Johnny Bucyk, Derek Sanderson, Dallas Smith, Fred Stanfield, Wayne Cashman, Rick Smith, Gary Doak, Don Marcotte, Gerry Cheevers

1970-'71
Coach: Tom Johnson
Lost Quarter-Finals to Montreal Canadiens (3–4)
Appearances by Ken Hodge, Phil Esposito, Ed Westfall, Ted Green, John McKenzie, Bobby Orr, Johnny Bucyk, Derek Sanderson, Dallas Smith, Fred Stanfield, Wayne Cashman, Eddie Johnston, Rick Smith, Don Marcotte, Gerry Cheevers

1971-'72
Coach: Tom Johnson
Won Stanley Cup Final over New York Rangers (4–2)
Appearances by Ken Hodge, Phil Esposito, Wayne Cashman, Johnny Bucyk, Fred Stanfield, John McKenzie, Ed Westfall, Don Marcotte, Derek Sanderson, Dallas Smith, Ted Green, Eddie Johnston, Gerry Cheevers

1972-'73
Coaches: Tom Johnson, Bep Guidolin
Lost Quarter-Finals to New York Rangers (1–4)
Appearances by Gregg Sheppard, Derek Sanderson, Johnny Bucyk, Bobby Orr, Wayne Cashman, Don Marcotte, Fred Stanfield, Dallas Smith, Ken Hodge, Phil Esposito, Gary Doak, Terry O'Reilly, Eddie Johnston, Jacques Plante

1973-'74
Coach: Bep Guidolin
Lost Stanley Cup Final to Philadelphia Flyers (2–4)
Appearances by Gregg Sheppard, Johnny Bucyk, Bobby Orr, Wayne Cashman, Don Marcotte, Dallas Smith, Ken Hodge, Phil Esposito, Terry O'Reilly, Bobby Schmautz, Gilles Gilbert

1974-'75
Coach: Don Cherry
Lost Preliminary Round to Chicago Blackhawks (1–2)
Appearances by Gregg Sheppard, Johnny Bucyk, Bobby Orr, Wayne Cashman, Don Marcotte, Dallas Smith, Ken Hodge, Phil Esposito, Terry O'Reilly, Bobby Schmautz, Gilles Gilbert, Gary Doak

1975-'76
Coach: Don Cherry
Lost Semi-Finals to Philadelphia Flyers (1–4)
Appearances by Johnny Bucyk, Jean Ratelle, Terry O'Reilly, Gregg Sheppard, Brad Park, Wayne Cashman, Ken Hodge, Don Marcotte, Dallas Smith, Gary Doak, Mike Milbury, Gerry Cheevers

1976-'77
Coach: Don Cherry
Lost Stanley Cup Final to Montreal Canadiens (0–4)
Appearances by Brad Park, Bobby Schmautz, Rick Middleton, Peter McNab, Terry O'Reilly, Gregg Sheppard, Wayne Cashman, Jean Ratelle, Gary Doak, Johnny Bucyk, Don Marcotte, Mike Milbury, Rick Smith, Gerry Cheevers

1977-'78
Coach: Don Cherry
Lost Stanley Cup Final to Montreal Canadiens (2–4)
Appearances by Brad Park, Bobby Schmautz, Rick Middleton, Peter McNab, Terry O'Reilly, Gregg Sheppard, Wayne Cashman, Jean Ratelle, Gary Doak, Don Marcotte, Mike Milbury, Rick Smith, Stan Jonathan, Gerry Cheevers

1978-'79
Coach: Don Cherry
Lost Semi-Final to Montreal Canadiens (3–4)
Appearances by Brad Park, Bobby Schmautz, Rick Middleton, Peter McNab, Terry O'Reilly, Wayne Cashman, Jean Ratelle, Gary Doak, Don Marcotte, Mike Milbury, Rick Smith, Stan Jonathan, Gerry Cheevers, Gilles Gilbert

1979-'80
Coaches: Fred Creighton, Harry Sinden
Lost Quarter-Finals to New York Islanders (1–4)
Appearances by Ray Bourque, Brad Park, Rick Middleton, Peter McNab, Terry O'Reilly, Wayne Cashman, Jean Ratelle, Gary Doak, Don Marcotte, Mike Milbury, Rick Smith, Stan Jonathan, Gerry Cheevers

1980-'81
Coach: Gerry Cheevers
Lost Preliminary Round to Minnesota North Stars (0–3)
Appearances by Don Marcotte, Brad Park, Peter McNab, Terry O'Reilly, Keith Crowder, Ray Bourque, Wayne Cashman, Steve Kasper, Rick Middleton, Mike Milbury, Stan Jonathan, Jean Ratelle, Rogie Vachon

1981-'82
Coach: Gerry Cheevers
Lost Division Final to Quebec Nordiques (3–4)
Appearances by Brad Park, Peter McNab, Terry O'Reilly, Keith Crowder, Ray Bourque, Wayne Cashman, Steve Kasper, Rick Middleton, Mike Milbury, Stan Jonathan, Jean Ratelle, Barry Pederson, Rogie Vachon

1982-'83
Coach: Gerry Cheevers
Lost Conference Final to New York Islanders (2–4)
Appearances by Ray Bourque, Barry Pederson, Peter McNab, Rick Middleton, Brad Park, Keith Crowder, Steve Kasper, Pete Peeters

1983-'84
Coach: Gerry Cheevers
Lost Division Semi-Finals to Montreal Canadiens (0–3)
Appearances by Ray Bourque, Barry Pederson, Rick Middleton, Keith Crowder, Steve Kasper, Terry O'Reilly, Mike Milbury, Pete Peeters

1984-'85
Coaches: Gerry Cheevers, Harry Sinden
Lost Division Semi-Finals to Montreal Canadiens (2–3)
Appearances by Ken Linseman, Keith Crowder, Rick Middleton, Terry O'Reilly, Ray Bourque, Steve Kasper, Mike Milbury, Pete Peeters

1985-'86
Coach: Butch Goring
Lost Division Semi-Finals to Montreal Canadiens (0–3)
Appearances by Randy Burridge, Keith Crowder, Steve Kasper, Barry Pederson, Ken Linseman, Ray Bourque, Mike Milbury

1986-'87
Coaches: Butch Goring, Terry O'Reilly
Lost Division Semi-Finals to Montreal Canadiens (0–4)
Appearances by Cam Neely, Randy Burridge, Keith Crowder, Steve Kasper, Ken Linseman, Ray Bourque, Mike Milbury, Rick Middleton

1987-'88
Coach: Terry O'Reilly
Lost Stanley Cup Final to Edmonton Oilers, (0–4)
Appearances by Ken Linseman, Glen Wesley, Cam Neely, Ray Bourque, Steve Kasper, Randy Burridge, Craig Janney, Keith Crowder, Rick Middleton, Andy Moog, Reggie Lemelin

1988-'89
Coach: Terry O'Reilly
Lost Division Finals to the Montreal Canadiens (1–4)

Appearances by Cam Neely, Ray Bourque, Randy Burridge, Craig Janney, Andy Moog, Reggie Lemelin

1989-'90
Coach: Mike Milbury
Lost Stanley Cup Final to Edmonton Oilers (1–4)
Appearances by Ray Bourque, Cam Neely, Randy Burridge, Don Sweeney, Craig Janney, Glen Wesley, Andy Moog, Reggie Lemelin

1990-'91
Coach: Mike Milbury
Lost Conference Finals to Pittsburgh Penguins (2–4)
Appearances by Ray Bourque, Craig Janney, Cam Neely, Don Sweeney, Glen Wesley, Randy Burridge, Andy Moog, Reggie Lemelin

1991-'92
Coach: Rick Bowness
Lost Conference Finals to Pittsburgh Penguins (0–4)
Appearances by Adam Oates, Ted Donato, Ray Bourque, Don Sweeney, Andy Moog

1992-'93
Coach: Brian Sutter
Lost Division Semi-Finals to Buffalo Sabres (0–4)
Appearances by Adam Oates, Cam Neely, Ray Bourque, Steve Heinze, Ted Donato, Don Sweeney, Glen Wesley, Andy Moog

1993-'94
Coach: Brian Sutter
Lost Conference Semi-Finals to New Jersey Devils (2–4)
Appearances by Adam Oates, Ray Bourque, Steve Heinze, Ted Donato, Don Sweeney, Glen Wesley

1994-'95
Coach: Brian Sutter
Lost Conference Quarter-Finals to New Jersey Devils (1–4)
Appearances by Adam Oates, Cam Neely, Ray Bourque, Steve Heinze, Ted Donato, Don Sweeney

1995-'96
Coach: Steve Kasper
Lost Conference Quarter-Finals to Florida Panthers (1–4)
Appearances by Adam Oates, Ray Bourque, Steve Heinze, Ted Donato, Don Sweeney

1997-'98
Coach: Pat Burns
Lost Conference Quarter-Finals to Washington Capitals (2–4)
Appearances by Joe Thornton, Sergei Samsonov, Ray Bourque, P.J. Axelsson, Kyle McLaren, Hal Gill, Ted Donato, Steve Heinze, Byron Dafoe

1998-'99
Coach: Pat Burns
Lost Conference Semi-Finals to Buffalo Sabres (2–4)
Appearances by Joe Thornton, Sergei Samsonov, Ray Bourque, P.J. Axelsson, Kyle McLaren, Hal Gill, Steve Heinze, Byron Dafoe

2001-'02
Coach: Robbie Ftorek
Lost Conference Quarter-Finals to Montreal Canadiens (2–4)
Appearances by Joe Thornton, Brian Rolston, Sergei Samsonov, P.J. Axelsson, Hal Gill, Don
   Sweeney, Kyle McLaren, Byron Dafoe

2002-'03
Coaches: Robbie Ftorek, Mike O'Connell
Lost Conference Quarter-Finals to New Jersey Devils (1–4)
Appearances by Joe Thornton, Brian Rolston, Sergei Samsonov, P.J. Axelsson, Hal Gill, Don
   Sweeney

2003-'04
Coach: Mike Sullivan
Lost Conference Quarter-Finals to Montreal Canadiens (3–4)
Appearances by Joe Thornton, Sergei Samsonov, Brian Rolston, Hal Gill, P.J. Axelsson, Ted
   Donato

2007-'08
Coach: Claude Julien
Lost Conference Quarter-Finals to Montreal Canadiens (3–4)
Appearances by Marc Savard, David Krejci, Andrew Ference, Milan Lucic, Zdeno Chara, P.J.
   Axelsson, Tim Thomas

2008-'09
Coach: Claude Julien
Lost Conference Semi-Finals to Carolina Hurricanes (3–4)
Appearances by Marc Savard, David Krejci, Andrew Ference, Milan Lucic, Zdeno Chara, P.J.
   Axelsson, Mark Recchi, Patrice Bergeron, Tim Thomas

2009-'10
Coach: Claude Julien
Lost Conference Semi-Finals to Philadelphia Flyers (3–4)
Appearances by Milan Lucic, Patrice Bergeron, Mark Recchi, Zdeno Chara, Johnny Boychuk,
   David Krejci, Marc Savard, Andrew Ference, Adam McQuaid, Tuukka Rask

2010-'11
Coach: Claude Julien
Won Stanley Cup Final over Vancouver Canucks (4–3)
Appearances by Brad Marchand, Mark Recchi, David Krejci, Patrice Bergeron, Zdeno Chara,
   Andrew Ference, Milan Lucic, Johnny Boychuk, Dennis Seidenberg, Adam McQuaid, Tim
   Thomas

2011-'12
Coach: Claude Julien
Lost Conference Quarter-Finals to Washington Capitals (3–4)
Appearances by Brad Marchand, David Krejci, Patrice Bergeron, Zdeno Chara, Andrew
   Ference, Milan Lucic, Johnny Boychuk, Dennis Seidenberg, Tim Thomas

2012-'13
Coach: Claude Julien
Lost Stanley Cup Final to Chicago Blackhawks (2–4)
Appearances by Brad Marchand, David Krejci, Patrice Bergeron, Zdeno Chara, Andrew

Ference, Milan Lucic, Johnny Boychuk, Dennis Seidenberg, Adam McQuaid, Torey Krug, Tuukka Rask

2013-'14
Coach: Claude Julien
Lost Second Round to Montreal Canadiens (3–4)
Appearances by Torey Krug, Brad Marchand, Patrice Bergeron, Jarome Iginla, Milan Lucic, Johnny Boychuk, Zdeno Chara, Tuukka Rask

2016-'17
Coaches: Claude Julien, Bruce Cassidy
Lost First Round to Ottawa Senators (2–4)
Appearances by Patrice Bergeron, David Pastrnak, Brad Marchand, Zdeno Chara, Adam McQuaid, David Krejci, Tuukka Rask

2017-'18
Coach: Bruce Cassidy
Lost Second Round to Tampa Bay Lightning (1–4)
Appearances by Patrice Bergeron, Brad Marchand, David Pastrnak, Torey Krug, Zdeno Chara, Adam McQuaid, Tuukka Rask

2018-'19
Coach: Bruce Cassidy
Lost Stanley Cup Final to St. Louis Blues (3–4)
Appearances by Patrice Bergeron, Brad Marchand, David Pastrnak, Torey Krug, Zdeno Chara, Tuukka Rask

2019-'20
Coach: Bruce Cassidy
Lost Second Round to Tampa Bay Lightning (1–4)
Appearances by Patrice Bergeron, Brad Marchand, David Pastrnak, Torey Krug, Zdeno Chara

Chapter Notes

Chapter 1

1. Cooney Weiland Page, hhof.com/Legends OfHockey/jsp/LegendsMember.jsp?mem= p197104&type=Player&page=bio&list=ByYear.
2. Stan Fischler, "Distant Replays: What If Replay Had Existed Way Back When?" *Boston Bruins: Greatest Moments and Players*, Sports Publishing, New York (2017), p. 111.
3. "Hockey Coach Dies at 80, After Illness," *The Harvard Crimson*, July 9, 1985.
4. Joe Pelletier, "Marty Barry," Greatest Hockey Legends (Blog), http://redwingslegends.blogspot.com/2008/03/marty-barry.html (retrieved February 25, 2019).
5. *Ibid.*
6. Joe Pelletier, "Nels Stewart," Greatest Hockey Legends (Blog), http://montrealmaroons.blogspot.com/2008/03/nels-stewart.html, March 31, 2008 (retrieved February 25, 2019).
7. *Ibid.*
8. "Nels Stewart, Classy Center, Goes to Boston Bruins Six," *Lewiston Daily Sun*, June 13, 19332 (retrieved October 2, 2019).
9. "Nels Played with His Brain," *The Montreal Gazette*, November 10, 1962 (retrieved October 2, 2019).
10. Kerry Keane, *Tales from the Boston Bruins Locker Room: A Collection of the Greatest Bruins Stories Ever Told*, Sports Publishing, New York (2017), p. 46.
11. Bronco Horvath AHL Hall of Fame page, ahlhalloffame.com/bronco-horvath.
12. Kevin Hunter, "Derek 'Turk' Sanderson: A Boston Legend," The Hockey Writers Archives, https://thehockeywriters.com/derek-turk-sanderson-a-boston-legend/, August 3, 2018 (retrieved March 1, 2019).
13. Dan Robson, "How Niagara Falls' Derek Sanderson Crashed and Rose Again," Sports Net News Site, https://www.sportsnet.ca/hockey/nhl/niagara-falls-derek-sanderson-crashed-rose/, October 7, 2017 (retrieved March 1, 2019).
14. Joe Pelletier, "Fred Stanfield," Greatest Hockey Legends (Blog), bruinslegends.blogspot.com/2008/10/fred-stanfield.html (retrieved Oct. 3, 2019).
15. *Ibid.*
16. Davig B. Lukow, "Steady Freddie: Stanfield a Winner On and Off the Ice," Best of WNY Website, http://www.bestofwny.com/sports/lukow/stanfield.htm (retrieved October 3, 2019).
17. *Ibid.*
18. Dave Stubbs, "Phil Esposito, Tony Esposito Share Stories, Laughs," NHL.com, March 5, 2017 (retrieved October 7, 2019).
19. "Phil Esposito Was Record-Setting Goal Scorer," YouTube, youtube.com/watch?v=nwv7p1s2t_1.
20. Stan Fischler, *Boston Bruins: Greatest Moments and Players*, Sports Publishing, New York (2017), p. 43.
21. Don Cherry, *Don Cherry's Sports Heroes*, Doubleday Canada, Toronto (2016), p. 63.
22. *Ibid.*
23. Stu Cowan, "Phil Esposito Is Still Bitter About Trade from Bruins," *Montreal Gazette*, June 16, 2013.
24. Craig Beauchemin, "From Battlefords to the NHL and Back Again," *Battlefords News-Optimist*, August 25, 2015.
25. *Ibid.*
26. *Ibid.*
27. Jean Ratelle Page, hhof.com/Legends OfHockey/jsp/LegendsMember.jsp?mem= p198504&type=Player& page=bio&list=.
28. "Bruins Legends: Jean Ratelle," NHL TV Website, www.nhl.com/bruins/video/bruins-legends-jean-ratelle/c-60755403.
29. *Ibid.*
30. Stan Fischler, "Distant Replays: What If Replay Had Existed Way Back When?" *Boston Bruins: Greatest Moments and Players*, Sports Publishing, New York (2017), p. 123.
31. Kerry Keane, *Tales from the Boston Bruins Locker Room: A Collection of the Greatest Bruins Stories Ever Told* (Sports Publishing, New York, 2017), p. 118.
32. Stan Fischler, "Distant Replays: What If Replay Had Existed Way Back When?" *Boston Bruins: Greatest Moments and Players*, Sports Publishing, New York (2017), p. 123.
33. Allan Kreda, "Rangers Greats Reunite to Honor Jean Ratelle," *New York Times*, February 24, 2018.

34. Stan Fischler, "Distant Replays: What If Replay Had Existed Way Back When?" *Boston Bruins: Greatest Moments and Players*, Sports Publishing, New York (2017), p. 219.

35. *Ibid.*

36. "Bruins Alumni: Peter McNab," Official NHL Website, https://www.nhl.com/bruins/video/bruins-alumni-peter-mcnab/t-277437088/c-60557903.

37. "Bruins Alumni: Barry Pederson," Official NHL Website, https://www.nhl.com/video/bruins-alumni-barry-pederson/c-57375703.

38. Steve Simmons, "Leafs' Steve Kasper Has no Nostalgia for Bruins Days," *Toronto Sun*, May 3, 2013.

39. Jim Iovino, "Kasper Made Big Mistake Benching Stars," LCS Guide to Hockey Website, ww.lcshockey.com/issues/35/feature3.asp (retrieved March 11, 2019).

40. Steve Simmons, "Leafs' Steve Kasper Has No Nostalgia for Bruins Days," *Toronto Sun*, May 3, 2013.

41. Bob Kravitz, "The Rat That Roared, Scored and Prospered," *Sports Illustrated*, November 25, 1985.

42. *Ibid.*

43. *Ibid.*

44. *Ibid.*

45. Matt Larkin, "All-Dirty/Skill Team: Who Blended Criminality and Talent Best?" *The Hockey News*, April 6, 2017.

46. Dave Stubbs, "Bruins Marchand Impressing Former Boston Center Linesman in Final," NHL Official Website, May 31, 2019 (retrieved October 10, 2019).

47. Rink Rats: Interview with Craig Janney, YouTube, youtube.com/watch?v=UzbTUe-2EEO, October 2, 2018.

48. Joe Pelletier, "Craig Janney," Greatest Hockey Legends (Blog), http://bruinslegends.blogspot.com/2007/12/craig-janney.html.

49. *Ibid.*

50. Rachel Alexander, "With Oates, Capitals Are in Good Hands, Center Helps Direct Team Back to Playoffs," *Washington Post*, April 11, 1998.

51. Rink Rats: Interview with Craig Janney, YouTube, youtube.com/watch?v=UzbTUe-2EEO, October 2, 2018.

52. Kostnya Kennedy, "Mystery Man," *Sports Illustrated*, July 25, 2012.

53. "Adam Oates: NHL's Fourth All-Time Assists Leader," YouTube, youtubecom/watch?v=0O6HWuW2fPo.

54. Brandon Champion, "Sharks Thornton Passes Gordie Howe on Assists List, Yzerman Next," https://www.mlive.com/sports/2019/02/sharks-joe-thornton-passes-gordie-howe-on-all-time-assists-list-steve-yzerman-is-next.html, February 12, 2019 (retrieved October 11, 2019).

55. "Thornton Traded to Sharks for Three Players," ESPN Online, https://www.espn.com/nhl/news/story?id=2242875, December 1, 2005 (retrieved March 15, 2019).

56. Genius website, https://genius.com/Gord-downie-you-me-and-the-bs-lyrics.

57. Patrice Bergeron, "Back Where We Belong," The Players Tribune Online Magazine, https://www.theplayerstribune.com/en-us/articles/patrice-bergeron-boston-bruins-nhl-playoffs, April 12, 2017 (retrieved March 18, 2019).

58. Marc Savard, "To Hell and Back," The Players Tribune Online Magazine, May 16, 2017 (retrieved March 22, 2019).

59. *Ibid.*

60. *Ibid.*

61. "Marc Savard, Hockey Stick Taping Nerd and 'Borrower' of Gretzky's Stick," YouTube, https://www.youtube.com/watch?v=qe6Y9tdrqUs.

62. John Bishop, "Hub, Meet Marc Savard," Official NHL Website, nhl.com/bruins/news/hub-meet-marc-savard/c-448548, December 14, 2007 (retrieved March 18, 2019).

63. Greg Wyshynski, "David Krejci on the NHL Playoff Format, False Teeth and Jaromir Jagr," ESPN Online, https://www.espn.com/nhl/story/_/id/26273460/david-krejci-nhl-playoff-format-false-teeth-jaromir-jagr, March 16, 2019 (retrieved March 21, 2019).

Chapter 2

1. Harry Oliver Page, legendsofhockey.net/LegendsOfHockey/jsp/LegendsMember.jsp?mem=p196703&page=bio&list=ByTeam&team=Calgary Tigers#photo.

2. Stan Fischler, "Distant Replays: What If Replay Had Existed Way Back When?" *Boston Bruins: Greatest Moments and Players*, Sports Publishing, New York (2017), p. 61.

3. Joe Pelletier, "Dit Clapper," Greatest Hockey Legends (blog), bruinslegends.blogspot.com/2007/02/dit-clapper.html.

4. Kerry Keane, *Tales from the Boston Bruins Locker Room: A Collection of the Greatest Bruins Stories Ever Told*, Sports Publishing, New York (2017), p. 44.

5. Kevin Shea, "One on One with Bobby Bauer," Official Hockey Hall of Fame Website, https://www.hhof.com/htmlSpotlight/spot_oneononep199601.shtml.

6. Stan Fischler, "Distant Replays: What If Replay Had Existed Way Back When?" *Boston Bruins: Greatest Moments and Players*, Sports Publishing, New York, (2017), p. 57.

7. *Ibid.*

8. *Ibid.*

9. Joe Pelletier, "Johnny Peirson," Greatest Hockey Legends (blog), bruinslegends.blogspot.com/2010/11/johnny-peirson.html.

10. Joe Beare, "Thinking About John Peirson," Official NHL Website, https://www.nhl.com/bruins/news/thinking-about-john-peirson/c-448132, June 6, 2007 (retrieved May 22, 2019).

11. Stan Fischler, "Distant Replays: What If

Replay Had Existed Way Back When?" *Boston Bruins: Greatest Moments and Players*, Sports Publishing, New York, (2017), p. 266.

12. Joe Pelletier, "Johnny Peirson," Greatest Hockey Legends (blog), bruinslegends.blogspot.com/2010/11/johnny-peirson.html.

13. Stu Hackel, "The Voice of the Bruins," *Sports Illustrated*, March 7, 1994.

14. Stan Fischler, "Distant Replays: What If Replay Had Existed Way Back When?" *Boston Bruins: Greatest Moments and Players*, Sports Publishing, New York (2017), p. 262.

15. Kerry Keane, *Tales from the Boston Bruins Locker Room: A Collection of the Greatest Bruins Stories Ever Told*, Sports Publishing, New York (2017), p. 82.

16. Stan Fischler, "Distant Replays: What If Replay Had Existed Way Back When?" *Boston Bruins: Greatest Moments and Players*, Sports Publishing, New York, (2017), p. 262.

17. *Ibid.*, p. 92.

18. *Ibid.*

19. Dominick Jansky, "Islanders of Yesteryear: Ed Westfal: 18," Lighthouse Hockey (Blog), https://www.lighthousehockey.com/2009/5/1/861487/islanders-of-yesteryear-ed, May 1, 2009 (retrieved Oct. 12, 2019).

20. Masterton Memorial Trophy Winners Page, Official NHL Website, https://www.nhl.com/news/nhl-bill-masterton-memorial-trophy-winners-complete-list/c-288418608.

21. "Former Bruin John McKenzie Is This Week's Talk of the Town," https://www.youtube.com/watch?v=udnDabxoUpU.

22. Stan Fischler, "Distant Replays: What If Replay Had Existed Way Back When?" *Boston Bruins: Greatest Moments and Players*, Sports Publishing, New York (2017), p. 234.

23. Ken Hodge Bio Page, hhof.com/Legends OfHockey/jsp/SearchPlayer.jsp?player=10649 (retrieved June 20, 2019).

24. Mathew Whitty, "Top NHL Players Who Were Hated by Their Own Team's Fans," The Sportster.com, https://www.thesportster.com/hockey/top-15-nhl-players-who-were-hated-by-their-own-teams-fans-2/, November 28, 2015 (retrieved Oct. 12, 2019).

25. Jerry Kirshenbaum, "The Wrath of Grapes," *Sports Illustrated*. January 15, 1979.

26. Joe Pelletier, "Terry O'Reilly," Greatest Hockey Legends (Blog), http://bruinslegends.blogspot.com/2006/05/terry-oreilly.html.

27. *Ibid.*

28. Dave Stubbs, "Five Questions with Terry O'Reilly," Official NHL Website, https://www.nhl.com/news/five-questions-with-bruins-legend-terry-oreilly/c-295790492, February 13, 2018.

29. *Ibid.*

30. "Bourque Calls O'Reilly 'The Ultimate Bruin,'" ESPN.com, http://static.espn.go.com/nhl/news/2002/1024/1450686.html, October 25, 2002 (retrieved October 12, 2019).

31. *Ibid.*

32. Neil Cote, "Schmautz Shooting for a Bruins Victory," *Boston Herald*, June 4, 2011.

33. Bobby Schmautz Page, Hockey Fights (NHL Forum), https://www.hockeyfights.com/forums/f18/bobby-schmautz-134893.

34. "The Nastiest Stick Men," Hockey Fights (NHL Forum), https://www.hockeyfights.com/forums/f18/nastiest-stick-men-110059.

35. Neil Cote, "Schmautz Shooting for a Bruins Victory," *Boston Herald*, June 4, 2011.

36. Garrett Hayden, "My Chat with Bruins Legend Rick Middleton," https://blackngoldhockey.com/2018/11/24/my-chat-with-bruins-legend-rick-middleton/, November 24, 2018 (retrieved May 22, 2019).

37. Daniel Oliver, "Hockey Hall of Fame Debates: Rick Middleton," https://thehockey writers.com/hockey-hall-of-fame-debates-rick-middleton/.

38. Greg Simon, "Nifty Choice by Bruins: Fall River's Alex Kogler Was Rick Middleton's Teammate at Providence," *The Herald News*, August 16, 2018.

39. Rick Middleton Page, http://nhlegendsof hockey.com/people/rick-middleton/.

40. Garrett Hayden, "My Chat with Bruins Legend Rick Middleton," https://blackngoldhockey.com/2018/11/24/my-chat-with-bruins-legend-rick-middleton/, November 24, 2018 (retrieved May 22, 2019).

41. "Cam Neely, What Really Counts," Famous Sports Stars, JRank.org, https://sports.jrank.org>pages>Neely--Cam--What-Really-Counts (retrieved October 16, 2019).

42. Joe Pelletier, "Cam Neely," Greatest Hockey Legends (blog), http://www.greatest hockeylegends.com/2013/07/cam-neely.html.

43. Stan Fischler, "Distant Replays: What If Replay Had Existed Way Back When?" *Boston Bruins: Greatest Moments and Players*, Sports Publishing, New York (2017), p. 149.

44. Joe Pelletier, "Glen Murray," Greatest Hockey Legends (blog), http://bruinslegends.blogspot.com/2013/06/glen-murray.html.

45. Matsuda, Gann, "Teamwork, Integrity and a Little Engineering Helped Retired LA Kings RW Glen Murray to Skate Again," Frozen Royalty (LA Kings Blog), https://frozenroyalty.net/2014/03/18/teamwork-ingenuity-and-a-little-engineering-helped-retired-la-kings-rw-glen-murray-to-skate-again/, March 18, 2014 (retrieved October 19, 2019).

46. Kevin Paul Dupont, "For Former Bruin Steve Heinze, a Day on the Ice is a Good Day," *Boston Globe*, January 1, 2016.

47. *Ibid.*

48. Ken Campbell, "Pastrnak Is the Man with the Golden Stick," *The Hockey News*, October 22, 2019.

49. "Dunkin X, David Pastrnak Penalty Box Regular," YouTube, https://www.youtube.com/watch?v=DHtapgcS2FY.

50. Ken Campbell, "Pastrnak Is the Man with

the Golden Stick," *The Hockey News*, October 22, 2019.

51. Mathew Castle, "3 Takeaways from the Bruins 5–1 Win Over the Sharks," Boston.com, October 30, 2019 (retrieved October 30, 2019).

Chapter 3

1. Stan Fischler, "Distant Replays: What If Replay Had Existed Way Back When?" *Boston Bruins: Greatest Moments and Players*, Sports Publishing, New York (2017), p. 173.
2. *Ibid.*, 253.
3. Joe Pelletier, "Herb Cain," Greatest Hockey Legends (Blog), http://bruinslegends.blogspot.com/2007/01/herb-cain.html.
4. *Ibid.*
5. Joe Pelletier, "Vic Stasiuk," Greatest Hockey Legends (Blog), http://bruinslegends.blogspot.com/2008/10/vic-stasiuk.html.
6. Vic Stasiuk Interview (following induction to the Alberta Sports Hall of Fame), www.youtube.com/watch?v=guZ1tYrw7ik.
7. *Ibid.*
8. "Philadelphia Fires Stasiuk," *Associated Press*, May 28, 1971.
9. Joe Pelletier, "Vic Stasiuk," Greatest Hockey Legends (Blog), http://bruinslegends.blogspot.com/2008/10/vic-stasiuk.html.
10. *Ibid.*
11. Stu Hackel, "Johnny Bucyk: 100 Greatest Hockey Players," NHL.com, January 1, 2017.
12. *Ibid.*
13. *Ibid.*
14. Joe Pelletier, "Johnny Bucyk," Greatest Hockey Legends (Blog), http://bruinslegends.blogspot.com/2007/01/johnny-bucyk.html.
15. Stan Fischler, "Distant Replays: What If Replay Had Existed Way Back When?" *Boston Bruins: Greatest Moments and Players*, Sports Publishing, New York (2017), p. 117.
16. "Bruiser and Playmaker Wayne Cashman," Original Hockey Hall of Fame, http://www.originalhockeyhalloffame.com/news-events/cashman.html.
17. Joe Pelletier, "Wayne Cashman," Greatest Hockey Legends (Blog), http://bruinslegends.blogspot.com/2006/05/wayne-cashman.html.
18. "Bruiser and Playmaker Wayne Cashman," Original Hockey Hall of Fame, http://www.originalhockeyhalloffame.com/news-events/cashman.html.
19. Jon Goode, "Catching Up with Don Marcotte," Southcoasttoday.com, March 27, 2005 (retrieved Nov. 4, 2019).
20. *Ibid.*
21. Christopher Bowden, "Defensive Standout Proves 2-Way Hockey Still Pays Off," *Christian Science Monitor*, March 22, 1982.
22. Michael Farber, "Three Little Words: Too Many Men," *Sports Illustrated*, May 9, 2014.
23. Jon Goode, "Catching Up with Don Marcotte," Southcoasttoday.com, March 27, 2005 (retrieved November 4, 2019).
24. "Boston Herald Talk of the Town: Former Boston Bruin Stan Jonathan," www.youtube.com/watch?v=WKSKql5VRHw (retrieved November 7, 2019).
25. Joe Pelletier, "Stan Jonathan," Greatest Hockey Legends (Blog), http://bruinslegends.blogspot.com/2006/06/stan-jonathan.html.
26. *Ibid.*
27. Mark Malinowski, "Getting to Know: Randy Burridge," *The Hockey News*, July 19, 2015.
28. Dave Sell, "Capitals' Burridge Prays the Wheels Stay On," *The Washington Post*, September 12, 1993.
29. Mark Malinowski, "Getting to Know: Randy Burridge," *The Hockey News*, July 19, 2015.
30. Nathaniel Popper, "Brains on Ice," *Boston Globe*, October 11, 2009.
31. "Hurricanes Add Samsonov to Scouting Department," nhl.com, September 16, 2014 (retrieved November 11, 2019).
32. "Bruins Alumni: PJ Axelsson," NHL.com, August 2, 2018 (retrieved November 12, 2019).
33. *Ibid.*
34. Stan Fischler, "Distant Replays: What If Replay Had Existed Way Back When?" *Boston Bruins: Greatest Moments and Players*, Sports Publishing, New York (2017), p. 191.
35. "Bruins Milan Lucic Calls Dalton Prout Punch 'Gutless,'" CBSsports.com, November 23, 2014.
36. "Inside Hockey: Ryan Miller Interview Bruins Sabres 11/12," https://www.youtube.com/watch?v=FvE82q4yKEM&feature=player_embedded.
37. Stan Fischler, "Distant Replays: What If Replay Had Existed Way Back When?" *Boston Bruins: Greatest Moments and Players*, Sports Publishing, New York (2017), p. 292.
38. Nick Schwartz, "A Strange History of Brad Marchand Kissing and Licking Players," *USA Today*, May 5, 2018.
39. *Ibid.*
40. "Brad Marchand on His Label as a Dirty Player: 'It's Disappointing,'" youtube.com/watch?v=39ZnPeB-ItM, February 6, 2018 (retrieved November 15, 2019).
41. Shawn Ferris, "Analytics Profile: Brad Marchand, the Results May Shock You," Stanley Cup of Chowder, September 5, 2018 (retrieved November 15, 2019).

Chapter 4

1. Dave Carignan, "This Week in Bruins History: Lionel Hitchman Second NHL Number to be Retired," Stanley Cup of Chowder, January 26, 2012 (retrieved November 15, 2019).
2. Dave Stubbs, "Bruins Legend Hitchman Deserves Hall Recognition," NHL.com, February 22, 2016 (retrieved November 16, 2019).
3. *Ibid.*

4. Joe Pelletier, "Lionel Hitchman," Greatest Hockey Legends (Blog), http://bruinslegends.blogspot.com/2009/12/lionel-hitchman.html.

5. Dave Stubbs, "Bruins Legend Hitchman Deserves Hall recognition," NHL.com, February 22, 2016 (retrieved November 16, 2019).

6. Stan Fischler, *Boston Bruins: Greatest Moments and Players*, New York: Sports Publishing (2017), p. 19.

7. Eddie Shore Player Bio, "Eddie Shore Was Bruins First Great Defenseman," https://www.youtube.com/watch?v=eODIX2Mq8jk.

8. Stan Fischler, *Boston Bruins: Greatest Moments and Players*, New York: Sports Publishing (2017), p. 21.

9. *Ibid.*, p. 22.

10. Stan Fischler, "If It Was Staggering, It Had to Be Eddie," *Sports Illustrated*, March 13, 1967.

11. Ecozens, "OTBH: Like a Flash (Hollett)," Stanley Cup of Chowder, August 21, 2013 (retrieved November 17, 2019).

12. Stan Fischler, *Boston Bruins: Greatest Moments and Players*, New York: Sports Publishing (2017), p. 182.

13. Mike Wyman, "The Golden Years: Murray Henderson," insidehockey.com (Blog), August 7, 2010 (retrieved November 17, 2019).

14. J. Amodea, "Murray Henderson Turns 90," hockeythenandnow.blogspot, September 26, 2011 (retrieved January 17, 2019).

15. Joe Pelletier, "Murray Henderson," Greatest Hockey Legends (Blog), http://bruinslegends.blogspot.com/2013/01/murray-henderson.html.

16. Mike Wyman, "The gold Years: Murray Henderson," insidehockey.com (Blog), August 7, 2010 (retrieved November 17, 2019).

17. Stan Fischler, *Boston Bruins: Greatest Moments and Players*, New York: Sports Publishing (2017), p. 167.

18. Joe Pelletier, "Fern Flaman," Greatest Hockey Legends (Blog), http://bruinslegends.blogspot.com/2007/01/fern-flaman.html.

19. *Ibid.*

20. Stan Fischler, *Boston Bruins: Greatest Moments and Players*, New York: Sports Publishing (2017), p. 195.

21. Bob Verdi, "The Verdict: Remembering Doug Mohns," NHL.com, February11, 2014 (retrieved November 23, 2019).

22. Kevin Shea, "One on One with Leo Boivin," Hockey Hall of Fame, April 25, 2008 (retrieved November 22, 2019).

23. *Ibid.*

24. Leo Boivin Biography Page, Hockey Hall of Fame, https://www.hhof.com/LegendsOfHockey/jsp/LegendsMember.jsp?mem=P198601&type=Player&page=bio&list=ByName.

25. Dallas Smith Page, Not in Hall of Fame (Blog), http://www.notinhalloffame.com/hockey/top-50-hockey-players-by-franchise/top-50-boston-bruins/6633-24-dallas-smith.

26. "Dallas Smith Will Sit Out Rest of Year," United Press International, March 3, 1977.

27. "Rangers Get Ex-Bruin, Dallas Smith," *New York Times*, December 20, 1977.

28. Stan Fischler, *Boston Bruins: Greatest Moments and Players*, New York: Sports Publishing (2017), p. 95.

29. Marvin Paye, "Ted Green, All-Star Bruins Defenseman Who Was Injured in Historic on-ice Fight, Dies," *Boston Herald*, November 2, 2019.

30. *Ibid.*

31. Joe Pelletier, "Gary Doak," Greatest Hockey Legends (Blog), http://bruinslegends.blogspot.com/2011/03/gary-doak.html.

32. "Cancer Claims Former Bruins Defenseman Gary Doak at 71," *Boston Globe*, November 17, 2018.

33. *Ibid.*

34. Ross Bonander, "Quotes of the Week: About Bobby Orr," The Hockey Writers, https://thehockeywriters.com/quotes-of-the-week-about-bobby-orr/, August 13, 2012 (retrieved November 26, 2019).

35. *Ibid.*

36. Stan Fischler, "Bobby Orr Deceived in Free Agency Departure to Blackhawks," NHL.com, June 28, 2017 (retrieved November 26, 2019).

37. Bobby Orr Quotes Page, https://www.brainyquote.com/authors/bobby-orr-quotes.

38. Joe Pelletier, "Rick Smith," Greatest Hockey Legends (Blog), http://www.greatesthockeylegends.com/2016/09/rick-smith.html.

39. "Rick Smith: The Accidental Stanley Cup Winner," The Original Hockey Hall of Fame Website, http://www.originalhockeyhalloffame.com/news-events/smith.html.

40. Joe Pelletier, "Rick Smith," Greatest Hockey Legends (Blog), http://www.greatesthockeylegends.com/2016/09/rick-smith.html.

41. Stu Hackel, "Brad Park: 100 Greatest NHL Players," NHL.com, January 1, 2017 (retrieved November 29, 2019).

42. *Ibid.*

43. *Ibid.*

44. Kerry Keane, *Tales from the Boston Bruins Locker Room: A Collection of the Greatest Bruins Stories Ever Told*, Sports Publishing, New York (2017), p. 112.

45. George Johnson, "Ray Bourque: 100 Greatest NHL Players," NHL.com, January 1, 2017 (retrieved December 4, 2019).

46. *Ibid.*

47. David Droschak, "Glen Wesley Tribute—Part 1: The Trade," NHL.com, February 2, 2009 (retrieved December 5, 2019).

48. *Ibid.*

49. *Ibid.*

50. Joe Pelletier, "Don Sweeney," Greatest Hockey Legends (Blog), http://bruinslegends.blogspot.com/2008/08/don-sweeney.html.

51. *Ibid.*

52. Michael Grange, "McLaren Sits Out for Hit on Zednik," *The Globe and Mail*, April 20, 2002.

53. Greg Beacham, "Kyle McLaren Ready to

Forget Boston," *Plainview Daily Herald*, January 23, 2003.

54. *Ibid.*

55. Hal Gill, "Four Pretty Good Hockey Stories," The Players Tribune (Blog), https://www.theplayerstribune.com/en-us/articles/hal-gill-nhl-stories, March 27, 2018, (retrieved December 9, 2019).

56. Dave Stubbs, "Five Questions with Hal Gill," NHL.com, October 17, 2017.

57. Brandon Share-Cohen, "Seven Cool Things About Zdeno Chara," The Hockey Writers (Blog), https://thehockeywriters.com/zdeno-chara-seven-things/, November 2, 2019 (retrieved December 10, 2019).

58. Andrew Thompson, "Former Boston Bruins Andrew Ference Calls It a Career," Causeway-Crowd.com, September 16, 2016.

59. Joe McDonald, "Andrew Ference Fined for Gesture," ESPN.com, April 21, 2011 (retrieved December 12, 2019).

60. Greg Wyshinski, "Andrew Ference Say NHL Must Reach Beyond 'Middle-Aged White Dudes,'" ESPN.com, March 26, 2018 (retrieved December 12, 2019).

61. Fluto Shinzawa, "Boychuk Is Next in Line on Bruins' Blue Line," *Boston Globe*, September 4, 2009.

62. *Ibid.*

63. "Boston Inks D Boychuk to Two-Year Contract," Associated Press, June 24, 2010.

64. "Blue Jackets Acquire Adam McQuaid from Rangers," Official Blue Jackets Website (NHL.com), February 25, 2019 (retrieved December 14, 2019).

65. "Adam McQuaid Putting Health First, Unsure of Future on the Ice," NBC Sports Boston, November 29, 2019 (retrieved December 14, 2019).

66. *Ibid.*

67. Fluto Shinzawa, "Glad Seidenberg Is on Their Side," *Boston Globe*, May 31, 2011.

68. Matt Kalman, "Seidenberg Deal a Good One for Bruins," ESPN.com, June 5, 2010 (retrieved December 15, 2019).

69. Joe Haggerty, "Dennis Seidenberg Announces Retirement from the NHL After 15 Seasons," NBC Sports Boston, October 24, 2019 (retrieved December 15, 2019).

70. Nik Decosta-Klipa, "Here's What Torey Krug Had to Say About His Helmet-Less Hit on Robert Thomas," Boston.com, May 28, 2019 (retrieved December 15, 2019).

71. Marina, "Torey Krug on Taking a Pay Cut to Stay in Boston—'It's Something I'm Interested In,'" Barstoolsports.com, September 5, 2019 (retrieved December 15, 2019).

Chapter 5

1. Kerry Keane, *Tales from the Boston Bruins Locker Room: A Collection of the Greatest Bruins Stories Ever Told*, Sports Publishing, New York (2017), p. 23.

2. *Ibid.*, p. 24.

3. Stan Fischler, *Boston Bruins: Greatest Moments and Players*, New York: Sports Publishing (2017), p. 275.

4. "Jim Henry: Sweet as Sugar, Gritty as Spinach Salad," Puckstruck, https://puckstruck.com/2017/10/23/jim-henry-sweet-as-sugar-gritty-as-a-spinach-salad/, October 23, 2017 (retrieved December 18, 2019).

5. Ken Campbell, "Top 100 Goalies: Don Simmons," *The Hockey News*, November 9, 2018.

6. George Grimm, *Guardians of the Goal: A Comprehensive Guide to New York Rangers Goaltenders*, New York: Sports Publishing (2019), Kindle version.

7. Ron Cook, "Eddie Johnston: A Hockey Life," *Pittsburgh Post Gazette*, July 26, 2009.

8. Shelly Anderson, "NHL Lifer Eddie Johnston Talks About Injuries, Bobby Orr, Trades and More," ESPN.com, November 16, 2015 (retrieved December 22, 2019).

9. "One on One with Gerry Cheevers," Hockey Hall of Fame, December 21, 204 (retrieved December 23, 2019).

10. *Ibid.*

11. Kerry Keane, *Tales from the Boston Bruins Locker Room: A Collection of the Greatest Bruins Stories Ever Told*, Sports Publishing, New York (2017), p. 38.

12. Kevin Van Steendelaar, "May 10, 1979: Boston Bruins Called for Too Many Men Against Montreal," Bleacher Report, May 10, 2009 (retrieved December 23, 2019).

13. "Bruins Academy: Gilles Gilbert," YouTube, posted November 15, 2017, https://www.youtube.com/watch?v=AsVuOiAoD8I.

14. Malcolm Moran, "Players: Bruins' Goalie Has Successful Style," *New York Times*, April 30, 1983.

15. *Ibid.*

16. Brian O'Connor, "Front 9 Q & A with Former Bruins Goaltender Reggie Lemelin," *North Shore Golf Magazine*, http://northshoregolfmagazine.com/front-9-q-a-with-former-bruins-goaltender-reggie-lemelin/ (retrieved December 24, 2019).

17. "Bruins Alumni: Reggie Lemelin," NHL.com, https://www.nhl.com/video/bruins-alumni-reggie-lemelin/t-277350912/c-62654203 (retrieved December 24, 2019).

18. *Ibid.*

19. Jared Clinton, "Top 100 Goalies: Reggie Lemelin," *The Hockey News*, November 9, 2018.

20. Lowetide, "Nation Profile: Andy Moog," Oilers Nation, https://oilersnation.com/2012/11/23/nation-profile-andy-moog/, November 23, 2013 (retrieved December 26, 2019).

21. Ryan Kennedy, "Top 100 Goalies: Andy Moog," *The Hockey News*, November 9, 2018.

22. *Ibid.*

23. Scott Frizzell, "Exclusive Interview with

Former Bruins Goaltender Byron Dafoe," *Boston Sports Extra*, April 15, 2018 (retrieved December 30, 2019).

24. *Ibid.*

25. Greg Balloch, "Byron Dafoe Chats About Modern Goaltending," *In Goal Magazine*, March 2015.

26. "Thomas Statement on White House Absence," NHL.com, January 23, 2012 (retrieved December 30, 2019).

27. Susan Mulligan, "Tim Thomas's White House Snub Wasn't Brave, It Was Just Rude," *U.S. News and World Report*, January 27, 2012.

28. Stephen Whyno, "Retired Goalie Tim Thomas Details Brain Damage from Hockey," *Associated Press*, December 12, 2019.

29. Kevin Woodley, "Rasky Business: The Skills Behind a Vezina winner," *In Goal Magazine*, September 2014.

30. "What Did Tuukka Rask Mean by His Post Game Comment?" NBC Sports Boston, January 1, 2019 (retrieved December 31, 2019).

Bibliography

"Absurd Goalie Monday: Byron Dafoe." Scotty Wazz Blog, http://scottywazz.blogspot.com/2010/07/absurd-goalie-monday-byron-dafoe.html, July 5, 2010 (retrieved Dec. 30, 2019).

"Adam McQuaid Putting Health First, Unsure of Future on the Ice." NBC Sports Boston, Nov. 29, 2019 (retrieved Dec. 14, 2019).

Adam Oates Bio Page. Hockey Hall of Fame Website, hhof.com/htmlInduct/ind12Oates.shtml.

"Adam Oates: NHL's Fourth All-Time Assists Leader." YouTube, youtubecom/watch?v=0O6HWuW2fPo.

Allen, Kevin, Duff, Bob, and Bower, Johnny. *Without Fear: Hockey's 50 Greatest Goaltenders.* Chicago: Triumph Books, 2002.

Amodea, J. "Murray Henderson Turns 90." Hockey Then and Now (Blog), Sept. 26, 2011 (retrieved Jan. 17, 2019).

Anderson, Shelly, "NHL Lifer Eddie Johnston Talks About Injuries, Bobby Orr, Trades and More." ESPN.com, Nov. 16, 2015 (retrieved Dec. 22, 2019).

Anderson, Shelly. "The Men Who Built the Penguins." Pittsburgh Hockey Now, Aug. 26, 2018 (retrieved Dec. 22, 2019).

Andy Moog Bio Page. British Columbia Hockey Hall of Fame, https://bchhf.com/portfolio-items/andy-moog/.

Art Ross Bio Page. Hockey Hall of Fame, https://www.hhof.com/LegendsOfHockey/jsp/LegendsMember.jsp?mem=p194510&type=Player&page=bio&list=ByYear.

Babe Pratt Bio Page. Hockey Hall of Fame, https://www.hhof.com/LegendsOfHockey/jsp/LegendsMember.jsp?mem=P196608&list=ByName.

Babe Siebert Bio Page. The Historical Website of the Montreal Canadiens, http://ourhistory.canadiens.com/player/Albert-Siebert.

Bailey, Arnold. "Pesky, Schmidt Share a Boston Bond for Life." *Sports Collector Digest,* Sept. 10, 2008.

Balloch, Greg. "Byron Dafoe Chats About Modern Goaltending." In Goal Magazine, Mar. 16, 2015 (retrieved Dec. 30, 2019).

Barry Pederson Bio Page. Hockey Hall of Fame, hhof.com/LegendsOfHockey/jsp/SearchPlayer.jsp?player=11272.

Beacham, Greg. "Kyle McLaren Ready to Forget Boston." *Plainview Daily Herald,* Jan. 23, 2003.

Bean, DJ. "Brad Marchand's Suspension History." NBCSports.com (retrieved Nov. 15, 2019).

Beare, Joe. "Thinking About John Peirson." Official NHL Website, https://www.nhl.com/bruins/news/thinking-about-john-peirson/c-448132, June 6, 2007 (retrieved May 22, 2019).

Beauchemin, Craig. "From Battlefords to the NHL and Back Again." *Battlefords News-Optimist,* Aug. 25, 2015.

Bergeron, Patrice. "Back Where We Belong." The Players Tribune Online Magazine, https://www.theplayerstribune.com/en-us/articles/patrice-bergeron-boston-bruins-nhl-playoffs, Apr. 12, 2017 (retrieved Mar. 18, 2019).

Bill Cowley Bio Page. Hockey Hall of Fame, hhof.com/LegendsOfHockey/jsp/LegendsMember.jsp?mem=p196801&type=Player&page=bio&list=ByName.

Bishop, John. "Hub, Meet Marc Savard." Official NHL Website, nhl.com/bruins/news/hub-meet-marc-savard/c-448548, Dec. 14, 2007 (retrieved Mar. 18, 2019).

"Blue Jackets Acquire Adam McQuaid From Rangers." Official Blue Jackets Website (NHL.com), Feb. 25, 2019 (retrieved Dec. 14, 2019).

"Bobby Bauer, 49, Ex-Hockey Star, Member of Kraut Line Dies-Won Lady Byng Trophy Award." *New York Times,* Sept. 17, 1964.

Bobby Orr Biography Page. BobbyOrr.com (The Official Site of Bobby Orr).

Bobby Orr Biography Page. Bobbyorr.net.

Bobby Orr Quotes Page. https://www.brainyquote.com/authors/bobby-orr-quotes.

Bobby Schmautz Page. Hockey Fights, https://www.hockeyfights.com/forums/f18/bobby-schmautz-134893.

Bobby Schmautz Stats Page. https://www.hockey-reference.com/players/s/schmabo01.html.

Bonander, Ross. "Quotes of the Week: About Bobby Orr." The Hockey Writers, https://thehockeywriters.com/quotes-of-the-week-about-bobby-orr/, Aug. 13, 2012 (retrieved Nov. 26, 2019).

Boston Bruins Coaches Page. https://www.hockey-reference.com/teams/BOS/coaches.html.

Boston Bruins Team History. NHL Official Website, nhl.com/bruins/team/history.

"Boston Herald Talk of the Town: Former Boston Bruin Stan Jonathan." YouTube, www.youtube.com/watch?v=WKSKql5VRHw (retrieved Nov. 7, 2019).

"Boston Inks D Boychuk to Two-Year Contract." *Associated Press*, June 24, 2010.

Bowden, Christopher. "Defensive Standout Proves 2-Way Hockey Still Pays Off." *Christian Science Monitor*, Mar. 22, 1982.

"Brad Marchand on His Label as a Dirty Player: 'It's Disappointing." youtube.com/watch?v=-39ZnPeB-ItM, Feb. 6, 2018 (retrieved Nov. 15, 2019).

Brian Leetch Bio Page. U.S. Hockey Hall of Fame Official Website, https://www.ushockeyhalloffame.com/page/show/833022-brian-leetch.

"Brian Rolston Slapshot on Giguere." YouTube, https://www.youtube.com/watch?v=AvPVRyYtzvc.

Bronco Horvath Page. AHL Hall of Fame Official Website, ahlhalloffame.com/bronco-horvath.

Bruce Cassidy Bio Page. NHL Official Website, https://www.nhl.com/bruins/team/exec-hockey-ops-bruce-cassidy.

"Bruins Alumni: Barry Pederson." NHL Official Website, https://www.nhl.com/video/bruins-alumni-barry-pederson/c-57375703.

"Bruins Alumni: Peter McNab." NHL Official Website, https://www.nhl.com/video/bruins-alumni-peter-mcnab/c-60557903, June 13, 2018 (retrieved Nov. 18, 2019).

"Bruins Alumni: PJ Axelsson." NHL Official Website, https://www.nhl.com/bruins/video/bruins-alumni-pj-axelsson/t-277443300/ c-60821703, Aug. 2, 2018 (retrieved Nov. 12, 2019).

"Bruins Alumni: Reggie Lemelin." NHL Official Website, https://www.nhl.com/video/bruins-alumni-reggie-lemelin/c-62654203, Nov. 6, 2018 (retrieved Nov.24, 2019).

"Bruins Legends: Jean Ratelle." NHL Official Website, https://www.nhl.com/video/bruins-legends-jean-ratelle/t-277350912/c-60755403, Jan. 4, 2020.

"Bruins Lucic Suspended One Game for Hit on Rinaldo." *The Canadian Press*, Dec. 19, 2011 (retrieved Nov. 14, 2019).

"Bruins Milan Lucic Calls Dalton Prout Punch 'Gutless.'" CBSsports.com, Nov. 23, 2014.

"Bruins Star McKenney Outlines Hockey Career." *Ottawa Journal*, May 28, 1957.

"Bruiser and Playmaker Wayne Cashman." Original Hockey Hall of Fame Museum Official Website, http://www.originalhockeyhalloffame.com/news-events/cashman.html.

Brunt, Stephen. *Searching for Bobby Orr.* Chicago: Triumph Books, 2006.

Buckley, Steve. "Big, Bad Bruin Johnny McKenzie Won His Biggest Fight Off the Ice." *Boston Herald*, June 6, 2018.

"Bun Cook: Developer of Slap Shot, Drop Pass." Original Hockey Hall of Fame Museum Official Website, http://www.originalhockeyhalloffame.com/news-events/bun_cook_article.html.

"Cam Neely. "What Really Counts." Famous Sports Stars, JRank.org, https://sports.jrank.org>pages>Neely—Cam—What-Really-Counts (retrieved Oct. 16, 2019).

The Cam Neely Foundation Home Page. https://camneelyfoundation.org/.

Campbell, Ken. "Pastrnak Is the Man with the Golden Stick." *The Hockey News*, Oct. 22, 2019.

_____. "Top 100 Goalies—Don Simmons." *The Hockey News*, Nov. 9, 2018.

"Canadiens Place Samsonov on Waivers." *The Hockey News*, Feb. 6, 2007.

"Cancer Claims Former Bruins Defenseman Gary Doak at 71." *Boston Herald*, Nov. 17, 2018.

Castle, Mathew. "3 Takeaways from the Bruins 5–1 Win Over the Sharks." Boston.com, Oct. 30, 2019 (retrieved Oct. 30, 2019).

Cecil Thompson Biography Page. Hockey Hall of Fame Official Website, https://www.hhof.com/LegendsOfHockey/jsp/LegendsMember.jsp?mem=p195903&type=Player&page=bio&list=.

Champion, Brandon. "Sharks Thornton Passes Gordie Howe on Assists List, Yzerman Next." MLive, https://www.mlive.com/sports/2019/02/sharks-joe-thornton-passes-gordie-howe-on-all-time-assists-list-steve-yzerman-is-next.html, Feb. 12, 2019.

Charles Adams Bio Page. Hockey Hall of Fame Official Website, https://www.hhof.com/LegendsOfHockey/jsp/LegendsMember.jsp?mem=b196001&type=Builder&page=bio&list=ByName.

Cherry, Don. *Don Cherry's Sports He*roes. Toronto: Doubleday Canada, 2016.

Claude Julien Bio Page. NHL Official Website, https://www.nhl.com/bruins/team/exec-hockey-ops-claude-julien.

Clinton, Jared. "Top 100 Goalies: Reggie Lemelin." *The Hockey News*, Nov. 9, 2018.

Coburn, Pam. *Hitch: Hockey's Unsung Hero: The Untold Story of Boston Bruin Lionel Hitchman.* Manotick, ON: Pamdre Publishing, 2019.

Cohen, Russ, Halligan, John, and Raider, Adam. *100 Ranger Greats: Superstars, Unsung Heroes and Colorful Characters.* New Jersey: John Wiley and Sons, 2009.

Colageo, Mike. "Former Bruins Coach, Hall of Famer, Dies at Cape Cod Home." *Southcoast Today*, Nov. 23, 2007.

Coleman, Charles L. *The Trail of the Stanley Cup, Vol. 2.* Toronto: Ino Dubellar Books, 1976.

Cook, Ron. "Eddie Johnston: A Hockey Life." *Pittsburgh Post Gazette*, July 26, 2009.

Cooney Weiland Bio. Bruins Legends (Blog), bruinslegends.blogspot.com/2007/12/cooney-weiland.html (retrieved Feb. 22, 2019).

"Cooney Weiland Dies at 80, Ex-Hockey Player and Coach." *New York Times*, July 7, 1985.

Cooney Weiland Page. Hockey Hall of Fame Official Website, hhof.com/LegendsOfHockey/jsp/LegendsMember.jsp?mem=p197104&-type=Player&page=bio&list=ByYear.

Cote, Neil. "Schmautz Shooting for a Bruins Victory." *Boston Herald*, June 4, 2011.

Cowan, Stu. "Phil Esposito is Still Bitter About Trade from Bruins." *Montreal Gazette,* June 16, 2013.

Craig Janney Bio Page. Hockey Hall of Fame Official Website, https://www.hhof.com/Legends OfHockey/jsp/SearchPlayer.jsp?player=10704.

Craig Janney Bio Page. U.S. Hockey Hall of Fame Official Website, https://www.ushockey halloffame.com/page/show/2724583-craig-janney.

Cy Denneny Bio Page. Hockey Hall of Fame Official Website, https://www.hhof.com/LegendsOfHockey/jsp/LegendsMember.jsp?mem=p195902&type=Player&page=bio&list=ByYear.

Dave Andreychuk Bio Page. Hockey Hall of Fame Official Website. https://www.hhof.com/htmlInduct/ind17Andreychuk.shtml.

Dave Andreychuk Foundation Page. https://www.daveandreychukfoundation.com/.

David Krejci Salary/Contract Information. https://www.spotrac.com/nhl/boston-bruins/david-krejci-1461/.

David Krejci Stats Page. https://www.hockey-reference.com/players/k/krejcda01.html.

Decosta-Klipa, Nik. "Here's What Torey Krug Had to Say About His Helmet-less Hit on Robert Thomas." Boston.com, May 28, 2019 (retrieved Dec. 15, 2019).

Derek Sanderson Page. Hockey Hall of Fame Official Website, https://www.hhof.com/LegendsOfHockey/jsp/SearchPlayer.jsp?player=14215.

Derek Sanderson Stats Page. https://www.hockey-reference.com/players/s/sandede01.html.

Dit Clapper Bio Page. Hockey Hall of Fame Official Website, https://www.hhof.com/LegendsOfHockey/jsp/LegendsMember.jsp?mem=p194701&type=Player&page=bio&list=ByName.

Dit Clapper Stats Page. https://www.hockey-reference.com/players/c/clappdi01.html.

Don Cherry Bio Page. http://www.famous canadians.org/don-cherry/.

Don McKenney Stats Page. Https://www.hockey-reference.com/players/m/mckendo01.html.

Don Sweeney Profile Page. NHL Official Website, https://www.nhl.com/bruins/team/exec-hockey-ops-don-sweeney.

Droschak, David. "Glen Wesley Tribute—Part 1: The Trade." NHL Official Website, https://www.nhl.com/hurricanes/news/glen-wesley-tribute-part-1-the-trade/c-471785, Feb. 2, 2009 (retrieved Dec. 5, 2019).

"Dunkin X, David Pastrnak Penalty Box Regular." YouTube, https://www.youtube.com/watch?v=DHtapgcS2FY.

Duplacey, James. and Zweig, Eric. *Official Guide to the Players of the Hockey Hall of Fame.* Richmond Hill, ON: Firefly Books, 2010.

Dupont, Kevin Paul. "For Former Bruin Steve Heinze, a Day on the Ice Is a Good Day." *Boston Globe,* Jan. 1, 2016.

Ecozens. "OTBH: Like a Flash (Hollett)." Stanley Cup of Chowder, Aug. 21, 2013 (retrieved Nov. 17, 2019).

Eddie Johnston Coaching Record. https://www.statscrew.com/hockey/stats/c-johnsed01c.

Eddie Shore Biography Page. Hockey Hall of Fame Official Website, https://www.hhof.com/LegendsOfHockey/jsp/LegendsMember.jsp?mem=p194705&type=Player&page=bio&list=ByYear.

Farber, Michael. "Three Little Words: Too Many Men." *Sports Illustrated,* May 9, 2014.

Ferguson, Bob. "Ex-Bruin Cowley Dies at Age 81." *Ottawa Citizen,* Jan. 2, 1994.

Ferris, Shawn. "Analytics Profile: Brad Marchand, The Results May Shock You." Stanley Cup of Chowder, Sept. 5, 2018 (retrieved Nov. 15, 2019).

Fischler, Stan. "Bobby Orr Deceived in Free Agency Departure to Blackhawks." NHL.com, June 28, 2017 (retrieved Nov. 26, 2019).

_____. "If It Was Staggering, It Had to Be Eddie." *Sports Illustrated,* Mar. 13, 1967.

Fischler, Stan. *Boston Bruins: Greatest Moments and Players.* New York: Sports Publishing, 2017.

Fischler, Stan, and Shirley. *The Hockey Encyclopedia.* New York: Macmillan, 1983.

"Former Bruin John McKenzie Is This Week's Talk of the Town." YouTube, https://www.youtube.com/watch?v=udnDabxoUpU.

"Former Bruin, John 'Pie' McKenzie Dead at 80." *Boston Globe,* June 10, 2018.

"Former Hockey Star Hooley Smith Dies." *Montreal Gazette,* Aug. 26, 1963.

"Former Phantoms Defenseman Dennis Seidenberg Retires After 16 Seasons." Lehigh Valley Phantoms, http://www.phantomshockey.com/former-phantoms-defenseman-dennis-seidenberg-retires-16-seasons/ (retrieved Dec. 15, 2019).

Frank Brimsek Biography Page. Hockey Hall of Fame Official Website, http://www.legends ofhockey.net/LegendsOfHockey/jsp/Legends Member.jsp?mem=p196604&page=bio&list.

Frank Frederickson Bio and Olympic Stats Page. https://www.sports-reference.com/olympics/athletes/fr/frank-fredrickson-1.html.

Frank Frederickson Bio Page. Hockey Hall of Fame Official Website, http://www.halloffame.mb.ca/honoured/1981/ffredrickson.htm.

Fred Stanfield Bio Page. Hockey Gods Website, hockeygods.com/images/16704-Fred_Stanfield_1972_Boston_Bruins.

Frizzell, Scott. "Exclusive Interview with Former Bruins Goaltender Byron Dafoe." Boston Sports Extra, Apr. 15, 2018 (retrieved Dec. 30, 2019).

Gerry Cheevers Biography Page. Hockey Hall of Fame (Official Website), https://www.hhof.com/LegendsOfHockey/jsp/LegendsMember.jsp?mem=p198501&type=Player&page=bio&list=.

Gill, Hal. "Four Pretty Good Hockey Stories." The Players Tribune (Blog), https://www.theplayers tribune.com/en-us/articles/hal-gill-nhl-stories, Mar. 27, 2018 (retrieved Dec. 9, 2019).

Gilles Gilbert Biography Page. http://www. hockeydraftcentral.com/1969/69025.html.

Goode, Jon. "Catching Up with Don Marcotte." Southcoasttoday.com, Mar. 27, 2005 (retrieved Nov. 4, 2019).

Grange, Michael. "McLaren Sits Out for Hit on Zednik." *The Globe and Mail,* Apr. 20, 2002.

Gregg Sheppard Page. Hockey Hall of Fame Official Website, https://www.hhof.com/Legends OfHockey/jsp/SearchPlayer.jsp?player=14296.

Grimm, George. *Guardians of the Goal: A Comprehensive Guide to New York Rangers Goaltenders.* New York: Sports Publishing, 2019.

Hackel, Stu. "Brad Park: 100 Greatest NHL Players." NHL Official Website, https://www.nhl. com/news/brad-park-100-greatest-nhl-hockey-players/c-285639546, Jan. 1, 2017 (retrieved Jan. 15, 2019).

_____. "Jagr: 100 Greatest NHL Players." NHL Official Website, https://www.nhl.com/ news/jaromir-jagr-100-greatest-nhl-hockey-players/c-285901906, Jan. 1, 2017 (retrieved Jan. 15, 2019).

_____. "Johnny Bucyk: 100 Greatest Hockey Players." NHL Official Website, https://www.nhl. com/news/johnny-bucyk-100-greatest-nhl-hockey-players/c-284246332, Jan. 1, 2017.

_____. "Phil Esposito: 100 Greatest Hockey Players." NHL Official Website, https://www.nhl. com/news/phil-esposito-100-greatest-nhl-hockey-players/c-284852638, Jan. 1, 2017 (retrieved Mar. 10, 2019).

_____. "The Voice of the Bruins." *Sports Illustrated,* Mar. 7, 1994.

Haggerty, Joe. "Dennis Seidenberg Announces Retirement from the NHL After 15 Seasons." NBC Sports Boston, Oct. 24, 2019 (retrieved Dec. 15, 2019).

Harry Oliver Bio Page. Manitoba Hockey Hall of Fame Official Website, http://www. mbhockeyhalloffame.ca/people/harry-oliver/.

Harry Oliver Page. Hockey Hall of Fame Official Website, https://www.hhof.com/Legends OfHockey/jsp/LegendsMember.jsp?mem=p196 703&type=Player&page=bio&list=ByYear.

Harry Oliver Stats Page. https://www.hockey-reference.com/players/o/oliveha01.html.

Harry Sinden Bio Page. NHL Official Website, https://www.nhl.com/bruins/team/exec-hockey-ops-harry-sinden.

Hayden, Garrett. "My Chat with Bruins Legend Rick Middleton." https://blackngoldhockey. com/2018/11/24/my-chat-with-bruins-legend-rick-middleton/, Nov. 24, 2018 (retrieved May 22, 2019).

Hiam, Michael. *Eddie Shore and That Old Time Hockey.* Toronto: McClelland & Stewart, 2011.

"Hockey Coach Dies at 80, After Illness." *The Harvard Crimson,* July 9, 1985.

Holzman, Morey. "Blackhawks: Cursed or Concoction?" *New York Times,* May 29, 2010.

Hunter, Kevin. "Derek 'Turk' Sanderson: A Boston Legend." The Hockey Writers Archives, https:// thehockeywriters.com/derek-turk-sanderson-

a-boston-legend/, Aug. 3, 2018 (retrieved Mar. 1, 2019).

"Hurricanes Add Samsonov to Scouting Department." NHL Official Website, https://www. nhl.com/news/hurricanes-add-samsonov-to-scouting-department/c-730636, Sept. 16, 2014 (retrieved Nov. 11, 2019).

"Inside Hockey: Ryan Miller Interview Bruins Sabres 11/12." YouTube, https://www.youtube. com/watch?v=FvE82q4yKEM&feature=player_ embedded.

Iovino, Jim. "Kasper Made Big Mistake Benching Stars." LCS Guide to Hockey Website, https:// www.lcshockey.com/issues/35/feature3.asp (retrieved March 11, 2019).

Jansky, Dominick. "Islanders of Yesteryear: Ed Westfall: 18." Lighthouse Hockey (Blog), https:// www.lighthousehockey.com/2009/5/1/861487/ islanders-of-yesteryear-ed, May 1, 2009 (retrieved Oct. 12, 2019).

Jean Ratelle Bio Page. Hockey Hall of Fame Official Website, https://hhof.com/LegendsOfHockey/ jsp/LegendsMember.jsp?mem=p198504&type =Player&page=bio&list=.

"Jim Henry: Sweet as Sugar, Gritty as Spinach Salad." Puckstruck, https://puckstruck. com/2017/10/23/jim-henry-sweet-as-sugar-gritty-as-a-spinach-salad/, Oct. 23, 2017 (retrieved Dec. 18, 2019).

Joe Mullen Bio Page. U.S. Hockey Hall of Fame, https://www.ushockeyhalloffame.com/page/ show/828897-joe-mullen.

Joe Pelletier's Greatest Hockey Legends Blog. https://www.greatesthockeylegends.com.

Joe Thornton Bio Page. Jock Bio Website, https:// www.jockbio.com/Bios/Thornton/Thornton_ bio.html.

John McKenzie Stats Page. https://www.hockey-reference.com/players/m/mckenjo01.html.

Johnson, George. "Ray Bourque: 100 Greatest NHL Players." NHL Official Website, https:// www.nhl.com/news/ray-bourque-100-greatest-nhl-hockey-players/c-285594564, Jan. 1, 2017 (retrieved Dec. 4, 2019).

Kalman, Matt. "Seidenberg Deal a Good One for Bruins." ESPN.com, June 5, 2010 (retrieved Dec. 15, 2019).

Keene, Kerry. *Tales from the Boston Bruins Locker Room: A Collection of the Greatest Bruins Stories Ever Told.* New York: Sports Publishing, 2017.

Ken Hodge Page. Hockey Hall of Fame Official Website, https://www.hhof.com/LegendsOf Hockey/jsp/SearchPlayer.jsp?player=10649.

Ken Hodge Stats Page. https://www.hockey-reference.com/players/h/hodgeke01.html.

Kendall, Brian. *Shutout: The Legend of Terry Sawchuk.* Toronto: Penguin Books Canada, 1996.

Kennedy, Kevin. "Johnny Boychuk." *The Hockey News,* Mar. 9, 2013.

Kennedy, Kostnya. "Mystery Man." *Sports Illustrated,* July 25, 2012.

Kennedy, Ryan. "Top 100 Goalies: Andy Moog." *The Hockey News,* Nov. 9, 2018.

Kevin Shea. "One on One with Bobby Bauer." Official Hockey Hall of Fame Website, https://www.hhof.com/htmlSpotlight/spot_oneononep199601.shtml.

Kirshenbaum, Jerry. "The Wrath of Grapes." *Sports Illustrated,* Jan. 15, 1979.

Kravitz, Bob. "The Rat That Roared, Scored and Prospered." *Sports Illustrated,* Nov. 25, 1985.

Kreda, Allan. "Rangers Greats Reunite to Honor Jean Ratelle." *New York Times,* Feb. 24, 2018.

"Krejci Wins NESN's Seventh Player Award." Official NHL Website, https://www.nhl.com/bruins/news/krejci-wins-nesns-seventh-player-award/c-449593, Apr. 2, 2009 (retrieved Mar. 21, 2019).

Kyle McLaren Professional Profile. https://www.linkedin.com/in/kyle-mclaren-95133673.

Larkin, Matt. "All-Dirty/Skill Team: Who Blended Criminality and Talent Best?" *The Hockey News,* Apr. 6, 2017.

Leo Boivin Biography Page. Hockey Hall of Fame Official Website, https://www.hhof.com/LegendsOfHockey/jsp/LegendsMember.jsp?mem=P198601&type=Player&page=bio&list=ByName.

Lowetide. "Nation Profile: Andy Moog." Oilers Nation, https://oilersnation.com/2012/11/23/nation-profile-andy-moog/, Nov. 23, 2013 (retrieved Dec. 26, 2019).

Lukow, David B. "Steady Freddie: Stanfield a Winner on and off the Ice." Best of WNY Website, http://www.bestofwny.com/sports/lukow/stanfield.htm.

Malinowski, Mark. "Getting to Know: Randy Burridge." *The Hockey News,* July 19, 2015.

"Marc Savard, Hockey Stick Taping Nerd and 'Borrower' of Gretzky's Stick." YouTube, https://www.youtube.com/watch?v=qe6Y9tdrqUs.

Marina. "Torey Krug on Taking a Pay Cut to Stay in Boston—'It's Something I'm Interested In.'" Barstoolsports.com, Sept. 5, 2019 (retrieved Dec. 15, 2019).

Mark Recchi Bio and Stats Page. The Historical Website of the Montreal Canadiens, http://ourhistory.canadiens.com/player/Mark-Recchi.

Mark Recchi Bio Page. Hockey Hall of Fame (Official Website), https://www.hhof.com/LegendsOfHockey/jsp/LegendsMember.jsp?mem=p201704&type=Player&page=bio&list=ByName.

Marty Barry Bio Page. Hockey Hall of Fame Official Website, https://www/hhof.com/LegendsOfHockey/jsp/LegendsMember.jsp?mem=p196501&page=bio&list=ByYear.

Matsuda, Gann. "Teamwork, Integrity and a Little Engineering Helped Retired LA Kings RW Glen Murray to Skate Again." Frozen Royalty, https://www.frozenroyalty.net/2014/03/18/teamwork-ingenuity-and-a-little-engineering-helped-retired-la-kings-rw-glen-murray-to-skate-again/, Mar. 18, 2014 (retrieved Oct. 19, 2019).

McDonald, Joe. "Andrew Ference Fined for Gesture." ESPN.com, Apr. 21, 2011 (retrieved Dec. 12, 2019).

Mickey Mackay Stats Page. https://www.eliteprospects.com/player/79227/mickey-mackay.

Mike Milbury Bio Page. U.S. Hockey Hall of Fame (Official Website), https://www.ushockeyhall.com/mikemilbury.

Moran, Malcolm. "Players: Bruins' Goalie Has Successful Style." *New York Times,* Apr. 30, 1983.

Mulligan, Susan. "Tim Thomas's White House Snub Wasn't Brave, it Was Just Rude." *U.S. News and World Report,* Jan. 27, 2012.

Navarro, Sharon. "A Trip Down Memory Lane: Terry O'Reilly 'Taz.'" Causeway Crowd (Blog), https://www.causewaycrowd.com/2012/10/18/a-trip-down-memory-lane-terry-oreilly-taz/.

"Nels Played with His Brain." *The Montreal Gazette,* Nov. 10, 1962.

Nels Stewart Page. Hockey Hall of Fame Official Website, https://www.hhof.com/LegendsOfHockey/jsp/LegendsMember.jsp?mem=p196222&type=Player&page=bio&list=.

"1996 Hockey Hall of Fame Inductees, Bobby Bauer, Veteran Players Category." Hockey Hall of Fame Official Website, https://www.hhof.com/htmlinduct/indWoind96c.shtml.

O'Connor, Brian. "Front 9 Q & A With Former Bruins Goaltender Reggie Lemelin." North Shore Golf Magazine, http://northshoregolfmagazine.com/front-9-q-a-with-former-bruins-goaltender-reggie-lemelin/ (retrieved Dec. 24, 2019).

Oliver, Daniel. "Hockey Hall of Fame Debates: Rick Middleton." https://thehockeywriters.com/hockey-hall-of-fame-debates-rick-middleton/.

"One on One with Gerry Cheevers." Hockey Hall of Fame Official Website, Dec. 21, 2014 (retrieved Dec. 23, 2019).

O'Neil, Donna. "Former Bruins Forward Jon McKenzie Teaches Musicians the Game of Hockey." Wicked Local News Site, https://www.medford.wickedlocal.com/article/20070404/NEWS/304049805, Mar. 28, 2007 (retrieved June 18, 2019).

Orr, Bobby. *Orr: My Story.* New York: G.P. Putnam and Sons, 2013.

Patrice Bergeron Bio Page. https://www.patricebergeron37.weebly.com/biography.html.

"Patrice Bergeron Recounts Injuries During Cup Finals." *The Chicago Tribune,* July 2, 2013.

Paul Coffey Bio Page. https://paulcoffey.ca/bio.php.

"Paul Stewart versus Bobby Schmautz." The Fan Grave (Blog), https://thefangrave.wordpress.com/2015/03/20/paul-stewart-vs-bobby-schmautz-3-20-80/.

Paye, Marvin. "Ted Green, All-Star Bruins Defenseman Who Was Injured in Historic On-Ice Fight, Dies." *Boston Globe,* Nov. 2, 2019.

Peter McNab Bio Page. Hockey Hall of Fame Official Website, https://www.hhof.com/LegendsOfHockey/jsp/SearchPlayer.jsp?player=13679.

Peter McNab Broadcasting Profile. https://www. altitudesports.com/on-air-talent/peter-mcnab.

Phil Esposito Page. Hockey Hall of Fame Official Website, https://www.hhof.com/Legends OfHockey/jsp/LegendsMember.jsp?type=Player &mem=P198401&list=ByYear.

"Phil Esposito Was Record-Setting Goal Scorer." YouTube, youtube.com/watch?v=nwv7p1s2t_1.

"Philadelphia Fires Stasiuk." *Associated Press*, May 28, 1971.

PJ Axelsson Stats Page. http://www.hockeydb. com/ihdb/stats/pdisplay.php?pid=15995.

Podnieks, Andrew. *Players: The Ultimate A-Z Guide of Everyone Who Has Ever Played in the NHL*. Toronto: Doubleday Canada, 2003.

Pollack, David. "Debate Persists on Suspension of San Jose Sharks Captain Joe Thornton." *Mercury News*, Nov. 8, 2010.

Popper, Nathaniel. "Brains on Ice." *Boston Globe*, Oct. 11, 2009.

Ray Bourque Family Foundation Website. https:// bourquefamilyfoundation.org/.

Red Beattie Page. Hockey Gods Website. http:// hockeygods.com/images/17650-Jack__Red__ Beattie_1935_Boston_Bruins.

Rick Middleton Page. http://nhlegendsofhockey. com/people/rick-middleton/.

"Rick Smith: The Accidental Stanley Cup Winner." The Original Hockey Hall of Fame Official Website, http://www.originalhockeyhalloffame. com/news-events/smith.html.

"Rink Rats: Interview with Craig Janney." You-Tube, youtube.com/watch?v=UzbTUe-2EEO, Oct. 2, 2018.

Robinson, Chris. *Great Left Wingers: Stars of Hockey's Golden Age*. Alberta, CA: Altitude Publishing, 2006.

Robson, Dan. "How Niagara Falls' Derek Sanderson Crashed and Rose Again." Sports Net News Site, https://www.sportsnet.ca/hockey/nhl/ niagara-falls-derek-sanderson-crashed-rose/, Oct. 7, 2017 (retrieved Mar. 1, 2019).

Rolby, Herb. "Ross Leaves Cowley Off Bruin Trip List, Draws Center's Ire." *Boston Daily Globe*, Apr. 6, 1947.

Rolston Hockey Academy Website. https:// rolstonhockeyacademy.com/about/staff/ brian-rolston/.

Roy Conacher Bio Page. Hockey Hall of Fame Official Website, https://www.hhof.com/ LegendsOfHockey/jsp/LegendsMember.jsp? mem=P199801&type=Player&page=bio&list= ByName.

Royle, Jen. "Talk of the Town: Ex-Bruin John McKenzie Looks Back on Hockey Career." *Boston Herald*, May 15, 2014.

Savard, Marc. "Hell and Back." The Players Tribune Online Magazine, https://www.the playerstribune.com/en-us/articles/marc-savard-bruins-hell-and-back, May 16, 2017 (retrieved Mar. 22, 2019).

Schwartz, Nick. "A Strange History of Brad Marchand Kissing and Licking Players." *USA Today*, May 5, 2018.

Sell, Dave. "Capitals' Burridge Prays the Wheels Stay On." *The Washington Post*, Sept. 12, 1993.

Seminara, Dave. "Over the Glass and Into Hockey Lore." *New York Times*, Dec. 23, 2009.

Sergei Samsonov Bio Page. NHL Official Website, https://www.nhl.com/hurricanes/team/ staff/hockey-operations.

Shea, Kevin. "One on One with Leo Boivin." Hockey Hall of Fame Official Website, Apr. 25, 2008 (retrieved Nov. 22, 2019).

Shinzawa, Fluto. "Boychuk Is Next in Line on Bruins' Blue Line." *Boston Globe*, Sept. 4, 2009.

_____. "Glad Seidenberg Is on Their Side." *Boston Globe*, May 31, 2011.

Simmons, Steve. "Leafs' Steve Kasper Has No Nostalgia for Bruins Days." *Toronto Sun*, May 3, 2013.

Simon, Greg. "Nifty Choice by Bruins: Fall River's Alex Kogler was Rick Middleton's Teammate at Providence." *The Herald News*, Aug. 16, 2018.

Sprague Cleghorn Bio Page. Hockey Hall of Fame Official Website, https://www.hhof.com/ LegendsOfHockey/jsp/LegendsMember.jsp? mem=p195803&type=Player&page=bio&list= ByYear.

"Stan Johnathan, Bobby Schmautz on the 1978 Stanley Cup Bruins." YouTube, https://www. youtube.com/watch?v=BIZGYyLB40E.

Steve Heinze Stats Page. https://www.hockey-reference.com/players/h/heinzst01.html.

Steve Kasper Stats Page. Hockey Hall of Fame Official Website, https://www.hhof.com/ LegendsOfHockey/jsp/SearchPlayer. jsp?player=10762.

Stubbs, Dave. "Bruins Legend Hitchman Deserves Hall Recognition." NHL Official Website, https://www.nhl.com/news/lionel-hitchman-worthy-of-hockey-hall-of-fame/c-279063520, Feb. 22, 2016 (retrieved Nov. 16, 2019).

_____. "Bruins Marchand Impressing Former Boston Center Linesman in Final." NHL Official Website, https://www.nhl.com/news/ boston-bruins-brad-marchand-impressing-former-boston-center-ken-linesman-in-cup-final/c-307631826, May 31, 2019 (retrieved October 10, 2019).

_____. "Five Questions with Hal Gill." NHL Official Website, https://www.nhl.com/news/five-questions-with-hal-gill/c-291984264, Oct. 17, 2017.

_____. "Five Questions with Terry O'Reilly." NHL Official Website, https://www.nhl.com/news/ five-questions-with-bruins-legend-terry-oreilly/c-295790492, Feb. 13, 2018.

_____. "Former Bruins Center Derek Sanderson Credits Dad for NHL Success." NHL Official Website, https://www.nhl.com/news/ ex-boston-player-derek-sanderson-credits-father-for-his-success/c-289949634, June 17, 2017 (retrieved March 1, 2019).

_____. "Phil Esposito, Tony Esposito Share Stories, Laughs." NHL Official Website, https:// www.nhl.com/news/phil-esposito-tony-esposito-share-stories-in-sunday-long-read/c-287373038, Mar. 5, 2017 (retrieved Oct. 7, 2019).

Sylvio Mantha Bio Page. The Historical Website of the Montreal Canadiens, http://ourhistory.canadiens.com/player/Sylvio-Mantha.

Ted Donato Bio Page. GoCrimson.com (Official Site of Harvard Athletics), https://www.gocrimson.com/sports/mice/coaches/donato_ted?view=bio.

Terry O'Reilly Bio Page. Hockey Gods Website, http://hockeygods.com/images/17754-Terry_O_Reilly_1972_Boston_Bruins.

Terry O'Reilly Page. www. hockeydraftcentral.com/1971/71014.html.

"Thomas Statement on White House Absence." NHL Official Website, https://www.nhl.com/news/thomas-statement-on-white-house-absence/c-613279, Jan. 23, 2012 (retrieved Dec. 30, 2019).

Thompson, Andrew. "Former Boston Bruins Andrew Ference Calls It a Career." Causeway Crowd.com, Sept. 16, 2016.

"Thornton Traded to Sharks for Three Players." ESPN Online, https://www.espn.com/nhl/news/story?id=2242875, Dec. 1, 2005 (retrieved Mar. 15, 2019).

Tim Thomas Bio Page. U.S. Hockey Hall of Fame Official Website, https://www.ushockeyhalloffame.com/timthomas.

Tom Johnson Bio and Stats Page. Hockey Hall of Fame Official Website, https://www.hhof.com/LegendsOfHockey/jsp/LegendsMember.jsp?mem=P197003&list=ByName.

"Top Ten Slapshots of All Time." *Sports Illustrated*, Mar. 8, 2013.

Torey Krug Bio Page. Online Sports Data Base, https://www.osdbsports.com/nhl/79/Boston_Bruins/3377/Torey_Krug.

Torey Krug College Profile Page. Michigan State (Official Website of Spartan Athletics), https://msuspartans.com/sports/mens-ice-hockey/roster/torey-krug/3186.

Van Steendelaar, Kevin. "May 10, 1979: Boston Bruins Called for Too Many Men Against Montreal." Bleacher Report, https://bleacherreport.com/articles/172173-may-10-1979-boston-bruins-called-for-too-many-men-against-montreal, May 10, 2009 (retrieved Dec. 23, 2019).

Vautour, Kevin. *The Bruins Book*. Toronto: ECW Press, 1997.

Verdi, Bob. "The Verdict: Remembering Doug Mohns." NHL Official Website, https://www.nhl.com/blackhawks/news/the-verdict-remembering-doug-mohns/c-704662, Feb. 11, 2014 (retrieved Nov. 23, 2019).

Vic Stasiuk Interview (Induction to Alberta Sports Hall of Fame). YouTube, www.youtube.com/watch?v=guZ1tYrw7ik.

Weber, Bruce. "Doug Mohns, NHL All-Star Who Played For 22 Seasons, Dies at 80." *New York Times*, Feb. 12, 2014.

Whyno, Stephen. "Retired Goalie Tim Thomas Details Brain Damage from Hockey." *Associated Press*, Dec. 12, 2019.

Wilbon, Michael and Breeana, Christine. "Peeters, Galley Hospitalized After Taking Shots to Head." *Washington Post*, Apr. 25, 1988.

Williams, Jeff. "Athlete in Friar History: Hal Gill." *The Cowl*, Dec. 9, 2019.

Willie O'Ree Bio Page. NHL Official Website, http://www.nhl.com/ice/page.htm?id=25345.

Willie O'Ree Bio Page. NHL Official Website, https://www.blackpast.org/african-american-history/o-ree-willie-1935/.

Wind, Herbert Warren. "The Old Kraut Revives the Bruins." *Sports Illustrated*, Jan. 28, 1957.

Woody Dumart Stats Page. https://www.hockey-reference.com/players/d/dumarwo01.html.

Wyman, Mike. "The Golden Years: Murray Henderson." Insidehockey.com (Blog), Aug. 7, 2010 (retrieved Nov. 17, 2019).

Wyshinski, Greg. "Andrew Ference Say NHL Must Reach Beyond 'Middle-aged White Dudes.'" ESPN Online, https://www.espn.com/nhl/story/_/id/22908289/nhl-andrew-ference-says-nhl-reach-middle-aged-white-dudes, Mar. 26, 2018 (retrieved Dec. 12, 2019).

Zeisler, Laurel. *Historical Dictionary of Ice Hockey*. Lanham, MD: Scarecrow Press, 2013.

Zwieg, Eric. "Babe Siebert's Sad Story." http://ericzweig.com/2018/07/17/babe-sieberts-sad-story/, July 17, 2018 (retrieved Jan. 3, 2020).

Index

Adams, Charles Francis 3, 4
Adams, Jack 60, 86, 118
Albany River Rats 31, 110
Alberta Senior Hockey League 138
Alberta Sports Hall of Fame 63
Allan Cup 35, 39, 57, 120, 137, 141, 157
Allen, Keith 63
American Hockey Association 116, 138
American Hockey League 12, 13, 14, 21, 32, 46, 49, 63, 81, 110, 141, 142, 144; Hall of Fame 141
Anaheim Ducks 71, 127
Anderson, Tom 58
Andreychuk, Dave 151
Arizona Coyotes 27, 113
Armstrong, Bob 13
Atlanta Flames 19, 87
Atlanta Thrashers 34, 104, 130, 131, 154
Aurie, Larry 6
Avco World Trophy (WHA) 91
Awrey, Don 90
Axelsson, P.J. 73–74

"Baby B's" (Providence Bruins) 160
Badali, Gus (agent) 123
Bailey, Ace 81, 140
Barber, Bill 92, 126
Barilko, Bill 88
Barrie Flyers 12, 42, 87
Barry, Marty 5, 6–7
Bartkowski, Matt 134
Barzal, Mat 113
Bathgate, Andy 12
Battlefords North Stars 19
Bauer, Bobby 9, 10, 11, 38–40, 42, 58, 59
Beattie, Red 37, 57–58
Belanger, Ken 71
Beliveau, Jean 38, 85, 147, 150
Bellevue Bulldogs 116
Berde, Gene 91
Bergeron, Patrice 31–33, 77, 155
Bergman, Julius 112
Berklee Ice Cats 45
"Big Bad Bruins" 1, 19, 43, 66
Big 4 Western League 137
"Big Three" (Montreal defensemen) 150
Bill Masterton Memorial Trophy 43, 52, 98
Birmingham Bulls 25
Blake, Toe 148
Boe, Roy 43
Boivin, Leo 41, 88–89, 91, 92
Boll, Jared 75
Bondra, Peter 28, 71

Bossy, Mike 25, 43, 50, 139, 159
Boston Arena (original home of the Bruins) 3
Boston College Eagles 26, 54, 153
Boston Garden 1, 4, 45, 47, 65, 68, 97, 109
Boston Olympics (hockey team) 84, 85
Boston Tigers 37
Bouchard, Pierre 68
Boucher, Billy 140
Boucher, Frank 120
Bourque, Ray 1, 22, 24, 47, 50, 52, 59, 71, 99–101, 103, 105, 150, 151, 152
Bower, Johnny 121, 124
Bowman, Scotty 122
Boychuk, Johnny 110–11
Brandon Elks 120
Brantford Lions 86
Brezhnev, Leonid (Soviet leader) 72
Brimsek, Frank 4, 6, 118–120
British Columbia Junior Hockey League 22
"Broad Street Bullies" 25, 157
Brooklyn Dodgers (baseball) 12
Broten, Neal 129
Brown, Keith 100
Bruins Team Name (origin) 3
Bucyk, Johnny 13, 16, 33, 43, 44, 46, 62, 63–65, 145
Buffalo Bisons 97
Buffalo Sabres 1, 16, 21; Hall of Fame 151
Burch, Billy 139–140
Bure, Pavel 71
Burns, Pat 29
Burridge, Randy 69–71
Burt, Adam 52
Byng Trophy 5, 12, 16, 19, 20, 39, 59, 65, 72, 150, 151, 153, 154, 155

Cain, Herb 61–62
Calder, Frank 37, 117, 141
Calder Cup 12, 13, 14, 61, 63, 113
Calder Trophy 12, 15, 19, 23, 24, 26, 32, 60, 66, 72, 73, 76, 88, 97, 100, 104, 111, 113, 133, 144, 153
Calgary Canadians 36
Calgary Flames 75, 101, 104, 109, 128, 151, 154, 155
Calgary Hitmen 110
Calgary Monarchs 116
Calgary Tigers 3, 36
Calgary Stampeders 44
California Golden Seals 63, 96
Callahan, Ryan 77
Campbell, Clarence (referee) 37
Campbell, Ken (writer) 56
Can-Am Enterprises (Bobby Orr) 95

Canadian-American Hockey League 6, 37, 39, 57, 136, 144
Canadian Hockey League 27
Capreol Caps 87
Carbonneau, Guy 73
Carolina Hurricanes 73, 101, 154
Carveth, Joe 60
Cashman, Wayne 21, 43, 51, 64–66, 96, 125
Cassidy, Bruce 159–160
Causeway Street (Boston Garden address) 1
Central Collegiate Hockey Association 114
Central Professional Hockey League 19, 85, 125
Chabot, Lorne 117
Chadwick, Ed 121
Chara, Zdeno 35, 103, 105–108, 109, 113
Cheevers, Gerry 42, 66, 123–125, 127, 159
Chelios, Chris 70
Cherry, Don 1, 12, 14, 18, 22, 46, 48, 50, 67, 68, 69, 84, 96, 97, 99, 156–157
Chevrefils, Real 42
Chiarelli, Peter 76, 103, 111, 113
Chicago Blackhawks 6, 13, 15, 17, 32, 44, 48, 59, 60, 61, 62, 73, 87, 94, 107, 119, 120, 122, 123, 137–138, 139, 145, 154, 160
Chicago Cougars 128
Cincinnati Swords 21
Clapper, Dit 5, 8, 10, 37–38, 57, 83
Clarke, Bobby 25, 70, 94, 97, 126
Cleary, Robert 6
Cleghorn, Sprague 78, 136
Cleveland Crusaders 124
Cleveland Indians (hockey) 7
Cobb, Ty (baseball) 80
Coffey, Paul 109, 151, 152
Colgate University Raiders 99
Colorado Avalanche 12, 100, 110, 151, 155
Colorado Rockies 49, 157
Columbus Blue Jackets 111, 112
Conacher, Charlie 59, 83, 84, 143
Conacher, Lionel 59, 83
Conacher, Roy 4, 9, 59–60, 83
Conn Smythe Trophy 133, 153
Cook, Bill 140–141
Cook, Fred "Bun" 140–141
Cooke, Matt 33
Cooper, Carson 86
Corson, Shayne 52
Cotton, Harold "Baldy" 84
Coutu, Billy 80
Cowley, Bill 4, 8–10, 60
"Crazy Eights Line" (Philadelphia Flyers) 153
Crowder, Bruce 51
Crowder, Keith 51, 70
Cude, Wilf 117
"Curse of Muldoon" (Chicago Blackhawks) 87
Cushenan, Ian 87
Cusick, Fred (broadcaster) 15, 40, 41

Dafoe, Byron 131–132
Dallas Stars 130, 133, 154, 155
D'Amico, John (referee) 67
Dandurand, Leo 142
Datsyuk, Pavel 114
Dayton Gems 68
Dean, Dizzy (baseball) 81
DeBrusk, Jake 160
DeGeer, Vern (writer) 78
Delvecchio, Alex 89

Demers, Jacques 54
Denneny, Cy 138–139
Detroit Falcons 137
Detroit Red Wings 5, 6, 7, 28, 42, 44, 57, 60, 62, 64, 81, 83, 84, 86, 89, 96, 98, 114, 118, 120, 126, 137, 144, 145, 149, 155
Detroit Vipers 72
Dionne, Marcel 50
Doak, Gary 89, 92–93
Donato, Ted 71–72
Dotchin, Jake 76
Downie, Gord (Tragically Hip) 30
Dryden, Ken 49, 69, 130, 149
Duchesne, Steve 27
Duff, Bob (writer) 122
Duggan, Tom (sports promoter) 3
Dumart, Woody 4, 9, 10, 11, 39
Dupuis Pascal 133
Durocheer, Leo 44
Duton, Red 141
"Dynamite Line" 5, 37

Eagleson, Alan (dispute with Bobby Orr) 95–96
Eastern Amateur Hockey League 13, 84, 85, 118
Eastern Professional Hockey League 20, 42, 157
Eaves, Patrick 76
ECAC Hockey 71, 99
Eddie Powers Memorial Trophy 14
Eddie Shore Award 75, 110
Edmonton Dominions 138
Edmonton Eskimos 78, 137
Edmonton Oil Kings 63
Edmonton Oilers 24, 25, 47, 72, 91, 149, 152
Edwards, Don 128
Egan, Pat 83
Eichel, Jack 28
Elizabeth C. Dufresne Trophy 19, 42, 91
Emma, David 54
Engelland, Derek 75
Esposito, Phil 11, 16–20, 33, 43, 45, 46, 47, 64, 90, 94, 100, 157
Esposito, Tony 17, 130
Essex 73s 51
Estevan Bruins 18, 89

Federov, Sergei 71
Fedyk, Brent 153
Ference, Andrew 108
Ferguson, John 44
Finley, Charlie 96
Fischler, Stan (writer) 79, 94
Fiset, Stephan 131
Fitzgerald, Ed (writer) 79
Flaman, Fern 84–86, 87
Fleury, Theo 155
Florida Panthers 34, 73, 105, 113, 133
Fogilin, Lee 25
Forrestal, John "Frosty" (trainer) 124
Forsberg, Peter 100
Fort Erie Meteors 69
Fox Sports Network 43
Francis, Ron 73
Frederickson, Frank 78, 136–137
Friesen, Jeff 107
Fuhr, Grant 129, 130, 155

Gaborik, Marian 106
Gainor, Dutch 5, 37

Galbraith, Percy 36
Gallery Gods 84, 85
Galt Blackhawks 13, 121
Gardiner, Herb 137
Gardner, Cal 11
Gary F. Longman Memorial Trophy 72
Gatineau Olympiques 35
Geiger, Jeff 25
Getliffe, Ray 61
Giacomin, Ed 122
Giguere, Jean Sebastain 31
Gilbert, Gilles 16, 125–126, 149
Gilbert, Rod 20, 153
Gill, Hal 105–106
Gillette Stadium 55
Gillies, Clark 43
Gilmour, Doug 111
Gionta, Brian 105
Girardi, Dan 56
Goal-a-Game Line "GAG" (New York Rangers) 20
Golden Hockey Stick Award 55, 154
Golden Horseshoe Junior Hockey League 69
"Gordie Howe Hat Trick" 56
Goring, Butch 47, 159
Gorman, Tommy 6, 61
Gracie, Bob 61
Grahame, Ron 66, 100
Great Depression 10, 57, 141
Green, Ted 43, 90–91
"Green Line" (Montreal Maroons) 61
Gretzky, Wayne 24, 28, 38, 50, 90, 127, 149, 152
Guelph-Biltmore Mad hatters 20
Guidolin, Bep 147

Hackett, Jeff 104
Hadfield, Vic 20, 21
Halifax Wolverines 9
Halward, Doug 68
Hamilton Bulldogs 156
Hamilton Red Wings 92
Hamilton Tigers 36, 139
Hanson Brothers (movie characters) 49
"Hap" Holmes Memorial Award 126
Happy Hooligan (Comic strip character) 141
Hart Trophy 7, 9, 11, 14, 20, 30, 58, 80, 95, 119, 127, 137, 139, 140, 148
Hartford Whalers 23, 89, 94, 101–102, 123, 125
Harvard Crimson Hockey 6, 71, 102, 158
Hasek, Dominic 55
Hawerchuk, Dale 23
Heinze, Steve 54–55, 71
Hell's Kitchen (NYC neighborhood) 150
"HEM Line" (Boston College) 54
Henderson, Murray 83–84
Henry, "Sugar Jim" 41, 120–121
Hershey Bears 12, 16, 40, 42, 61, 84, 110
Hewitson, Bobby (referee) 8
Hextall, Dennis 92
Hill, Mel "Sudden Death" 9, 60
Hitchman, Lionel 78–79, 136
Hobey Baker Award 26, 114
Hockey Hall of Fame (Toronto) 6, 7, 10, 12, 18, 21, 23, 28, 37, 49, 53, 78, 86, 89, 98, 100, 120, 125, 129, 136, 137, 138, 139, 140, 141, 143, 144, 145, 146, 147, 148, 149, 150, 151, 152, 153, 154, 155
Hockey Night in Canada 157
Hockeyfights.com 74, 124
Hodge, Charlie 149

Hodge, Ken 11, 16, 35, 45–46, 49
Hodge, Ken, Jr. 46
Hollett, Flash 4, 81–82, 87
Holmgren, Paul 25
Horeck, Pete 86
Horvath, Bronco 13–14, 62, 64
Hossa, Marian 106
Howe, Gordie 10, 29, 62, 63, 85, 89
Hull, Bobby 13, 17, 66, 67, 121
Hull, Brett 27, 28
Hull Olympiques 156
Hunwick, Matt 33

Iginla, Jarome 155
Ilves Tampere (SM Liiga) 133
Imlach, Punch 16
Inkerman Rockets 88
International-American Hockey League 7, 70, 72, 118, 121, 126, 137, 141
Ivan, Tommy 86

Jack Adams Award 156
Jackie Robinson (baseball) 146
Jackson, Art 143
Jackson, Busher 142–143
Jackson, Percy 117
Jagr, Jaromir 55, 154–155
James, Angela 155
Janney, Craig 26–27, 28, 101
Jennings, William 91
Jennings Trophy 129, 130
Jerwa, Joe 57
Jillson, Jeff 104
John P. Bucyk Trophy 108
Johnson, Mark 127
Johnson, Norm 42
Johnson, Tom 147, 157–158
Johnston, Eddie 94, 122–123
Jonathan, Stan 68–69
Joseph, Curtis 27
Julien, Claude 113, 156, 160

Kamloops Blazers 155
Kansas City Pla-Mors 62
Karakas, Mike 118
Kasper, Steve 24–25, 51, 68
Keats, Duke 137–138
Keenan, Mike 27
Keene, Kerry (writer) 118
Kennedy, Forbes 124
Kenora Thistles 143
Kentucky Thoroughblades 106
"Kid Line" (Maple Leafs) 143
King Clancy Memorial Trophy 109
Kingston Canadians 24
Kingston Frontenacs 157
Kissinger, Henry (US Secretary of State) 124
Kitchener Greenshirts 10, 57
Kitchener-Waterloo Dutchmen 39, 83
Kobasew, Chuck 109
Kogler, Alex 50
Kolzig, Olaf 131
Komarov, Leo 76
"Kraut Line" 9, 10, 11, 39, 59
Krejci, David 34–35, 55
Krug, Torey 114–115
Krupp, Uwe 112
Kurri, Jari 152

L.A. Blades 42, 48
Labine, Leo 41–42
Lafleur, Guy 67, 126
Lake Erie Monsters 110
Lalime, Patrick 107, 131
Lalonde, Newsy 6
Lapointe, Guy 149–150
Lapointe, Martin 32
Larkin, Matt (writer) 25
Laroque, Georges 107
Las Vegas Thunder 70
Leach, Reggie 126
Leduc, Albert 39
Leetch, Brian 21, 152–153
Lehkonen, Artturi 111
Lemelin, Reggie 128–129, 130
Lemieux, Mario 123, 151
Leslie Jones Collection (Boston Public Library) 1, 4, 11, 38, 41, 117, 119
Lester B. Pearson Award 20
Lester Patrick Trophy 6, 53, 146, 153
Lewis, Herbie 6
Lidstrom, Niklas 73
Lindros, Eric 29, 153
Linseman, Ken 24–26
Longueuil Chevaliers 150
Los Angeles Kings 24, 51, 53, 54, 55, 71, 75, 100, 131, 149, 155
Lubbock Cotton Kings 27
Lucic, Milan 72, 74–75
Lunqvist, Henrik 73
Lynn, Patrick 11

MacKay, Mickey 138
Mackell, Fleming 41
MacTavish, Craig 49
Madison Square Garden 150
Madison Square Garden Incident 22, 47, 98–99
Madison Square Garden Network 18
Magnuson, Keith 68
Maine Mariners 25, 126, 158
Maki, Chico 147
Maki, Wayne 91
Manilow, Barry ("Looks Like We Made It," song) 105
Manitoba Hockey Association 137
Manitoba Junior Hockey League 143
Manitoba Sports Hall of Fame 91, 121
Mantha, Georges 142
Mantha, Sylvio 142
Maple Leaf Gardens (Toronto) 60
Marchand, Brad 32, 75–77
Marcotte, Don 66–68
Maritime Senior Hockey League 9
Mark Messier Trophy 155
Marker, Bob 61
Marotte, Gilles 15
Martin, Pitt 15
Martin, Rick 69
Matthews, Auston 95
May, Brad 55
McAuley, Ken 63
McAvoy, Charlie 160
McDavid, Connor 95
McDonald, Bucko 93
McDonald, Jiggs 43
McInnis, Marty 54
McKenney, Don 12–13, 42, 84, 146
McKenzie, John "Pie" 16, 44–45, 65

McLaren, Kyle 102–104
McNab, Peter 21–22, 47
McQuaid, Adam 109, 111–112
McReavy, Pat 60
Mellanby, Scott 131
Melnyck, Gerry 44
Melville Millionaires 79
Memorial Cup 5, 12, 19, 39, 42, 51, 67, 74, 87, 90, 143, 156
Messier, Mark 21, 25, 152
Messier Trophy 108
Michigan State Spartans Hockey 114
Middleton, Rick 22, 49–50, 68, 71
Migay, Rudy 124
Mikita, Stan 16, 87, 107
Milbury, Mike 98–99, 158–159
Miller, Ryan 75
Milwaukee Brewers (baseball) 146
Minneapolis Millers 5, 7, 116
Minnesota Fighting Saints 96
Minnesota North Stars 16, 43, 87, 89, 106, 125, 149, 159
Minnesota Wild 31
Mohns, Doug 87–88
Montreal Arena (Home of Montreal Wanderers) 3
Montreal Canadiens 3, 4, 5, 6, 7, 8, 16, 23, 24, 31, 34, 36, 37, 39, 42, 48, 61, 78, 89, 102, 105, 116, 121, 130, 138, 139, 142, 143, 145, 147, 148, 149, 150, 155, 156, 157, 158, 159
Montreal Forum (Home of Canadiens) 13, 143
Montreal Junior Canadiens 40
Montreal Junior Royals 122
Montreal Maroons 4, 6, 7, 57, 61, 78, 136, 141, 142
Montreal Wanderers 3
Moog, Andy 128–130
Morel, Dennis (referee) 47
Morenz, Howie 5
Mount Royal Intermediate League 6
Mullen, Joe 150–151
Mulligan, Susan (journalist) 132
Murray, Glen 53–54
Murray, Rob 160
Muskegon Lumberjacks 153
Myre, Phil 126

Namath, Joe 15
Nashville Predators 106
National Hockey Association 3, 136, 137, 139
National Hockey League 3
National Italian-American Hall of Fame 18
Neale, Harry 98
Neely, Cam 1, 23, 24, 28, 43, 51–53, 71, 74, 93, 101, 151
NESN (Sports Network) 15, 23, 27, 49
Nesterenko, Eric 42
New Brunswick Hawks 123
New England Hockey Conference 45
New England Hockey Writers Association 6
New England Whalers 91
New Haven Nighthawks 46
New Jersey Devils 22, 31, 106, 127, 129, 151, 156
New Westminster Royals 144
New York Americans 8, 37, 81, 142, 143
New York Islanders 1, 23, 31, 43, 99
New York Rangers 1, 4, 5, 12, 13, 15, 18, 20, 21, 29, 33, 44, 47, 49, 61, 66, 71, 89, 96, 104, 112, 114, 141, 144, 145, 148, 150, 152, 153, 158
Niagara Falls Flyers 14, 16, 42, 67

Nieuwendyk, Joe 101
1920 Summer Olympics (Antwerp, Belgium) 137
1923 Stanley Cup Playoffs 78
1924 Stanley Cup Playoffs 3, 36, 142
1924 Winter Olympics (Chamonix, France) 141
1926 Stanley Cup Playoffs 140
1929 Intra-League Draft 6
1929 Stanley Cup Playoffs 3, 4, 5, 36, 37, 81, 116, 139, 156
1930 Stanley Cup Playoffs 5, 6, 36, 37, 142
1931 Stanley Cup Playoffs 142
1933 Stanley Cup Playoffs 140
1934 All-Star Team 5
1936 Stanley Cup Playoffs 6
1937 Stanley Cup Playoffs 7
1939 Stanley Cup Playoffs 6, 10, 61, 81, 83, 119, 156
1940 Stanley Cup Playoffs 144
1941 Stanley Cup Playoffs 6, 9, 10, 61, 83, 119, 158
1943 Stanley Cup Playoffs 143
1945 Stanley Cup Playoffs 83, 145
1952 Stanley Cup Playoffs 62, 120
1953 Stanley Cup Playoffs 86
1955 Stanley Cup Playoffs 62
1957 Stanley Cup Playoffs 40, 88, 145
1958 Stanley Cup Playoffs 13, 88, 145
1959 Stanley Cup Playoffs 13
1960 U.S. Hockey Team 6
1962 Stanley Cup Playoffs 121
1965 Intra-League Draft 124
1967 NHL Expansion Draft 147
1970 Stanley Cup Playoffs 14, 16, 65, 67, 91, 96, 124
1972 Stanley Cup Playoffs 14, 65, 67, 97, 124, 158
1972 Summit Series (Canada vs. USSR) 157
1974 Stanley Cup Playoffs 19
1975 Amateur Draft 68
1976 Stanley Cup Playoffs 20
1976 Summer Olympics (Montreal) 106
1977 Amateur Draft 126
1977 Stanley Cup Playoffs 69
1978 Stanley Cup Playoffs 49, 68
1979 Stanley Cup Playoffs 18, 69
1979 Stanley Cup Semi-finals Game 7 (Too Many Men on the Ice) 67–68, 125, 126
1981 Stanley Cup Playoffs 130
1983 NHL Entry Draft 52
1983 Stanley Cup Playoffs 130
1984 Stanley Cup Playoffs 25
1986 IIHF World Junior Championships 25
1986 NHL Entry Draft 26
1987 NHL Entry Draft 101
1988 NHL Entry Draft 54
1988 Stanley Cup Playoffs 24, 25, 26, 70, 101, 129, 159
1988 Winter Olympics (Calgary) 130
1990 Stanley Cup Playoffs 27, 102–103, 129, 158
1991-'92 All-Star Game 70
1991 Stanley Cup Playoffs 106, 123
1992 NHL Players Strike 130
1992 Stanley Cup Playoffs 123
1992 Winter Olympics (Albertville, France) 71
1994-'95 NHL Lockout 130
1994 Stanley Cup Playoffs 28
1995 NHL Entry Draft 34
1996 NCAA Frozen Four 132
1997 NHL Entry Draft 29, 72
Nolan, Ted 75
Norris, Jack 15, 18
Norris Trophy 88, 91, 95, 98, 100, 108, 146, 147, 152, 153

Northern Ontario Hockey Association 60
Northern Ontario Junior Hockey League 87
Nosek, Tomas 29
Nova Scotia Sport Hall of Fame 7

Oakland Seals 94
Oates, Adam 27–28, 151
Oates Sports Group 28
Obama, Barrack (U.S. president) 75
O'Connell, Mike 104
Oklahoma City Blazers 19, 65, 89
Oliver, Harry 141
Olympic Saddledome (Calgary) 128
Ontario Hockey Association 8, 10, 12, 13, 14, 20, 39, 45, 51, 94, 143
Ontario Hockey League 29, 49, 53, 96, 111, 123
Ontario Major Junior Hockey League 24, 152
O'Ree, Willie 42, 146–147, 155
O'Reilly, Terry 24, 26, 46–48, 67, 159
Orr, Bobby 4, 14, 15, 17, 18, 19, 22, 43, 45, 47, 49, 64, 66, 83, 89, 90, 93–95, 96, 97, 98, 100, 122–123, 157
Orr Hockey Group 95
Oshawa Generals 14, 47, 49, 65, 157
Ottawa Commandos 120
Ottawa New Edinburghs 78
Ottawa Senators 5, 28, 33, 71, 78, 106, 131, 137, 138, 139
Ottawa 67's 10, 25, 159
Owen Sound Greys 5

Pacific Coast Hockey Association 3, 137, 138
Pacific Coast Hockey League 10, 57, 144
Pacigic Grain Seniors 116
Pacioretty, Max, (Chara incident) 108
Palffy, Ziggy 53
Parent, Bernie 147–148
Park, Brad 18, 20, 21, 43, 65, 96–98, 149
Pastrnak, David 32, 55–56, 77, 160
Patrick, Lynn 40, 59, 85
Pederson, Barry 22–23, 50, 56, 101
Peeters, Pete 116, 126–127
Peirson, Johnny 40–41
Penniston, Don 40
"Perfection Line" 32, 77
Perrault, Bob 122
Perron, David 114
Peterborough Petes 51, 68, 70
Philadelphia Arrows 6
Philadelphia Blazers 14, 45
Philadelphia Flyers 24, 25, 66, 104, 110, 113, 126–127, 128, 146, 147, 148, 153, 157
Philadelphia Ramblers 144
Pickering Panthers 152
Pilous, Rudy 96
Pittsburgh Hornets 7, 63, 91, 124
Pittsburgh Penguins 15, 43, 53, 89, 106, 123, 151, 152, 154
Pittsburgh Pirates (hockey) 137, 138
Plante, Jacques 16, 122, 123, 147–149
Port Arthur Bruins 88
Port Colborne Sailors 8
Portland Winter Hawks 101, 131
Potvin, Denis 19, 25, 43, 97, 159
"Poverty Pond" (Toronto) 143
Pratt, Babe 85, 143–144
President's Trophy 99, 155, 158, 160
Propp, Brian 25, 126

Prout, Dalton 75
Providence Bruins 35, 160
Providence Collee Friars 105
Providence Reds 12, 39, 85, 118
Provonost, Marcel 94
Prust, Brandon 75
Punch Imlach Memorial Award (Sabres) 70

Quackenbush, Bill 86
Quebec Aces 63, 146
Quebec Major Junior Hockey League 24, 35, 75, 100, 128, 150, 156
Quebec Nordiques 31, 107, 123, 150, 156
Quintal, Stephane 28

Ranford, Bill 28
Rask, Joonas 133
Rask, Tuukka 133–135
"Rat Patrol" 25
Ratelle, Jean 18, 20–21, 43, 46, 47, 49, 68, 69, 96, 97
Raycroft, Andrew 133
Raynor, Chuck 120
RCAF Hockey 84
Recchi, Mark 151, 153–154
Red Deer Rustlers 101
Red Wings Hall of Fame 7
Regan, Larry 12
Richard, Henri 85
Richard, Maurice 8, 60, 120
Rickles, Don (comedian) 124
Riggin, Pat 127, 128
Rinaldo, Zac 75
Roach, Mickey 82
Robinson, Larry 48, 90, 150
Robitaille, Luc 53
Rochester Americans 13, 14, 121, 124, 157; Hall of Fame 125
Roenick, Jeremy 99
Rolston, Brian 30–31
Ross, Art 3, 8, 9, 57, 59, 60, 61, 79, 82–83, 84, 95, 117, 118, 140, 156
Ross Trophy 30, 61, 154
Roy, Patrick 100, 129
Royal Canadian Air Force 39
RPI Engineers 27, 28
Ruff, Lindy 52
Ruth, Babe (baseball) 118, 139, 143
Rutherford, Jim 101, 102
Ryan, Bob (writer) 79
Ryan, Ron 99

"S-Line" (Montreal Maroons) 7, 140, 141, 142
St. Catharines Teepees 15, 121
St. Louis Blues 12, 15, 27, 28, 43, 71, 89, 114, 148, 150, 160
St. Louis Braves 15
St. Louis Cardinals (baseball) 10
St. Louis Eagles 8
St. Michaels Majors 39, 42, 123
St. Paul Saints 121
St. Thomas Stars 29
Sakic, Joe 100
Salo, Sami 76
Samsonov, Sergei 31, 71–72, 102
Samuelson, Ulf 52
San Diego Gulls 21
San Jose Sharks 27, 29, 66, 104

Sanderson, Derek 14–15, 41, 64, 66, 67
Sands, Charlie 61
Sarnia Legionnaires 17
Saskatchewan Junior Hockey League 19, 48
Sault Ste. Marie Greyhounds 29
Savard, Andre 21
Savard, Marc 29, 33–34
Savard, Serge 150
Sawchuk, Terry 64, 120, 121, 124, 144–145
Schmautz, Bobby 48–49
Schmidt, Milt 4, 10–11, 39, 44, 58, 59, 87, 89, 145
Schultz, Dave 49, 66
"Scooter Line" (Chicago Blackhawks) 87
Seidenberg, Dennis 112–114
Selke, Frank J. 8, 143
Selke Trophy 19, 24, 31, 32, 73
Selkirk Fishermen 36
Senior, Bob 95
Seventh Player Award 19, 35, 51, 56, 69, 70, 75, 77, 92, 103, 104
Shanahan, Brendon 27
Shelley, Jody 55
Sheppard, Gregg 18–19
Sherbrooke Castors 128
Shore, Eddie 4, 10, 37, 57, 78–81, 83, 86, 140, 142
Siebert, Babe 7, 116, 140, 141
Simmons, Don 121–122
Sinden, Harry 16, 17, 19, 23, 46, 68, 70, 91, 92, 94, 102, 124, 157, 158, 159
Six Nations Reserve (Ontario) 68, 69
Smeaton, Cooper (referee) 8
Smith, Dallas 89–90
Smith, Hooley 7, 141–142
Smith, Rick 95–96
Smythe, Conn 82, 84, 117
Smythe Trophy 148
"The Soo" 17
Sorel Blackhawks 100
Souray, Sheldon 150
Spezza, Jason 106
Springfield Coliseum 81
Springfield Indians 13, 81, 121
Staal, Eric 95
Stamkos, Steven 29
Stanfield, Fred 11, 15–17, 44, 45, 65, 125
Stanley, Allan 145–146
Stasiuk, Vic 13, 42, 62–63, 64
Stasny, Anton 123
Stasny, Marion 123
Stasny, Peter 107, 123
Stevens, Kevin 24
Stevens, Scott 28
Stewart, Bill (referee) 6
Stewart, Gaye 86
Stewart, Nels 7–8, 141
Stewart, Paul 48
Stewart, Ron 145
Sudbury Wolves 53, 111
Sundin, Mats 73
Sutter, Brian 100
Svoboda, Peter 70
Swedish National Team 73
Sweeney, Bob 101
Sweeney, Don 93, 102–103
Syracuse Stars 82

Tacoma Rockets 104
Talbot, Jean-Guy 90

Tampa Bay Lightning 18, 56, 66, 76, 151, 154, 155
Tappanzzini, Jerry 146
TD Garden 33, 49, 68
Team Canada Hockey 23, 32, 39
Team USA Hockey 25, 31, 54, 106
Thomas, Robert 114
Thomas, Tim 132–134
Thompson, Cecil "Tiny" 37, 116–118
Thornton, Joe 29–30, 53, 72, 107
"Three-Gun Line" 9
Tim Horton Memorial Award 70
Tocchet, Rick 28
Topps Hockey Cards 1
Toronto Arenas (hockey team) 138
Toronto Granites 141
Toronto Maple Leafs 7, 8, 11, 12, 13, 24, 25, 39, 44, 52, 61, 82, 84, 85, 86, 88, 105, 117, 120, 121, 122, 123, 124, 133, 144, 145, 149, 151, 157
Toronto Marlboros 83, 97, 143
Toronto Nationals 60
Toronto Native Sons 86
Toronto St. Patricks 4, 139
Toronto Young Rangers 83
The Tragically Hip ("50 Mission Cap," song) 88
Trois-Rivieres Draveurs 100
Trois-Rivieres Lions 20
Trottier, Bryan 25, 43, 159
Tulsa Oilers 138
2000 NHL Expansion Draft 55
2001 NHL Entry Draft 113
2002 NHL Entry Draft 110
2002 Summer Olympics (Salt Lake City) 32
2003 Western Hockey League Draft 74
2004 NHL Entry Draft 35
2004 NHL Lockout 32, 105, 109, 132, 153
2004 Stanley Cup Playoffs 109, 151, 155
2004 YoungStars Game 31
2006 NHL Entry Draft 76
2006 Stanley Cup Playoffs 102, 154
2006 Winter Olympics (Turin, Italy) 73
2009 Stanley Cup Playoffs 105
2011 Stanley Cup Playoffs 32, 34, 35, 65, 74, 75, 76, 111, 112, 113, 132, 133, 154
2012 All-Star Skills Competition 107
2013 Stanley Cup Playoffs 32, 154
2014 NHL Entry Draft 55
2016 Bruins Alumni Game 55
2018 IIHF World Championship 35
2019 All-Star Skills Competition 56
2019 Stanley Cup Playoffs 32, 108, 114, 160
2020 NHL All-Star Game 56

"Uke Li" 13, 62, 64
United States Amateur Hockey Association 7
U.S. Hockey Hall of Fame 26, 99, 133, 151, 159
United States Hockey League 62
University of Vermont Catamounts Hockey 132

Vachon, Rogie 126, 149
Vadnais, Carol 18, 20, 90

Vanbiesbrouck, John 132
Vancouver Canucks 23, 33, 48, 52, 76, 101, 112, 130
Vancouver Giants 74
Vancouver Lions 57
Vancouver Millionaires 138
Vancouver Minor Hockey Association 74
van Hellemond, Andy (referee) 47
van Riemsdyck, James 28
Vegas Golden Knights 29
(The) Ventures, "Nutty" (Bruins TV theme) 1
Verbeek, Pat 75, 129
Vernon, Mike 128
Vezina Trophy 116, 117, 127, 128, 131, 133, 135, 145, 148, 149, 158
Victoria Cougars 22, 137
Voorhees, Jason 1

Warroad Lakers 121
Washington Capitals 11, 28, 87, 96, 127, 131, 160
WBZ Radio (Boston) 41
Weber, Shea 107
Weicker, Lowell (Connecticut governor) 101
Weiland, Cooney 5–6, 37, 57, 158
Wesley, Glen 101–102
Western Canada Hockey League 3, 4, 6, 22, 36, 42, 45, 48, 85, 104, 106, 109, 110, 127, 131, 137, 138, 141, 146, 155
Western Canada Junior Hockey League 44
Westfall, Ed 42–44, 67, 89, 91
Wharam, Kenny 87
Wheeler, Blake 28
Wilson, Dunc 43
Wilson, Eli 134
Wilson, Woodrow (U.S. president) 58
Windsor-Essex Hall of Fame 51
Winnipeg Braves 90
Winnipeg Falcons 137
Winnipeg Jets 27
Winnipeg Lombards 120
Winnipeg Maroons 121
Winnipeg Warriors 122
Wirtz, Bill (Bobby Orr trade) 95
Wiseman, Eddie 9
World Hockey Association 15, 16, 18, 21, 25, 51, 91, 96, 124, 125, 128, 148, 149
World War I 13, 57, 137, 138
World War II 8, 39, 40, 57, 60, 81, 83, 93, 119, 120, 143
Worsley, Gump 125, 129, 149
WSBK TV (Boston) 1, 15, 41
Wyshynski, Greg (writer) 34

Yarmouth Mariners 24
Yashin, Alexei 106
Yastrzemski, Carl 91
Young, Garry 95

Zboril, Jakub 75
Zednik, Richard 103
Zweig, Eric (writer) 122